30 Key Questions that Unlock Management

30 Key Questions that Unlock Management

BRIAN SUTTON AND ROBINA CHATHAM

IT Governance Publishing

IT Governance Publishing
IT Governance Limited
Unit 3, Clive Court
Bartholomew's Walk
Cambridgeshire Business Park
Ely
Cambridgeshire
CB7 4EH
United Kingdom

www.itgovernance.co.uk

First published in the United Kingdom in 2012
by IT Governance Publishing.

ISBN 978-1-84928-344-1

FOREWORD

Your first thought might be '... *another management book* ...'. But let me assure you, this book is different from all the other management books I have ever read.

Like most managers, I find that much of my time is taken up by merely *reacting* to developments in the business; I constantly find myself running faster just to stay in the same place. To make matters worse, I and many of my colleagues have developed some sort of Pavlovian response to BlackBerrys beeping and flashing, rushing to fulfil perceived expectations, and exposing ourselves to unnecessary and scattered workflow. Under this sort of pressure, it is easy to lose contact with the basis of the business, i.e. the roots of how the business makes money. We spend too much time reacting to the imperatives of the present and too little time thinking constructively about how to build a better future.

With their new book, Brian and Robina have managed to create a DIY guide to help busy managers mitigate these problems. Since all companies are different (at least to a certain extent), and the actual problem areas you and I have to deal with are not the same either, the modular structure of this book comes in really handy. You are not forced to read the book from beginning to end; nor are you required to wade through complex management theory divided into subjects that have little relevance to the real problems that you face on a daily basis.

This is a book for real managers grappling with real managerial problems. The structure and associated Mind Maps® help you to find answers quickly to your particular problem. Just read the section that provides you with the information that you need right now. And as an added bonus, each question is wrapped up with easy practical advice showing you clearly the steps you can take immediately to deal with your issue and improve your performance.

Maybe I should close with a health warning. This book can be a real eye-opener; it makes you question how you and your colleagues behave and it makes you look more carefully at things you have previously taken for granted. I feel sure that, like me, you will find that making relatively minor changes to some facets of your behaviour can make you and your business more effective.

A fantastic read – and full of advice that really works!

Robert Ruehl

Director

Pan-European Retail Multiple

PREFACE

Most people who find themselves in a management position for the first time are lost and ill-prepared. The challenge of stepping up to management is not something that can be overcome by attending a course or reading a book that abstractly talks about planning or motivation or delegation. There is a big difference between understanding the theory of how something works and being able to apply those ideas in practice.

We work extensively with mid- and senior-level managers in all industry sectors and across national boundaries and cultures. We find the same issues whether we are working with IT folk, scientists, engineers, finance professionals, academics or sales people – they all ask us the same questions and they always start with the words 'How do I ...?'

But we have come to realise that generally, while they may have the book knowledge of what to do, they just have no idea of how to go about doing it. And we have also learned to listen to the subtext of the question. When people ask us:

> *How do I delegate a task to my subordinate?*

they are not looking for an explanation of the process; they already know the process. What they are really asking is:

> *How do I delegate to this person who used to be my friend but now works for me and I have realised is using our friendship to avoid things they don't want to do?*

Similarly a plea of:

> *I don't understand my boss*

is often code for:

> *How do I tell my boss I don't know what they want me to do without looking stupid or incompetent?*

or:

How do I give a subordinate the chance to do an important presentation without my boss thinking that I am lazy or abdicating responsibility?

We know from long experience that these questions, and many more like them, are the real management challenges that people face. We also know that it is extremely difficult to find practical answers to questions like these when you look at a management text organised in terms of theoretical topics.

When you engage with someone as their manager, you are not simply directing work; you are engaged in creating and sustaining an environment within which those people can deploy their various talents to collectively achieve great outcomes – outcomes that make a real difference in the lives of our customers and constituents.

Managers need to realise that success comes more through your ability to create and sustain positive emotional spaces for your people than from implementing best-practice processes.

Every situation that we face as a manager will have an element of uniqueness; every interaction will be coloured by the hopes, fears and aspirations of both parties. What makes management so difficult is that all too often we are blissfully unaware of our own driving forces, let alone those that drive the people we are managing.

We have built this book around 30 of the questions that we hear most in our work. These are 30 questions that can unlock understanding of what makes people tick and how you can release their full potential.

To help you navigate your way through the book, we have structured the questions into five themes as illustrated in the Mind Map on the following page.

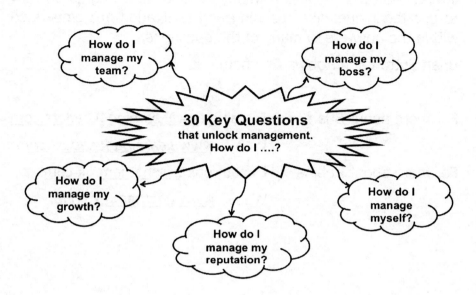

Each section will start with a more detailed Mind Map showing the killer questions that are linked to that theme. Each question is dealt with concisely, using the same format, so that you can rapidly find the help you need.

It is not our intention that you should read this book from front to back, but rather that you use it as a repository of helpful hints and tips – just enough, just when you need it and in a format that helps you see what is important and what is merely interesting.

We suggest that you start by familiarising yourself with the Mind Map and question structure. Then, when you need help, just pick out the one or two questions that most closely approximate to your specific challenge and read just what you need to get you started with solving your issue.

You will find that all the questions are structured around real dilemmas and situations that you meet in the workplace. We have not, for instance, included a question on how to coach, because coaching is a technique, a type of management intervention that applies to many situations. Thoughts on how to use techniques like coaching and facilitation are embedded within the answers to many of the questions.

Brian Sutton and Robina Chatham

For more about Brian	E-mail brian@Learning4Leaders.com
	Web *www.Learning4Leaders.com*
For more about Robina	E-mail robina@chatham.uk.com
	Web *www.chatham.uk.com*

ABOUT THE AUTHORS

Dr Brian Sutton has over 30 years' management and leadership experience. He has developed comprehensive information systems (IS) strategies, conducted large-scale re-engineering initiatives and led major organisational change. He regularly contributes articles to professional journals and speaks at major professional gatherings. He holds a Doctorate in Corporate Education, a Master's degree in Information Systems Management from the London School of Economics, and has worked extensively in both the private and public sectors in Europe and the United States. He was formerly a Professor of Systems Management in the Information Resources Management College of the National Defence University in Washington DC and is currently a visiting professor with the Institute for Work-based Learning at Middlesex University. He now runs his own learning consultancy, Learning4Leaders, that is focused on increasing the effectiveness of senior leaders.

Dr Robina Chatham has 14 years' experience in IT, culminating with the position of CIO for a leading merchant bank. She is qualified as both a mechanical engineer and a neuroscientist. Previous books include *Corporate Politics for IT Managers: How to get Streetwise* and *Changing the IT Leader's Mindset: time for revolution rather than evolution*, the latter being co-authored with Brian. She has written a number of book chapters, numerous academic papers, and articles for trade journals and magazines. She is a visiting fellow at Cranfield School of Management, and also runs her own training consultancy specialising in helping senior managers to develop political acumen, to master the art of influencing others, and hence, to increase their personal impact at board level.

ACKNOWLEDGEMENTS

We would like to offer our sincere thanks to all the people who have attended our educational programmes around the world. You have inspired and motivated us to produce this work; the shape and content of this book came about as a direct result of your questions. So when we sat down to write this book, we did not ask ourselves 'What do we know that we wish to tell other people?' Instead, we have built this book around your questions and the answers that you inspired in us, as we struggled to find the best ways of guiding you in your unique challenges. Without you, this book would never have seen the light of day.

To those of you who are familiar with our work, we hope that you will find renewed value in hearing again the ideas that we tried so hard to convey as we answered your questions. To those who are coming to us for the first time, we hope that some of the questions will inspire you to see and be different and to find new understanding in your working relationships.

We must also give a huge vote of thanks to Kate Greaves, a true friend and wonderful professional who spent many hours reading and commenting on the early drafts of this book. Kate, without your wisdom and advice, this book would be but a pale shadow of its current form. Thank you.

We are most grateful to Robert Ruehl for his encouragement throughout and for providing the foreword to this book, and to Chris Evans DPSM MBCS; ir. H.L. (Maarten) Souw RE, ICT Auditor, UWV, and Keith Bedingham, Chairman of Verax International, for their helpful reviews of the manuscript.

Last, but by no means least, we need to say a huge thank you to our respective partners, Angela and John. They are a constant support, and without their patience and understanding we could never have completed this book.

CONTENTS

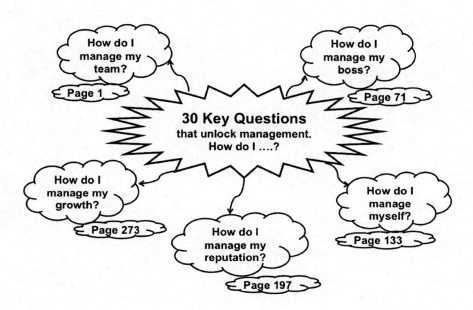

HOW DO I MANAGE MY TEAM?

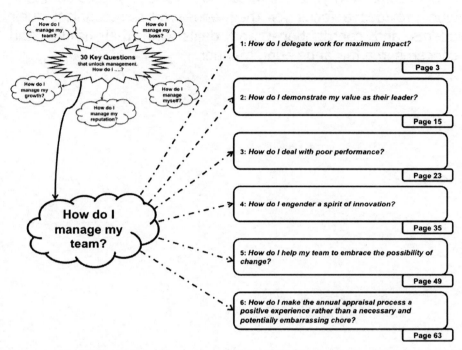

1: *How do I delegate work for maximum impact?*

Page 3

2: *How do I demonstrate my value as their leader?*

Page 15

3: *How do I deal with poor performance?*

Page 23

4: *How do I engender a spirit of innovation?*

Page 35

5: *How do I help my team to embrace the possibility of change?*

Page 49

6: *How do I make the annual appraisal process a positive experience rather than a necessary and potentially embarrassing chore?*

Page 63

The term 'team' is much overused and in most organisational settings is a synonym for – a bunch of people who happen to work for me by virtue of my position in the organisational hierarchy. But a team has the capacity to be far more than just a bunch of people.

Your job as a manager is to harness the capabilities of your 'bunch of people' and give them both a sense of direction and a modicum of freedom, so that they become a mutually supportive collective that takes a pride in achieving significant and measureable outcomes.

Leading a team is not just a matter of saying and doing the right things – how you behave and the values that you live by speak more eloquently and carry more weight than you may think. In this section, we start to give you tools that will help you to see and be different.

We will answer *six* key questions about how to build better relationships with your team, so that they see you as someone who provides a focus for their endeavours, recognises their talents and contributions, and deals with their issues and concerns in a fair and caring manner.

1: HOW DO I DELEGATE WORK FOR MAXIMUM IMPACT?

Why should I be asking this question?

Hands up all of you who don't have enough to do. We guess that not many hands went up. In fact, most of you probably have far too much to do, feel stressed that you can't keep up with all the demands on your time and seldom leave the office at the appointed hour.

We believe that if you did an honest audit of how you spend your time, you would find that about a third is spent doing tasks that you really shouldn't be doing and about another third is spent in meetings where you make little or no contribution. All of this means that, on average, only about a third of your available time is spent doing meaningful things that might actually produce value for your organisation or develop the people under your care. Let's look in a little more detail at the first two categories.

So why do you spend time doing things that don't necessarily need to be done by you? There are a number of reasons; maybe they are things you were good at before you got promoted and you feel that you do them best, or perhaps you just like doing them. Alternatively, you may find a certain therapeutic value in 'busy work', stuff that produces a physical output without much in the way of mental input. You could say that the time that you spend doing all of the above represents your *potential* energy, time that you could free up in order to do something more beneficial.

Now let's look at the third of your time that you spend in meetings, or dealing with organisational noise that has little or no relevance to your day job. This includes drafting long and complicated responses to e-mails on which you were just a 'cc' addressee, and attending meetings where you have no useful input but you feel that your organisational position demands that you are seen to be present, or you don't want to risk missing something. Generally, we find that this sort of frantic organisational arm-waving depletes your time and energy, but usually fails to produce anything in the way of valuable organisational results. You could say that this represents your *kinetic* energy, energy that you could redirect towards more purposeful ends.

The chances are that you have considerable stores of untapped *potential* and *kinetic* energy. The scientists among you will know that you cannot create new energy, but you can certainly redirect the energy that you have. The good news is that the number-one way of redirecting management energy is the art of delegation.

The impact of the issue

All managers have a duty to develop their people, so that they can achieve their full potential and, in so doing, contribute to the broader business success. This element of the manager's role is a form of organisational stewardship that requires a level of selflessness and a willingness to see the key role of management as developing people. Alas, in our experience, we find that many managers strike the wrong balance between task and people focus. It may be that they have had little exposure to people management skills in their education and have achieved their position as a result of excellent performance in their functional specialism. But, as a manager, your organisational value lies not in what you can do, but, rather, in what you can enable others to do; this is rooted in your ability to delegate.

Managers who fail to delegate, or who delegate poorly, are failing their organisation and failing in a duty of care to their people. Failure to delegate appropriately will lead to:

- people not realising their talents and underperforming;

- people not knowing what they are supposed to be doing;

- people working at cross purposes or in general confusion;

- missed deadlines, increased stress and burn-out;

- a vacuum when you need to move on and no one has the skills to succeed you. Indeed, one of the biggest issues that organisations face at all levels of management is succession.

Making sense of it all

Delegation is about giving up part of your job with the two prime objectives of:

- growing your subordinates;

- creating space in your own diary, so that your own boss can grow you by delegating part of their job to you.

If these are not your objectives, you will be effectively 'dumping' or 'offloading'; and just as you don't like to be dumped on, it is not nice to do it to others.

Delegation is really important; you have to find a way to do it and make it work for you and your people. Understanding why managers avoid delegation is the first step towards developing your own coping strategies. There are three principal psychological barriers to delegation:

- *It often involves giving up jobs that you like doing* – this is the difference between being efficient and being effective. You may scrub floors efficiently, but being effective is about directing your efforts to the right job.

- *It usually involves overcoming the fear of losing control* – we tend to think (sometimes rightly) that nobody else can do the job as well as us. When we give a task to someone, we then unfairly judge the quality of what they produce and often end up redoing all or part of it to our own exacting standards – this creates needless extra work and stress that could have been avoided.

- *There is a need to balance two, potentially competing, psychological contracts* – one with your own leadership or customer who wants the outcome of your delegated task, and one with the person you delegated to who is looking to you for help and development. These contracts tend to be implicit, rather than explicit, and we are often lax at making sure that everyone's expectations are aligned.

In addition to the psychological barriers, there is also the practical barrier that delegation takes time and effort. You need to select the right person, brief them properly, spend extra time guiding their efforts and reviewing their progress, and, finally, you need to check their output. This all takes time and, unless you create the time and space to do it properly, the chances are that your delegation process will just end in frustration and confusion.

Even when you manage to overcome the psychological and practical barriers that stop most managers from delegating, you are still faced with the issue of organisational responsibility. You need to remember that you can delegate tasks and the authority to do those tasks, but you can't delegate accountability. You are the manager if it all goes wrong; you are accountable because you have managed unwisely – pointing downwards and claiming 'the dumb cluck let me down' is just another way of saying 'I'm a useless manager who doesn't know what I am doing and can't see what is happening around me'. The buck stops with you; if you delegate and someone screws up, that someone is you.

So now let's look at some things that you can start to do now that will help you overcome all the barriers and become great at the art of delegation.

Practical advice

You need to:

- Start with the outcome: paint a clear picture of what needs to be achieved and how success will be measured.

- Brief people fully: make sure that constraints and boundaries are explained and that they have access to the information needed.

- Wind backwards from the deadline: if the output is needed by close of business next Friday, you need to set a deadline of close of business Wednesday. Remember, they probably haven't done this before, and so they will need more time and you will need time to check and possibly polish the output.

- Ensure that they have the appropriate skills – train and coach them (as appropriate).

- Direct, guide, excite and empower them (as appropriate).

- Open any doors that need to be open, so that they have access to the people and resources that they will need. Remember, unless you inform others what is going on, they may not get timely access to people and information.

- Never be tempted to take the job back.

- Praise, encourage, reward and provide feedback (as appropriate).

- Take your hands off, but keep your eyes open – be available for advice and check on key points (as appropriate).

Who you delegate to is just as important as how you delegate. You need to be careful that your chosen person has not only the skills and knowledge, but also the desire to take on the task. Not every task can, or should, be delegated and not everyone is ready to be delegated to. Use the skill/will matrix in

Figure 1 to assess how you should approach each potential delegatee.

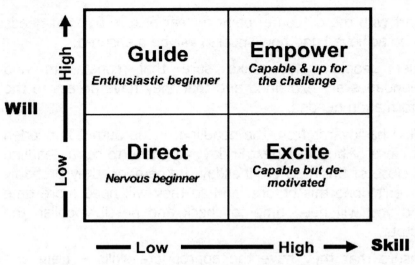

Figure 1: Skill versus will matrix[1]

Direct – these are people with low levels of skill and experience who are not used to taking on additional responsibility. If you delegate to these people, you should start with relatively straightforward, well-bounded tasks that are likely to recur soon, so that they can get additional practice at the same sort of activity. You will need to:

- Tell them what to do and how to do it.

- Check their understanding.

- Provide clear rules and deadlines.

- Give them just enough training just as they are about to take on the task.

- Provide frequent feedback against progress.

- Supervise closely – praise and nurture.

---

[1] The skill versus will matrix is credited to Max Landsberg in his book *The Tao of Coaching: Boost Your Effectiveness at Work by Inspiring and Developing Those Around You,* first published by HarperCollins in 1996.

Guide – these people are ready and eager for the challenge, but don't have the skills and knowledge required to perform well. They probably don't realise how little they know and, in their eagerness, are likely to charge into things and often make mistakes, mistakes that they may not recognise. They still needs lots of direction, but you will need to be subtle about how you do it as they tend to be impatient:

- Explain what you need them to do and suggest in broad terms how they may go about it. Suggest they bring back a detailed plan of action before they start work.

- Check their plan and confirm their understanding of what outcomes need to be produced.

- Check their understanding by asking them to think through what might go wrong and where they may need help.

- Identify people they can talk to who have done something similar.

- De-risk while learning takes place and mistakes are likely.

- Monitor, provide feedback and praise.

- Control without demotivating, and relax the frequency and depth of your controls as progress is made.

Excite – these people are well able to do the required task, but are reluctant to step up to the plate. They may have had a previous bad experience, or may not have learned to trust you. Managers often ignore, or sideline, this sort of person as being too difficult. These are key resources and need to be engaged for their benefit and the benefit of the team. You will need to:

- Explain what needs to be achieved and why they are well suited to the task.

- Spend time with them to identify the reasons for their reluctance. Is it a question of your management style, or some previous bad experience or some other personal factors?

- Energise and engage them – use them as a sounding board for ideas, show that you value their input, and include them in scoping the task and defining the outputs and quality criteria to be used.

- Develop a coaching relationship with the objective of their personal growth. Remember that the relationship between coach and coachee must be elective and trust based. You may be their manager, but you may not be the best person to coach them.

- Monitor and provide frequent feedback and praise.

- Ensure that they get wider recognition for their efforts – involve them in presentations to clients or senior leaders. Sing their praises to the rest of the team.

Empower – these people are ready and eager for the challenge; if you don't harness their energy, they will probably find a way to go around you. These are candidates for your succession planning. You should go beyond just delegating tasks to these people – you need to delegate decision making, as this is a key management skill. With these people you need to:

- Talk about the desired outcomes and ask them how they would achieve them.

- Use analytical and explorative questions to check that they have considered every angle in relation to the problem or opportunity.

- Involve them in decision making and the identification of additional resources.

- Give them responsibility for getting other people up to speed and provide the necessary training.

- Adopt a coaching style in order to grow your subordinate.

- Praise, don't ignore.

- Don't over manage.

Further food for the curious

- Keller Johnson L. Are You Delegating So It Sticks? *Harvard Business Review*, Sept. 2007:

  - This short paper sets out five big ideas to help you become more effective in delegation.

- Delegation: Gaining Time for Yourself. Book chapter excerpted from *BR Essentials – Time Management*, May 2005:

  - This is a good primer that links the related arts of delegation and time management, and provides practical tips and advice.

Things for you to work on now

Key questions to ask yourself
• If I had an extra day per week, what could I do with it that would produce long-term benefit for the company and me? • If I had one day fewer per week, what tasks could I give up, or give to someone else, without degrading the overall performance of my department? • If I had to nominate one of my team to step into my job, who would I choose and why? • What are the three or four key characteristics and behaviours that I need to see in a team member before I can start to trust and rely on them? • What have I done recently to make sure that all my team members understand those three or four characteristics that I really value?

Mini exercises you can try immediately

- Carry out a personal audit of how you have spent your time over the last two weeks. Now focus in on the actual time you spent doing tasks that produce outputs that are needed by internal or external customers. Score each of these tasks using a 1 to 5 scale, where 5 means only you could possibly do it and 5 means pretty much anyone in your team could have done it. All the tasks that scored 3 or below are strong candidates for delegation and you should make a personal commitment to find a way of delegating these tasks.

- Look at the time you spent developing members of your team – make a commitment to double the time you devote to these activities over the next two weeks and monitor how your team respond to this new approach.

- Identify two members of your team to whom you can start to delegate tasks. Use the skill/will matrix to assess how you should work with each of them. After two weeks, add another team member into the mix of people you are growing – make sure that over the next three months you spend time developing each and every member of your team. Make a new personal rule – no favourites.

Links to other questions

You may want to take a look at:

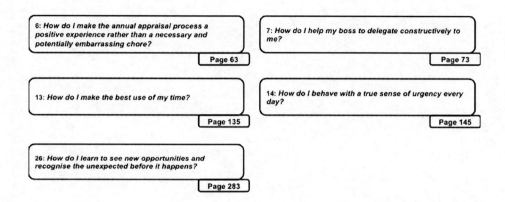

6: *How do I make the annual appraisal process a positive experience rather than a necessary and potentially embarrassing chore?*

Page 63

7: *How do I help my boss to delegate constructively to me?*

Page 73

13: *How do I make the best use of my time?*

Page 135

14: *How do I behave with a true sense of urgency every day?*

Page 145

26: *How do I learn to see new opportunities and recognise the unexpected before it happens?*

Page 283

2: HOW DO I DEMONSTRATE MY VALUE AS THEIR LEADER?

Why should I be asking this question?

We often get promoted to a managerial position because we are good at our job within our functional discipline – this may be a technical job, a clerical role or something practical. The role of a manager is very different from that of 'doer'. Often we are expected to perform as a manager with little training or guidance; we may be expected to manage former 'workmates' and, particularly within technical disciplines, staff often have little respect, or regard, for the managerial role. As we become more focused on management activities, we also become more distant from our technical roots and may find ourselves managing people who know much more than we do about the technical aspects of their job – but we still need to earn their respect.

Management is an art, rather than a science; it is not just about process and procedure: it is about communication, influence, teamwork, and the ability to inspire and motivate others. It is about keeping your eyes open and your hands off, rather than your eyes down and your hands on. It is about asking the right questions, rather than searching for or providing the right answers.

The impact of the issue

If your staff don't respect you or your role as a manager, you will not get the best out of them and sometimes you will get the very worst due to boredom, frustration, or simply because 'they can't be bothered'.

Organisations end up losing valuable team members while gaining poor managers. A recent study cited the impact on productivity to be down by some 75–80% when a manager didn't have the respect of their team members. The principal reasons included:

- Poor communication – staff did not know what was expected of them, or how they were meant to do it.

- Lack of teamwork – effort was expended in 'doing their own thing'; there were no guiding principles to bring the individual members of the team together.

- Lack of a shared and compelling vision – there wasn't anything for the team members to believe in; no group purpose or vision to see where they were heading.

- Lack of urgency – there was no drive, energy or motivation to perform and achieve.

Making sense of it all

The following mini case study puts the issue into context.

> *The story is about George, a middle manager working within the information technology (IT) department of a retail bank. The IT department underwent a major reorganisation and, in his new role, George inherited a team of 17 very intelligent and highly skilled 'super techies'. These people were exceedingly independent and had the reputation of being 'unmanageable'. They viewed their own management as a hindrance, rather than a help.*
>
> *George was well aware that he needed to make an immediate impact and create a positive impression in the eyes of his new team. He also needed to demonstrate the value of his managerial position. His predecessor had had a tough time being ignored, sidelined and sniped at and, although his predecessor was not a bad guy, he had never established his worth in the eyes of his team.*

Within a few weeks, George had them 'eating out of his hand', talking to him, asking for his help on various political issues , involving him and doing anything he asked of them. How did he achieve this?

As everyone knows, reorganisations generally involve a physical component, i.e. where people sit. There was one particularly sought-after area within the large and essentially open-plan office: it was a south-facing window location that was somewhat 'off the beaten track'. Everyone wanted to sit there and, predictably, the most competitive of George's colleagues acquired this space for his team. At management level, George's entire peer group had their own offices dotted around the big open-plan area and although responsibilities were changing, status was not; therefore none of them was required or expected to move office. George played on a colleague's weakness – his ego – and offered to swap his own larger office for his colleague's smaller one in exchange for the best physical location for his team. George instantly won his team's respect and admiration; he never told them how he had achieved this feat, but merely quipped that it was 'for him to know and them to wonder'. It was at this point that they started to understand what the role of a manager was all about and how George could be of use to them.

Practical advice

George did not try to compete with his team technically; he valued their technical expertise and took an interest in what they were doing. Similarly, they valued his leadership skills and learned the purpose and value of the managerial role.

Table 1: Dos and don'ts of management

Do	Don't
• Value your staff and take an interest in them personally. • Demonstrate, through action, that you can do things for them that they could never hope to achieve through their own efforts. • Ensure they have the tools, resources and necessary training to do the things you ask of them. • Delegate by talking about desired outcomes, rather than being prescriptive about actions. • Look for opportunities to praise. • Give the credit to your team and open doors for them to demonstrate their capability in more senior circles. • Monitor their progress, coach and develop	• Try to be one of the lads, but neither should you distance yourself. • Do their jobs for them, micro-manage them or abdicate responsibility. • Shut them out, or overtly take credit for their successes. • Expect your staff to read your mind. • Be too prescriptive about how to achieve a certain task – leave room for creativity and innovation, and give them the opportunity to do it their way. • Look for opportunities to criticise. • Blame your team when things go wrong – you can delegate authority, but not accountability. • Say one thing, but do another.

them and give them feedback.	• Lie to them – you will be found out and it will destroy trust.
• Nurture and reward talent, and involve them in selecting and growing new talent.	• Play one team member off against another.
• Build mutual trust through supportive actions.	
• Be open and honest.	

Further food for the curious

- Collins J. Level 5 Leadership. *Harvard Business Review*, Jan. 2001:

  – An excellent insight into what makes a leader truly great – a paradoxical mixture of personal humility and professional will.

Things for you to work on now

Key questions to ask yourself

- How do my staff view my role as their manager? What do they think I spend my time doing? Do they feel I justify my salary?

- What do my staff think of me personally? What do they say about me when I am not in earshot? Do they feel they can talk to me about their problems, or ask for help when they need to?

- Do I genuinely care about me team? What do I do to encourage and develop them?

- What behaviours earn me respect? What more could I do?

- What behaviours earn me trust? What more could I do?

- Do I show favouritism, or do I treat everyone equally?

- Do I unconsciously recruit in my own likeness, or do I genuinely value diversity in all its forms?

- Do they feel they have grown in the last year – if so, what can they do now that they couldn't do a year ago and what specific action of mine was the key enabler of that growth?

Mini exercises you can try immediately

- Do the rounds every morning for a month and see the difference. Ask how they are getting on; take an interest in their work and them as individuals. Take a note of key people and events in their lives. Ask questions like 'How did Andrea get on with her A levels?', etc.

- Take each member of your team aside and ask them what more you could do to help them deliver in their roles, liberate their talent and develop their skills.

- Be opportunistic – continually look for opportunities to go that extra mile for your team.

- Keep them informed – messages from on high, insights about the company, your industry sector and the market you operate in.

- Tell the truth and nothing but the truth, recognising, however, that you will sometimes need to be economical with the truth. If you can't tell them, be honest and tell them that you can't tell them.

- Always speak well of others in front of your team – that way they will think you will speak well of them (rather than badly) when they are not within earshot.

Links to other questions

You may want to take a look at:

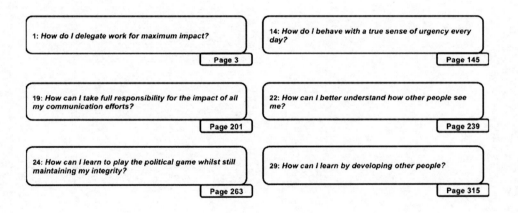

1: *How do I delegate work for maximum impact?*

Page 3

14: *How do I behave with a true sense of urgency every day?*

Page 145

19: *How can I take full responsibility for the impact of all my communication efforts?*

Page 201

22: *How can I better understand how other people see me?*

Page 239

24: *How can I learn to play the political game whilst still maintaining my integrity?*

Page 263

29: *How can I learn by developing other people?*

Page 315

3: HOW DO I DEAL WITH POOR PERFORMANCE?

Why should I be asking this question?

We are all being expected to do more with less. The pressure to produce and deliver is probably greater today than it ever has been before and, if certain individuals are not pulling their weight, then those that do so are under even greater pressure.

Poor performers inject most of the mistakes and errors into a task, which usually has a knock-on effect down the line, resulting in rework and fire-fighting. It is estimated that rework and fire-fighting increase costs by a factor of 10.

In addition, poor performers can invade an organisation like a virus; they get passed around from pillar to post as each manager, in turn, tries to rid themselves of the problem by passing the poor performer on to some other unsuspecting manager. As a consequence, poor performers often have a history of glowing recommendations and appraisals, because no one is likely to take on what is known to be a problem person. When successive managers fail to address the poor performance issue and duck the problem, it becomes very difficult, if not impossible, to take the person through formal disciplinary procedures when they do eventually get a manager with the courage to do so.

The impact of the issue

In virtually every organisation, people are your biggest budget item and, if we are honest, we could all point the finger at certain individuals who we do not perceive to be 'pulling their weight'.

Dealing with poor performance is difficult, time-consuming and fraught with danger; hence it is often avoided. For many organisations, in particular the more traditional and longer-standing ones, dealing with poor performance is one of the principal 'zones of uncomfortable debate', i.e. a key issue that needs to be addressed, that is holding the organisation back, but which is just too uncomfortable to talk about.

Making sense of it all

There are two key aspects that contribute towards one's performance: capability and attitude. When we talk about capability, we are considering the holistic combination of a person's knowledge, skills and experience. When we talk about attitude, we are considering their willingness to contribute, to collaborate and to learn — all of which should be done with a positive intent for the greater good.

When dealing with poor performance, it is important to distinguish between temporary glitches and long-term degradation. The former needs to be nipped in the bud swiftly and simply by following the steps you will find at the beginning of the practical advice section.

In the case of long-term degradation in performance, it is important to understand the root causes and to work with the person to reverse the trend. The model in Figure 2 helps us to make sense of a situation and identify the root cause.

Problem children — these people are your biggest challenge; they have neither the capability nor the right attitude. They could be young, insecure and just starting out, they could be approaching retirement and marking time, or they may have been left in the wrong job for too long and become disillusioned. Whatever the reason, they will need coaching, counselling and motivating in order to move them to a better place.

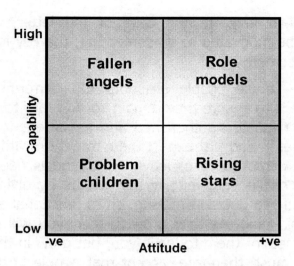

Figure 2: Performance portfolio

Rising stars – these are your people with the right attitude, but without the necessary capability. They may be youngsters just starting out, members of your team who have just taken on a new role, or possibly people who have been promoted too soon. Training and development may be the answer in the case of the former. In the case of the latter, you may need to consider adjustment to their role, or even changing it for a more suitable one. Either way, employees in this category need to be nurtured and protected. It is important to recognise that whenever someone takes on a new role, they will, by definition, be lacking capability, so the key issue is how quickly they can adjust and get up to speed. People who find themselves on the management fast-track tend to be those who demonstrate a clear capacity for rapid adjustment to new demands and an ability to very quickly achieve a high level of competence.

Fallen angels – these people have the capability, but the wrong attitude. You will need to uncover the reason for the negative attitude and then tackle the issue head on. They may be underutilised and bored, they may be in the wrong job and, hence, unhappy, they may be distracted by a personal issue, or simply just plain lazy. In the case of the latter, virtually everyone can be motivated to do something; the key is finding out what that something is.

Role models – these people are your top performers; the challenge here is to ensure they remain so. In order to achieve this, they will need to be cherished and rewarded. If you let complacency set in and just expect them to get on with it, they will either get demotivated or leave. Role models need to be stretched and challenged; initially this will be by giving them greater exposure to decision making, cross-functional activities and forward planning. As they grow further, you will need to find opportunities for them to leave you, but grow in the wider business. You must, therefore, accept that people in the role-model sector will, and indeed must, leave you and that your job is to make sure that when they move on, they do so within the company and they do so for a more challenging job.

In the following section, we will give practical advice on how to deal with the four different types of performance.

Practical advice

Before you can start to deal with any performance issue, there are a few questions you need to ask yourself, and a few things that you need to ensure are in place:

- Have you clearly communicated what is expected in terms of outcome, i.e. what needs to be achieved, when it needs to be achieved and how success will be measured?

- Does the person have the appropriate skills, or have they undergone the necessary training to enable them to complete the task?

- Do they have access to the information and resources they need?

- Challenge your own leadership ability; could part of the problem lie at your doorstep?

- Have you delegated with sufficient clarity?

- Have you been there to provide support and guidance when needed?

- Have you adequately prioritised, so that they understand what is important and why?

- Is this a real issue and not one of personality clash or difference in style?

- Do you have the real-time evidence to support your claim of poor performance? You must ensure that you are not relying upon hearsay.

Having satisfied the above, you need to tackle the issue in a timely manner, i.e. shortly after it occurs. Don't wait for appraisal time – this is far, far too late. You should immediately take the following steps in this order:

- Tell them very clearly that their performance is not of an acceptable standard.

- Give them the opportunity to explain why their performance was not up to standard. If, for example, something dreadful had happened to a family member the previous day, you would feel very foolish if you had just laid into them for not performing at their best.

- Be very clear about why the performance is substandard and the impact of their performance on others and the wider context of the organisation as a whole.

- Say how you feel about the situation.

- State, explicitly, what is at stake.

- If appropriate, be honest about your own part in creating the issue.

- Give them the opportunity to explain the situation from their point of view. Keep quiet and actively listen to what they have to say.

- Confirm a common understanding of the issue and then agree a sequence of steps necessary to rectify the situation.

- Agree any follow-up actions that you, the manager, need to take.

- Make sure that they have a workable plan for what they need to do and agree when and how you will check on their progress. Thank them for their input.

- Keep clear records to aid follow-up activities and support future conversations.

- Keep on top of the situation – do not expect a quick fix, but also do not let it slip off your priority list.

Now we will move on to consider how best to deal with the issue of long-term degradation in performance. We need to use a feedback and developmental approach appropriate to the person's capability and attitude, and will use the model outlined in the previous section to structure our advice.

Dealing with your problem children – the first step is to find out what the problem is with your problem child. Are they a nervous starter or long-serving cynic? Have they been over-promoted, or ended up in a role that bores them to tears? Once you have identified the root cause, you will need to determine the most appropriate corrective action. This may include any one or a number of the following:

- Training – would the person benefit from either skill-based training or behavioural training?

- Coaching – would this person benefit from being asked some probing questions to challenge their thinking and behaviour, in particular some reflective questions to get them thinking about why they did what they did. You should also encourage them to honestly examine the motives that underpinned their actions. Finally, you need to help them think through the impact that their poor performance is having on others.

- Mentoring – are they lacking in self-confidence and in need of reassurance or affirmation from someone with greater experience?

- Motivation – could you enhance their role in any way to make it more appealing?

- Counselling – do they need professional help to resolve a personal issue?

- Consider a change in job role – are they in the right job? Have they been over-promoted, and are they struggling with both the task and their emotions as a consequence?

- If none of the above strategies achieve the desired result, you may need to take people through formal disciplinary procedures. Ensure that you follow the formal process, as laid down by your HR (human resources) department, starting with an informal verbal warning and progressing, if need be, to formal written warnings.

- As a last resort, you might need to consider managing them out of the organisation or towards early retirement. Here is where you may benefit from the assistance of your HR department and outplacement organisations.

Dealing with your rising stars – the first step is to understand their potential. Are they bright, able and quick to learn, or do they get there through tenacity and hard work? Once you have established their potential and what interests and motivates them, you will be able to agree an appropriate developmental plan. Your prime tools will include:

- Training – this may be skill-based or behavioural training.

- Coaching – would this person benefit from being asked some probing questions to clarify their understanding of what is expected of them and how confident they feel in achieving it, some explorative questions to open their mind to new possibilities, or some fresh questions to challenge their basic thinking and 'eternal truths'?

- Mentoring — would this person benefit from mirroring someone with greater experience or guidance in their judgement of situations and their consequential decision making?

Dealing with your fallen angels — the first step is to uncover the root cause of the bad attitude. Is it because they are bored, unhappy, disgruntled, feeling bullied or just plain lazy? Have they been ignored, forgotten about or ended up in the wrong job? You may wish to consider:

- Coaching — would this person benefit from being asked some probing questions to invite more detail in relation to their attitude problem, some reflective questions to get them thinking about why they behave the way they do and to examine their motives, some affective questions to consider the impact their attitude is having on others, or some explorative questions to open their mind to new perspectives?

- Mentoring — could the issue be one of lack of self-confidence? If so, they may be in need of affirmation or guidance from someone with greater experience than themselves.

- Counselling — do they need professional help to resolve a personal issue?

- Do they feel bullied? — if so, the problem may well lie at your doorstep (*see 'My boss is a bully, what can I do, how do I cope?'*).

- Job enrichment — could you enhance or supplement their role to make it more fulfilling/appealing?

- Consider a change in job role — do they need greater responsibility or a new challenge?

The final quadrant of the model deals with people you have classified as role models. You would not expect to have performance issues with these people, but that does not mean that you can afford to ignore them. With these people, your focus should be on maintaining and sustaining actions and providing intellectual and professional challenge.

Ensuring your role models remain just that – such valuable members of your team will need to be cherished, nurtured and rewarded. If you don't, they will either leave, or become fallen angels. Focus on the following actions:

- Provide opportunities for personal development and preparing them for the next step up.

- Give them frequent and positive feedback – ensure that they know that they are doing a good job, and that they know how much you value and appreciate them.

- Coach them – specifically in areas where they will need to exercise judgement and decision making. Stretch them and encourage them to aim for higher goals; challenge them to think the unthinkable and to generate new insights.

- Reward their achievements and celebrate their successes.

- Give them opportunities to represent you in discussions with other departments/businesses.

- Help them to develop their circle of influence, and to develop wider knowledge of the business and its operating environment.

- Involve them in discussions about strategic direction and planning the development of junior colleagues.

- Identify opportunities for them to act as coaches for junior colleagues.

- Could you enhance their job in any way to increase their job satisfaction?

Any discussions about performance issues will be emotionally charged. Therefore, it is imperative that you remember the importance of tone, body language and facial expression. Make use of silence to help both of you to get in touch with what you really want to say, and ensure there is space for reflection and active listening. Ensure at all times that you engage in a genuine two-way conversation, rather than letting your discussions deteriorate into a one-way monologue.

Get to know your staff; understand both their hearts and their minds. Ensure the dialogue is ongoing. Use active questioning to establish what excites and what frustrates them. Actively listen to the nuances and subtext to get beneath the surface. Develop a strong interest in motivational psychology. Be prepared to accept short-term pain for long-term gain. Your reward will be motivated, energised and loyal staff.

Further food for the curious

- Scott S. *Fierce Conversations: Achieving Success at Work and in Life, One Conversation at a Time*. The Penguin Group, New York (2002):
  - An enlightening and practical book on achieving results through skilful and courageous dialogue.

Things for you to work on now

Key questions to ask yourself

- Am I concerned about the performance of any member of my team? The answer is probably yes, otherwise you would not be reading this question.

- If so, how have I dealt with the situation in the past? What is my approach towards dealing with poor performance?

- If you do have poor performers, how has this been handled within the appraisal process and formal HR procedures?

- What is the general attitude and approach towards

poor performance in my company?

- Honestly consider if you, yourself, could be part of the problem.

Mini exercises you can try immediately

- Use the attitude versus capability matrix to analyse the performance of your team. Categorise each member of your team and then plot them on the matrix. How many do you have in each category? (Your analysis is for your eyes only – keep it safe from prying eyes.)

- Draw up and agree a plan for dealing with one of your 'fallen angels'. Analyse the experience – what went well and what didn't go so well? Now refine your approach and repeat with another of your fallen angels.

- Draw up and agree a plan for dealing with one of your 'rising stars'. Analyse the experience – what went well and what didn't go so well? Now refine your approach and repeat with another of your rising stars.

- Having learned from these two groups, you are now ready to tackle your 'problem children'.

Links to other questions

You may want to take a look at:

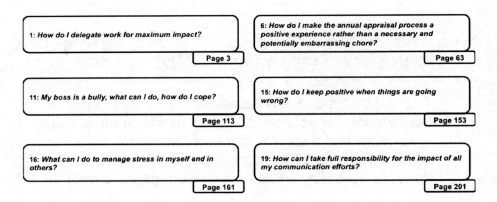

4: HOW DO I ENGENDER A SPIRIT OF INNOVATION?

Why should I be asking this question?

It is common to presume that innovation is always the result of a bright idea and that such bright ideas only occur inside the heads of seriously clever people, people who are not in any way like us, people who are collected together in a special department, often called 'research and development'.

Nothing could be further from the truth. Increasingly, we see innovation not as something that occurs inside the heads of smart people, but rather as something that happens in the spaces between inquisitive people. What really makes innovation work is connecting people, especially people who think differently and have different skills and experience. Innovation is not the same as creativity – the focus is not on conjuring up something amazing out of nothing, but rather on finding new ways of plugging together existing knowledge to deliver new and exciting outcomes.

We often hear people say 'Oh, I'm not a creative person', or 'I'm no good at thinking strategically', or 'I've never had an original idea'. The manager's job is to help people to rise above such self-limiting statements of personal inadequacy. We are all innovators in our own way and, when we engage constructively with people who see the world in a slightly different light from ourselves, we open up the possibility of producing great new insights and new ways of working.

The impact of the issue

Our organisations face many challenges; doing more with fewer resources, changing demographics, skills shortages, environmental pressures, evolving legislative structures and financial pressures to name but a few. One thing is for sure, doing more of the same, or getting better at what we currently do, is not a sustainable model. This is not a new phenomenon and is captured nicely by one of the greatest thinkers of our time:

> *The significant problems that we face cannot be solved with the same level of thinking that created them.*
>
> **Albert Einstein**

Or, to put it in the form of a mantra increasingly popular with senior leaders:

> *If you always do what you always did, you will always get what you always got.*

Innovation is about finding combinations of new and existing insights that generate new possibilities for our customers to fulfil their 'jobs to be done'.

Making sense of it all

Being great at innovation is not a matter of luck. Organisations and teams that are good at innovating tend to have a characteristic culture, a culture that values constructive questioning, healthy co-operation and an openness to new experiences and ways of thinking. Innovations are most likely to happen when a team has:

- A shared purpose that inspires them and ignites action. Interestingly, such a purpose is seldom created as a result of a top-down edict; it comes through curiosity, questioning and challenging each other to achieve something special.

- A willingness to truly co-operate, to give freely of personal resources to help others to develop and test their ideas. This requires an emphasis on the greater good, rather than on local and/or short-term gains, and it involves collaboration and a preparedness to compromise on individual interests in order to achieve the best overall result.

- An openness to engage with people who think and see the world differently. We often ignore things that are right in front of our eyes because we have long considered them to be irrelevant, but someone new to a situation sees everything for the first time and sees with a mind that has different values and experiences. We increase our chance of seeing anew when we cross organisational or industry boundaries – innovations nearly always come by applying something from one field or scientific discipline to another field or scientific discipline. People who can span boundaries are critical to increasing innovation.

Innovation also needs to be managed differently than business as usual. In business as usual, the emphasis has to be on right first time and every time. However, in order to innovate, we must experiment, and when we experiment, we must expect to fail. So, managing for an innovative culture means that we must strive for ultimate success, while embracing the possibility of many small failures along the way. We should embrace those failures and view them as a learning opportunity.

In essence, we normally strive to perfect what we already know. By contrast, innovation usually involves grappling with unknown quantities and unpredictable consequences; under these circumstances, hitting the jackpot first time is unlikely and perfection is well downstream.

For innovation to thrive, we need to cultivate a culture that values people who try, however imperfectly, to seize the unknown. Figure 3 depicts the three pillars of an innovative culture built upon the solid foundations of a highly tuned productive capacity.

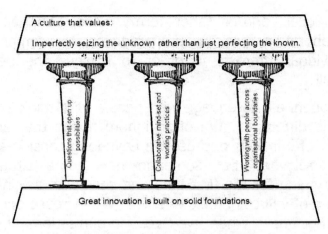

A culture that values:

Imperfectly seizing the unknown rather than just perfecting the known.

Questions that open up possibilities

Collaborative mind-set and working practices

Working with people across organisational boundaries

Great innovation is built on solid foundations.

Figure 3: Three pillars of capability

The three core capabilities that underpin innovation are:

- *Questions that open up possibilities.* Every innovation starts with a question, and the very best innovations emerge when we ask questions that challenge conventional wisdom and open the possibility of being different. The problem is that, most of the time, most of us are not very good at asking questions. Or, when we do ask questions, we use our questions as a weapon to put people down, rather than as a mechanism to lift people up. Consider the following points:

  - Research shows that poorly performing teams tend to ask 1 question for every 20 statements. High-performing teams have a ratio much closer to 1 to 1.

  - A good question can act as an igniting catalyst for a team and challenge and inspire them – a bad question can debilitate them and freeze them into inactivity.

  - The best questions are future-focused and challenge existing thinking, collective wisdom and organisational or industry paradigms; they may shake deeply held personal values or beliefs.

- *Collaborative mind-set and working practices.* To collaborate means to work with others on a joint project. To co-operate means to be of assistance, or willing to assist. In order to stimulate innovation, collaboration has to be much more than just working together; it must embrace a sense of shared purpose, mutual responsibility and commitment to achieve win–win outcomes:

- Too much of our organisational behaviour is based on advocacy – this leads to a feeling that in order to win, others must lose.

- Being collaborative doesn't mean going with the flow or being unwilling to challenge what is expected. Collaboration works best when we listen respectfully, value and build on the ideas of others, and be willing to back winning ideas even when to do so may require personal courage and commitment. We show our desire to collaborate when we start using the word 'AND', rather than the word 'BUT', when discussing new ideas.

- People collaborate most effectively when there is a common work product and a shared pride in the outcome. We need to see a willingness to volunteer to give our own scarce resources for the good of someone else's idea.

- *Working with people across organisational boundaries*. The truly great innovations in the world usually came about when we suddenly found a new way of seeing something that had always been there in front of us. Often, we see something being used for one purpose and start to ask the question of how that idea could be adapted to serve a completely different purpose. In order to increase the probability of this sort of breakthrough, we need to increase the amount of time that we spend with people who have a totally different experience to our own, and therefore interpret situations differently and see the world with different eyes. In short, we need to get out of our comfort zone and spend less time surrounded by people who think and act just like us. Think about the following observations:

- A great organisational paradox is that breakthrough innovations and novel combinations are most likely to occur when you put people together who bring ideas from different sectors or scientific disciplines, and yet in our organisations we group people, so that they are surrounded by people who think and act just like them.

- People who see, or experience, something for the first time are likely to ask apparently facile questions that lead to great new insights.

- We too often ignore insights from lower down the organisational totem pole, or from people with fewer qualifications than ourselves. Insight can, and does, come from anywhere – great innovators are constantly looking for different perspectives.

Practical advice

We will split our practical advice into three sections to reflect the three distinct capabilities that are so important for stimulating innovation. Let's start with ways to stimulate questions that open up possibilities:

- Think of questions as a way to kick-start thinking and learning – ask open, non-leading questions and phrase them in the future tense. Look for questions that challenge deeply held beliefs.

- Rather than telling people what to do, try describing an outcome that you would like to achieve and then ask questions like:

  - What would it feel like to work in that kind of environment?

  - If we had this in place, what would we be able to do that we can't do now?

  - What do we need to put in place now to start moving us in this direction?

- What can you do individually that could support us all in this change?

- Ask your team what one thing we could do that would transform the service we give to our customers:

  - Get your team to prioritise the ideas.

  - Get them to work up some of the ideas into a practicable proposal.

  - Get them to vote on which of the ideas are the most likely to be successful.

  - See if you can start an experiment to check out the validity of the most popular idea – see how many people are prepared to invest some of their own spare time on the project.

  - Once you have a working hypothesis, get the team to present it to management and see if you can get funding to take it further. Treat it like making a pitch to the bank manager for funding to start a new business.

Now let's look at some things you can do to create or support a collaborative mindset and collaborative working practices. The first thing to realise is that stimulating collaboration starts with your recruitment and induction processes:

- When recruiting, we tend to look for people who can do the things we do and appear to be enthusiastic about how we do it. We are attracted to people who think like we do and hold similar values to ourselves. The problem with this is that we run the risk of hiring a bunch of people just like us; this is commonly referred to as the 'comfortable clone syndrome'. When we recruit, we have an opportunity to bring in fresh ideas and new thinking – so actively look for people who:

  - ask you why you do things the way you do and look unimpressed when you explain why;

- people who have a passion for something and are looking for an opportunity to try it out in your company;

- people who ask you challenging questions during the interview — if they are confident enough to question you in an interview situation, the chances are they will continue to question you and everything once they are on the team. People who ask constructive questions are worth their weight in gold.

- Our induction processes tend to focus on getting people to understand our processes, systems, values and beliefs. The idea is that the quicker we can get people to be just like us, the better. Actually, while we want new recruits to understand what we are trying to achieve, we should be slightly more wary about indoctrinating them into our ways, especially when a key element of their role is to be innovative in the solutions they produce. Try some of the following:

  - Don't be too concerned if people appear to be slow at learning your processes or reluctant to embrace your ways. Instead of pushing harder to make them conform, ask them questions to understand their concerns and reservations.

  - Focus on introducing new team members to peers who have a track record of questioning and producing good ideas.

  - After two to three weeks, ask your new people what one process or practice they find most frustrating and why. Allow them to suggest better ways to achieve the same objectives. Get them to run a short workshop with a handful of your best thinkers to discuss the process or practice and how it could be better.

  - Try to create a peer-to-peer network that spans all sections of the business — arrange regular meetings and encourage people to freely discuss the issues they are facing – try to get informal groups to work together to develop and test new ideas in action.

- Collaboration is not about meekly doing what you are asked to do and joining in – it is about volunteering for a task because you are inspired by the possibility of producing a new level of service or a previously unimagined product. Before people can volunteer, they need to know what is going on and they need to be engaged. Try some of the following ideas:

    - Create an intranet site, or collaboration space, where your team members can post their ideas. Establish a process where they can vote for the ideas they think are the best.

    - Allow your team members to volunteer their services to develop the ideas that are top of the list.

    - Encourage your team members to always ask 'Why?'.

Finally, let's look at some of the things you can do to stimulate working across organisational boundaries and bringing ideas in from the outside:

- Get some magazines and journals from completely different disciplines – if you are an engineer, perhaps you could get professional journals on medicine, the bio-tech industry, oil exploration, toys and gaming, furniture design, geology, photography, etc. Encourage your team members to look through the articles and each month organise a short 30-minute discussion around the article that people found most fascinating. Get them to work up three things that made this story so compelling – then challenge them to think of ways in which you could apply similar insight to your own industry.

- Arrange a short-term transfer for one of your team into a completely different role in another part of the organisation.

When they come back, get them to brief your team on their experience. Suggest that they focus most on:

- How are the people in the other role different?

- What are their main priorities?

- What are the big assumptions that appear to underpin their decision-making?

- What do they worry about most?

- What do they consider to be their biggest success in the last 12 months and why are they so proud of it?

- What three things do they do that our team should try to copy?

- What three things do they do that our team should try to avoid doing ourselves?

• Find opportunities for you to visit different industries and see how they do things. Think of it as a benchmarking exercise where the aim is to see how people work collaboratively, rather than trying to copy their process. Focus on the following areas:

- How does someone with a good idea bring it to the attention of the management?

- What percentage of the ideas that they are working on came from outside their organisation (a process increasingly known as open innovation)?

- When they have a problem they can't solve, how do they look for potential solution providers? Some organisations call this process scouting, i.e. looking for third-party providers who can bring new insight to an existing problem.

- What is their process for assessing the potential value of new ideas?

- Who decides who works on the key projects? What potential is there for people to volunteer their services or get involved with things that interest them?

Further food for the curious

- Johnson S. *Where Good Ideas Come From; the Natural History of Innovation*. London, Allen Lane, a division of Penguin (2010):

    - A fascinating read that charts the genesis of many great innovations and points to five key principles that underpin the development of all great ideas.

- Gratton L. Hot Spots: *Why Some Companies Buzz with Energy and Innovation and Others Don't*. Prentice Hall. London (2007):

    - This book points to four conditions that increase the likelihood that spontaneous innovation will flourish in organisations.

Things for you to work on now

Key questions to ask yourself
<ul><li>What structures do you have in place to help members of your team engage with people from different departments, industries or professions?</li><li>How many ideas come from outside your immediate team?</li><li>How can you encourage people who don't work for you to contribute towards solving your problems or producing new ideas?</li><li>How can you create a mechanism where team members have an element of choice about which projects to invest their personal resources in?</li></ul>

- Is it feasible for you to create an internal open market for ideas, where your team members can vote for those ideas that they feel are the biggest winners?

- How do people interact with each other within your organisation – is their approach more competitive or more collaborative?

- What is the attitude of your organisation towards failure?

- How easily could you articulate your current 'shared purpose'?

Mini exercises you can try immediately

- In your meetings, start to keep a tally of the ratio of questions to statements and the ratio of supportive comments to negative, or blocking, comments.

- Work over a period of weeks to adjust the balance, so that people are more supportive of each other and ask more incisive questions.

- Arrange for a total outsider to sit in on your next team problem-solving session – take careful note of the different perspective that this brings and see how this impacts on the conversations you have.

- Count the number of open versus closed questions and leading versus non-leading questions that you and others ask.

- Look at your recruitment process – do you seek clones or do you seek diversity? What could you do to generate the selection of greater diversity in terms of background, approach and thinking style?

- Look at your current induction process and see what you can change so that you value the ideas that new people bring and give them a chance to share their experience.

- Organise a day a month in a different department or organisation for a period of at least six months.

- Book yourself on a study tour.

- Take out a subscription to a magazine or journal in a field of interest different from your own.

Links to other questions

You may want to take a look at:

20: *How do I increase my circle of influence?* Page 211	**23:** *How can I be seen as someone who helps change happen?* Page 251
26: *How do I learn to see new opportunities and recognise the unexpected before it happens?* Page 283	**27:** *What can I do to get better at seeing the big picture and thinking strategically?* Page 293

5: HOW DO I HELP MY TEAM TO EMBRACE THE POSSIBILTY OF CHANGE?

Why should I be asking this question?

For many people, the prospect of organisational change can trigger a strong, even overwhelming, sense of anxiety. In extreme cases, a department, or even a whole organisation, can drift into a state of listless near-paralysis. These are the conditions that often result in entrenched resistance to the idea of change and can be the death knell for new ways of working, or the adoption of new behaviours. As a manager, your job is to guide your people through these turbulent times.

Most organisational change initiatives fail to produce the outcomes that were hoped for at the outset. Sometimes this is because the environment moves on again and the change is no longer relevant, but, more often, the issue is that not enough people really appreciated the need to change before significant damage occurred. Once we get to that stage, change is like pushing a rock uphill; it is difficult, exhausting and essentially futile and, if you let up for a moment, it will roll back and squash you.

To be successful at preparing people for change, you have to start the process before they even get the idea that a change may be needed. In the same way that a gardener spends time enriching and preparing the soil in flower beds long before the time comes to plant out the seedlings, you, as a manager, need to work to create a state of readiness for change. You need to give your team the tools and the attitudes to see the positives in prospective changes and the will to take action and make those changes a working reality.

The impact of the issue

Change is now an ever-present feature of organisational life, yet our understanding of how to bring about change in human systems is still tenuous, and many managers feel ill-equipped to deal with the human fallout from their change initiatives.

The thinking behind how we bring about and manage organisational change has moved on considerably in the last 20 years and now most managers appreciate that change is a process, but most of the models used to guide managers view change as something that you do to other people, or other systems. Yes, the models emphasise the importance of taking people with you, having a vision, communicating urgency, building a network of committed people, etc. yet, laudable though all this is, they are still stuck in the belief that change is something we do to others. The reality is that where human behaviour is concerned, change can only come from the inside; each and every individual must come to the decision to change for themselves, and for each person, the trigger for that change will be different.

When faced with change, a very few people will find it exciting and exhilarating, and a similarly small proportion will become very active and vocal opponents of anything that looks different. But the *normal* reaction to change is *ambivalence*. Let's be clear about this; ambivalence does not mean *don't care*. To be ambivalent is 'to simultaneously hold two opposed and conflicting attitudes or emotions'. Because change is all around us, most people have learned to be ambivalent until they understand how the proposed change will affect them at a personal level. So we have a position where people cannot motivate themselves to change, unless and until their very personal ambivalence is resolved.

So at any given time, most of the people who work for you will be ambivalent to change – this means that they are subconsciously caught in a conflict of opposed attitudes and emotions that results in competing commitments. These competing commitments will undermine morale and performance and could, ultimately, paralyse any change initiative.

Making sense of it all

People react to change, or the threat of change, at an emotional level. Change evokes strong emotions and that internal turmoil tends to produce observable behaviour patterns. Much of the thought about human change comes from working with people undergoing profound change; often this work has been done by clinical psychologists working with people coping with bereavement, terminal illness or substance abuse and dependency. These ideas are then picked up, generalised and reshaped to fit the world of organisational behaviour.

The most widely known model comes from pioneering work carried out by Elizabeth Kübler-Ross and published in her book *On Death and Dying* (1969). In this she identifies five stages of transition for people facing death, namely: denial, anger, bargaining, depression and, finally, acceptance. She was at pains to stress that the order of these stages is not necessarily chronological; nor will everyone experience all five stages. It is also not a linear process – people don't progress neatly from one stage to the next; they experience setbacks and can flip from stage to stage.

The model was quickly appropriated by organisational psychologists and subsequently expanded, and is often now termed the *change cycle* or the *change roller coaster*. A typical representation of the roller coaster is shown in Figure 4.

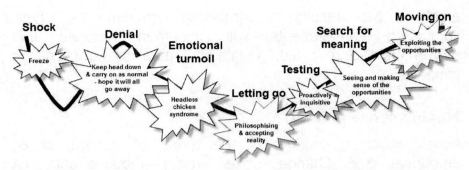

Shock

Freeze

Denial

Keep head down
& carry on as normal
- hope it will all
go away

Emotional
turmoil

Headless
chicken
syndrome

Letting go

Philosophising
& accepting
reality

Testing

Proactively
inquisitive

Search for
meaning

Seeing and making
sense of the
opportunities

Moving on

Exploiting the
opportunities

Figure 4: Behaviour through the transition curve[2]

There can be no doubt that the Kübler-Ross curve is a valuable insight into the human response to change, but, sadly, the change roller-coaster concept has been widely shared by people with no understanding of where it comes from or its underpinning philosophy – the result is that too many managers wrongly believe that this is some form of mechanistic process where everyone goes through all the stages in this order, and that their role as a manager is to help their people get through the stages as quickly as possible. Such a belief is less than helpful and can do irreparable harm to people who are in a vulnerable emotional state.

The reality is that most people experience change and the change cycle in many different layers for the different changes that we are facing. Most of us can cope with a few changes at one time, but for each of us there comes a time when we reach a tipping point where we fail to cope. At this point, we can become overwhelmed with ambivalence as a sort of defence mechanism.

More recent work has focused on trying to understand the root causes of personal ambivalence or, in the words of Kegan and Laskow Lahey, competing commitments. This is the idea that

---

[2] Behaviour through the transition curve is based on an adaptation of the grief cycle, devised and published by Elizabeth Kübler-Ross in her seminal work *On death and dying* in 1969, first published in the UK by Tavistock Publications Ltd in 1970.

people's backgrounds, early experiences, education, etc. cause them to adopt 'big assumptions' about how the world works – these mental frameworks are often unexamined and unconscious, but they colour everything we see and generate the internal competing commitments. A competing commitment may blindside us to the need for change, or paralyse us into a state of confused inaction where we know that we need to change, but cannot find the motivation to do so, or to maintain our course of action.

Current thinking indicates that in order for people to find the motivation to change, they need help to surface and confront their competing commitments. It is becoming clear that people don't change because they hear your words, no matter how eloquent and persuasive they may be; they change when they take part in a discussion about their own competing commitments and the roots of their ambivalence. This sort of discussion is called *change talk* and is at the heart of a technique practised by clinical psychologists called *motivational interviewing*. Getting people to engage in *change talk* is a critical element of motivational interviewing. While we recognise that it is unrealistic, and possibly dangerous, to expect managers to become amateur clinical psychologists, it is reasonable to expect managers to understand that their role is not to *talk at their people* about change, but rather to *openly engage their people* in *change talk* in such a way as to allow them to surface and explore their own competing concerns and commitments, and through this understanding find a route to their own motivation to change.

Practical advice

If you have had any change management training, you have probably come to view organisational change as a process. Typically that process will have four or five stages. The model in Figure 5 has been mapped against the eight factors for successful change that are set out in Kotter's book *Our Iceberg is Melting*.

1. Set the scene • **Create a sense of urgency** • **Pull together the guiding team**	**2. Decide what to do** • **Develop the change vision and strategy**
3. Make it happen • **Communicate for buy-in** • **Empower others to act** • **Produce short-term wins**	**4. Make it stick** • **Don't let up** • **Create a new culture**

Figure 5: Model for implementing change

Helpful and insightful though this is, you must remember that this is a model of how you implement change, not how people respond to change.

If we are looking for a model that maps against this change process, but explicitly deals with human reaction to change, we would be better to take the five-stage model that underpins motivational interviewing and the world of competing commitments. This model helps those making the organisational change to keep on track and to embrace best practice in change management. It identifies the five stages of change as being:

- pre-thinking
- thinking
- deciding
- doing
- maintaining.

The model reminds you of your role as the leader of your people during change.

The manager's role and approach differs in each of the stages – yes, you need to do all the things associated with the process model of change, but, in addition, you should be working on a one-to-one basis with your people to help them understand their motivations and engage in *change talk*. Here is some general guidance on how to approach each of the stages:

- *Pre-thinking stage* – when people are in this stage, they are not yet considering change, or are unwilling, or unable, to accept that change may be necessary. The manager's role is to:

  - Start to raise doubt in their minds that things can go on as they are.

  - Give them information about the risks and problems we face; give concrete examples of how the same sorts of problems have beset other departments, companies or industries and the consequential fallout from these issues. Involve them in brainstorming and prioritising the risks that could impact your change initiative.

  - Bring an awareness of the outside to the inside. This form of open and honest communication about the changing world and our place in it will reduce the shock that we tend to experience at the start of the change curve.

- *Thinking stage* – now people can see the possibility of change, but are ambivalent about the change. They cannot find within them the motivation to begin the change journey and remain uncertain and unconvinced that it is the right thing for them. This is the time when you need to engage in real change talk:

  - Bring the reasons for ambivalence to the surface.

- Discover together the big assumptions that we hold about how things work and what our place is in the scheme of things.

- Avoid being judgemental.

- Don't take sides, but do encourage people to challenge their own beliefs and support them in the process through reflective questioning, affirmation and summarising. This will help people to get through the denial phase of the change curve.

- *Deciding stage* – they are now convinced of the need to change and are motivated to do so, but remain unclear about what they need to do and how they should go about it. This is a critical stage and the manager now has a role in:

  - helping them think through what they might do first – maybe create a simple plan of things they can do tomorrow or next week; avoid the long term and keep things low key;

  - exploring with them through questioning and active listening what they might do if things don't go to their plan;

  - using reflective listening and affirmation to help them through the emotional turmoil of the change curve.

- *Doing stage* – they are now actively taking steps to achieve the change, but their steps are hesitant and faltering – they have not stabilised themselves into new routines and patterns of thinking, and are prone to doubt and uncertainty. As a manager you can help by:

  - helping them to be realistic about what they can achieve and to plan in terms of small steps;

  - using open questions and affirmation to help them develop coping strategies when they experience frustration and setbacks;

- helping them look for opportunities to reinforce positive behaviours and anchor them in their daily routines;

- discussing openly things that are good about the new ways of working and things that are not so good; avoid being judgemental;

- giving them support and guidance and the resources they need to experiment with new ideas and ways of working. They are now letting go of their old ways and key elements will be the space to try out new things and help when they hit speed bumps and roadblocks.

- *Maintaining stage* – they have now achieved the change goals they set themselves and are working to sustain the new patterns of behaviour and ways of thinking and seeing the world. As a manager, your role now is to help by:

  - maintaining supportive contact;

  - monitoring progress against personal objectives and helping to set new short- and medium-term goals;

  - helping them to find new meaning and motivation as they settle into new working patterns and practices;

  - helping them to increase their circle of influence, so that they can create a new support network for themselves.

As you try to help your staff through the phases of change, you will find that you increasingly need to call upon and develop four key skills. Fortunately these are not new skills; they are the same skills that you use to coach, provide feedback, delegate and facilitate group problem solving. They are:

- Open-ended questioning – this is how you get *change talk* going. Use question structures such as:

  - How would you like things to be different?

  - What would you be able to achieve if we could take 'x' out of the way?

- What are the good things about the current situation and what are the not so good things about it?

- Affirming statements – this is an important skill and is not just about saying nice things or stroking people. Your aim is to:

  - Recognise strength when you see it; sometimes it is easier for you to see that they have made a big step than it is for them to see that they have moved.

  - Share with them the things that they have done that you really appreciate and would like them to do more of. Get them to give similar feedback to you.

  - Once you have built a trusting relationship, you can move on to talk about the things that they are doing that are less effective and that you would like them to do less of. Similarly, you can have a discussion about the effectiveness of your own behaviours.

  - Build their confidence in their own ability to change.

  - Be genuine and make sure that your actions, words and body language all match.

- Reflective listening – when you ask questions you need to become very good at listening. You also need to show that you are listening and understanding them by reflecting back what you hear:

  - In the first instance, stick to simple reflection – repeat and rephrase what they have told you, sticking as closely to their words as possible.

  - Later, and if you suspect that there may be a deeper meaning behind the words being used, you can start to work towards amplified reflection. This is where you paraphrase and then use gentle probing or analytical questions to find out what's going on below the surface. In such cases, how you say things is as important as what you say – avoid any form of words that might convey judgement, or cast doubt on their right to hold and express the views that they have.

- Summarising – this is a special case of reflective listening and generally is used as a transition point in a conversation. You might use structures such as:

    - Let me see if I understand what you are saying …

    - I think what you are saying is … in which case that might lead us to wonder about how we might …

Practise these four key skills, but remember the context in which you use them.

Further food for the curious

- Kegan R and Laskow Lahey L. The Real Reason People Won't Change. *Harvard Business Review* (2001):

    - This article introduces the idea of competing commitments; subconscious hidden goals that compete with their stated commitments. It is an interesting paper that will make you examine why you believe the things you do, how you came to believe them and how those beliefs can constrain your options for action.

- Miller WR and Rollnick S. *Motivational Interviewing*, 2nd edition. New York, Guildford Press (2002):

    - This is not for the faint-hearted, but for anyone who is serious about finding out more on the subject of motivational interviewing, this is a great place to start.

- Kotter JP. *Our Iceberg is Melting*. London, Macmillan (2006):

    - This is a retelling of the *Heart of Change* as a metaphor. It is simple to read and engaging, while losing none of the theoretical underpinning of his work. It is an ideal text to give to your team members to help them focus on the stages of change and the challenges of gaining wide acceptance that change needs to happen.

Things for you to work on now

Key questions to ask yourself

- How much time do I actually spend listening to the concerns of my team members? Not just fobbing them off, but really listening.

- How good am I at picking up on the concerns and feelings of the people in my team and immediate working environment?

- If this is not a natural ability for me, who can I turn to that I trust who has a natural sense of empathy, and how can I work with them to compensate for my own lack of awareness?

- What are my own 'big assumptions' and consequential competing commitments?

- How much of my time do I spend getting people ready for the possibility of change?

Mini exercises you can try immediately

- Do a personal audit on a recent change that has impacted your team. What was your role in that change? How did people react to the change and to your role? Was the pattern of the change 'decide – announce – defend', or was it more in the form of 'consult – decide – sell'?

- Read the recommended article 'The real reason people won't change' – study the table that takes you through the questions to uncover your competing commitments and their underpinning big assumptions. Do the exercise for yourself.

- Now you have a clearer idea of your own competing commitments, reflect on how your own big assumptions can get in the way of you seeing opportunities to change and be different.

- Practise reflective listening when talking to one of your team members about a new skill or task you want them to step up to. Afterwards, ask them for feedback on how they felt when you summarised their thoughts and made affirmative statements.

Links to other questions

You may want to take a look at:

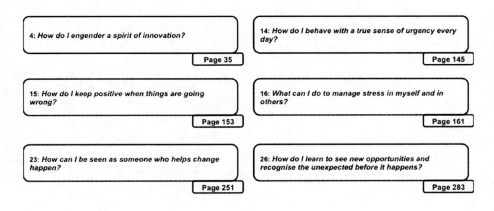

4: *How do I engender a spirit of innovation?*

Page 35

14: *How do I behave with a true sense of urgency every day?*

Page 145

15: *How do I keep positive when things are going wrong?*

Page 153

16: *What can I do to manage stress in myself and in others?*

Page 161

23: *How can I be seen as someone who helps change happen?*

Page 251

26: *How do I learn to see new opportunities and recognise the unexpected before it happens?*

Page 283

6: HOW DO I MAKE THE ANNUAL APPRAISAL PROCESS A POSITIVE EXPERIENCE, RATHER THAN A NECESSARY AND POTENTIALLY EMBARRASSING CHORE?

Why should I be asking this question?

We all need feedback – to motivate us and to help us develop and improve our skills. It also has the added bonus of giving us a feel-good factor. Feedback takes two prime forms – formal and informal. Formal feedback normally takes the form of an annual appraisal, while informal feedback is something that should be done as part of every boss/subordinate interaction.

Formal feedback should be no surprise if informal feedback has been done regularly, consistently and properly; however, this is often not the case and, hence, formal mechanisms are put in place to ensure that it is done at least periodically. The 'catch 22' is that if managers do not engage in informal feedback, the annual appraisal process becomes all the more difficult; and if you find the informal process a challenge, the formal annual interview and report will be an even more daunting prospect.

You need to develop a mind-set that views performance management as something that takes place every day – not once a year. If you can operate this way then the annual appraisal becomes a two-way contract that sets out what you need your staff to do and what you commit to do in order to help them achieve these goals.

The impact of the issue

The consequences are that for many organisations the appraisal process becomes a tick in the box exercise monitored and controlled by HR, with the purpose and potential benefits long forgotten. It becomes a dreaded chore, to be agonised over or paid lip service to, and ends up serving no useful purpose.

Even when a manager attempts to do the job properly, often their hands are tied by a legacy of avoided, incomplete or glowing appraisals overestimating an employee's positive attributes and sidestepping the negative ones.

Making sense of it all

The following mini case study puts the issue into context.

Bob was a particularly intelligent, committed and well-liked member of his team and had a history of very positive appraisals, and promises of promotion and pay rises. The promotion and pay rises had, however, never materialised, he became confused and disillusioned and the rest of the team was very much on his side. A new manager took it upon themselves to find out why this apparent anomaly existed and address the problem.

Part of Bob's role was to 'police' technical standards and he inevitably had to say 'no' from time to time; in the process, he had upset a few powerful individuals and been accused of having a somewhat brusque manner and a cutting sense of humour.

Bob's previous manager had ducked the issue at appraisal time and simply told Bob what he wanted to hear, effectively sweeping the issues under the carpet. By contrast, Bob's new manager was totally open and honest with him about their findings; Bob thanked them for being truthful and asked if they would help him overcome the issues raised.

> *Bob's manager role-played various scenarios with him and showed him how to say 'no' positively and constructively; they gave him opportunities to test out his new approach on 'green field' customers, monitored his progress, gave him frequent and specific feedback and, six months on, got him his promotion and pay rise. This had a hugely positive impact on both Bob and the whole of the team. Their productivity was estimated to have risen by over 50%.*

Practical advice

Providing developmental feedback is a key management skill and one that needs to be learned. Training, reviewing both good and bad examples, and on-the-job coaching will all help. Some people will, inevitably, find it easier than others – if it doesn't come naturally to you, it just means you will have to work a little harder.

When giving feedback, the following points are important:

- Focus on both the positive and the negative – we all need encouragement, to feel valued and appreciated. In addition, if we are to progress, we also need to understand our areas for improvement.

- Look at performance outcomes, rather than the inner person – always separate behaviour from the person. You are entitled to comment on behaviour; indeed, as a manager, it is part of your job to encourage certain behaviours and change others. But always treat the person with respect and as an adult. Help them to see how their performance impacts on the people they interact with and how their performance contributes to the whole.

- It is only when they feel attacked as a person that people get defensive – if you limit your comments to aspects of their behaviour, they will usually work with you to solve the problem.

- Focus on the specific, rather than the general – 'I liked it when you offered to help Tom with his filing', rather than 'There was a very friendly atmosphere'. In that way, people can learn from it and do it again. You cannot 'do' a friendly atmosphere again, but you can help someone with their filing again. If you make a general observation, follow it up with a specific example.

- Use observation, rather than interpretation – what you saw them do or heard them say, rather than what you interpreted by their behaviour, e.g. 'You started looking through your other papers', rather than 'You had no intention of listening to me'.

- Use descriptions, rather than judgements – describe what you saw/and or heard and how that made you (and/or others) feel. Remember, feelings are the intangible facts and deserve consideration, e.g. 'When you shout in meetings, people can get really scared', rather than 'You deliberately try to frighten people'.

- Focus on questions, rather than statements – questions give the recipient the responsibility of reaching their own conclusions and force them to think about the issues, e.g. 'How do you think Bob felt when you started looking through your papers?' or 'What effect do you think it has when you shout at your staff?'

- Use comparisons, rather than damnation – make evaluations against agreed criteria, past performance or competitive benchmarks. Explore any discrepancies without assigning blame. Identify 'high' and 'low' points of performance and the specific behaviours that appear to contribute to, or limit, success. Make suggestions regarding possible means of improving performance. Never compare performance with that of another member of the team.

Before concluding your discussions, check that the messages have been understood and received as intended – watch body language and ask them to summarise what has been agreed. Remember that this is an opportunity to build trust, respect and reciprocity – ask them what they need from you and agree how you need to provide that support and by when.

Table 2: Helpful and unhelpful feedback

Helpful feedback	Unhelpful feedback
<ul><li>Is easy to understand and put into context</li><li>Is specific and direct – examples and consequences</li><li>Matters – it is important enough to comment on</li><li>Focuses on behaviour that can be changed</li><li>Is 'owned' by you (i.e. clearly labelled as yours; what you believe, how you feel)</li><li>Leaves choices for the recipient e.g. 'Could do' rather than 'Should do'</li><li>Is delivered with honesty and kindness</li><li>Is timely – it needs to be given as soon as possible after the event; the impact reduces if you delay</li></ul>	<ul><li>Is coded or out of context</li><li>Is general or vague</li><li>Is unimportant or trivial</li><li>Imposes your own values, e.g. 'That was really stupid'</li><li>Makes judgements about attitudes, impact and intentions and decides for them what they ought to change</li><li>Is based on hearsay, e.g. 'Fred thinks that you ...'</li><li>Is too prescriptive – focus on outcomes rather that process; people need to be free to do things their way</li><li>Results in hurt feelings, emotional barriers and defensive behaviours</li></ul>

Finally, remember that nothing contained within an appraisal should be a surprise to the recipient. Feedback should be a continual process – it should be regular and timely. The formal appraisal process should be an opportunity to review and summarise all that has already been said over the past appraisal period, but, more importantly, it should be viewed as an opportunity to discuss future growth and learning.

Further food for the curious

- Gillen T. *Performance Management and Appraisal*. CIPD toolkit, 2nd edition. Chartered Institute of Personnel and Development, London (2007):
  - A comprehensive and practical resource.

Things for you to work on now

Key questions to ask yourself
<ul><li>How do I feel about the prospect of doing performance appraisals?</li><li>Are some of my team easier to appraise than others?</li><li>How much time do I spend on my appraisals? Is this too much or too little?</li><li>Do I focus too much attention on the positive aspects or too much on the negative, or is it about right?</li><li>Do I know what a good appraisal and a poor appraisal look like?</li><li>Think about your own last appraisal – was it a good experience? Did you learn something about yourself? Did it build on the trust and respect you hold for your boss? If not – work out what went wrong and don't do it to other people!</li></ul>

Mini exercises you can try immediately

- Reread some of the appraisals you have written in the past – how would they score in terms of the practical advice given above? Ask yourself how you would feel if you were on the receiving end of this appraisal – would this have been your intention?

- Keep a log of when you give feedback to your staff and look at the trends and patterns. How often, to whom, positive or negative?

- Find someone to be your co-coach and practise giving feedback to each other.

Links to other questions

You may want to take a look at:

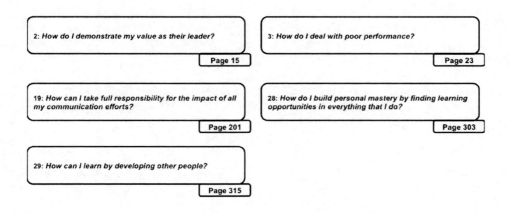

2: How do I demonstrate my value as their leader?
Page 15

3: How do I deal with poor performance?
Page 23

19: How can I take full responsibility for the impact of all my communication efforts?
Page 201

28: How do I build personal mastery by finding learning opportunities in everything that I do?
Page 303

29: How can I learn by developing other people?
Page 315

HOW DO I MANAGE MY BOSS?

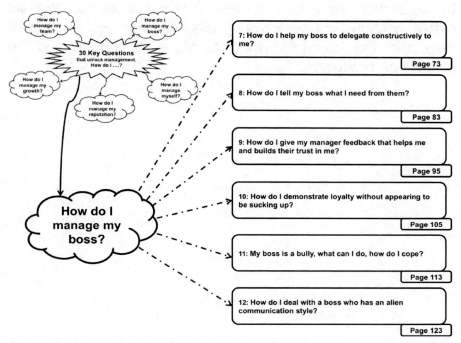

7: How do I help my boss to delegate constructively to me?

Page 73

8: How do I tell my boss what I need from them?

Page 83

9: How do I give my manager feedback that helps me and builds their trust in me?

Page 95

10: How do I demonstrate loyalty without appearing to be sucking up?

Page 105

11: My boss is a bully, what can I do, how do I cope?

Page 113

12: How do I deal with a boss who has an alien communication style?

Page 123

You may not have any choice about who your boss is, but you have far more control than you may think about how your boss treats you.

Your boss may be good or bad, supportive or destructive, open and friendly, or secretive and manipulative. Whatever their traits, one thing is for sure – they behave differently with different people. How they behave with you depends on how you manage your interactions and how much responsibility you take for creating a positive working relationship.

It is a truism that you tend to get the boss you deserve. When you work on developing your relationship with your boss, you are not just furthering your own ends, but also working to promote the worth and value of your whole team. Remember that in looking after the interests of your team, you are also increasing your own referential power base; so what is good for them is also good for you.

In this section, we answer *six* key questions about how to build better relationships with your boss, so that you are seen, respected and valued for what you do, what you say and the results you produce.

7: HOW DO I HELP MY BOSS TO DELEGATE CONSTRUCTIVELY TO ME?

Why should I be asking this question?

At the end of a working day, do you feel exhausted or fulfilled, or maybe a little of both? Think about the things that bring about each of these contrasting states – many of us associate feelings of exhaustion with doing repetitive work, dealing with trivia and mundane tasks, lack of variety, etc. Whereas when we experience new situations, can exercise some imagination in how we deal with issues and have flexibility about how and when we provide solutions, we feel more valued and fulfilled.

Maybe you have also noticed that when your boss hands out interesting and difficult challenges, they always seem to go to the same select few people. It appears that the favoured few get the cream and everyone else gets to pick up the routine grunt work. How did they get into that inner circle? How can you get in there, too?

The good news is that you don't have to sit and wait and hope that your manager may notice you and see your talents and think 'Gosh, I must give them more interesting work'. You can take action today that helps your boss to see you and understand how best to use your talents. Just as you can delegate to others, you can use the same process in reverse to help your boss to delegate to you.

The impact of the issue

We have seen in previous questions the benefits for you and your team when you delegate. Remember, one of the key reasons for delegating was to create space for your boss to delegate part of their job to you. But you don't want any old mundane tasks; what you need is tasks and graduated responsibility that provides you with the opportunity to:

- pick up new skills and knowledge, so that you increase your employability and value to the company;

- gain experience in decision making and understand how those decisions impact on company performance;

- get visibility in the organisation, so that important people can see your capabilities for themselves;

- start to grow your sphere of influence and your broader business understanding;

- add variety to what you do and increase your degree of job satisfaction;

- see how other departments and other leaders work and make decisions;

- learn about your business and its customer value proposition, so that you can keep your own team focused on doing the right thing.

It's not enough that you do a great job; you have to be seen to be doing a great job and you need, most of all, to be seen by people whose opinion matters. Like it or not, your boss is the shop window through which people will see you.

You need to ask yourself the question 'When people look at the window that is my boss, are the curtains closed, or are they open with the ray of sunshine illuminating me?' Helping your boss to delegate wisely to you is your way of opening the curtains and making sure that the sunlight lands on you.

Making sense of it all

The chances are that your boss is run off their feet, and so busy reacting to events that they don't have time to sit back and think about how they can develop you and, perhaps more importantly from their point of view, how they can use you to make their own life easier.

Before your boss will delegate important and interesting stuff to you, they have to learn to trust you. This is a slow process and trust is built one step at a time. Let's look at a simple example.

You are responsible for compiling the monthly customer quality statistics, usually a 10 to 15-page report. You know that your boss does something with this and extracts some data to put in a one-page PowerPoint® presentation that goes in the operational-board briefing pack on the 28th of each month. You don't know what the board does with this or, indeed, if anyone ever reads it or acts upon it. You could go to your boss and say something like 'I have been thinking about the quality stats and I wonder if there is anything I can do to present them in a way that is more useful to you when you have to compile the board briefing pack?' You could then follow up with some questions like 'What do the board do with the numbers? What could we do to give them greater insight? Is there anything that they are particularly concerned about that we could shed more light on by collecting or analysing the data in a different way?'

By taking this style of approach with your boss, you are achieving several things:

- You are showing that you are thinking and interested in what happens to your output when it leaves you.

- You show that you have an appreciation of what your boss does and that you could do more to take some of their load.

- You are helping them to think about how they could provide their own boss with better, more insightful information in a way that may not mean any more work for your boss, but which could give them considerable kudos.

- You are learning about how your boss thinks and what sorts of ideas they are prepared to take upwards.

- You can share your new understanding with your own team, so that they can better see the value that they are contributing to the business.

- At the very least, your boss is likely to show you what they do with your report and how they convert your data into their board report – if your boss does show you what they do with it, then it is your opportunity to offer to draft next month's report for them.

By using strategies like this, you can influence the sort of work that comes your way and, at the same time, build a trusting relationship with your boss.

Practical advice

People often make the mistake of thinking that managers delegate to the person most competent and able to do the job. Wrong – in most cases they delegate to the person that they have a trust-based relationship with. Trust takes time to build and it generally doesn't come through showing that you are smart, able or energetic. Trust comes when you get to know someone, show them that you have the same values as they do, demonstrate personal loyalty and mutual respect. Once you have a trust-based relationship, it becomes easy for them to turn to you, it also allows them to let down their guard with you and admit their own vulnerabilities. Interestingly, it also makes them far more likely to turn a blind eye if and when you don't perform quite as well as you should have done.

The best way to influence what tasks come your way is to make getting to know your boss your number-one priority – find out what makes them tick and use that knowledge to build rapport and trust.

- Learn to read their moods and behaviours and the secret code embedded in their speech. What words, expressions or actions wind them up? What sort of activities and problems tweak their interest and get them excited?

  - Tailor your dialogue, so that you make opportunities to link your efforts to the things that excite your boss.

  - If you have done something that is necessary, but you know that your boss finds it boring – don't bore them. Just give them the headline news and move on quickly to something that they show an interest in.

- Find out what is the most important thing to them. Is it company reputation, personal reputation, quality, customer satisfaction, etc? Every manager has one or more hot topics that always get their instant attention. Find out what does it for your boss:

  - Whatever you do or talk about, find a way of linking it back to one of your boss's hot buttons

  - If you can think of something novel that would make their worries go away permanently, you will be a hero and find that you are quickly embraced into your boss's inner circle.

- Do some gentle investigation – what are the one or two biggest calamities that have happened on your boss's watch? What caused them? Are the roots of those issues still a present danger? If so – make sure that you don't ever say, or do, anything that reminds them of that discomfort.

- Get to know how they like to receive information – are they a detail person who wants facts, facts, facts, or do they think in terms of the bigger picture?

  - If they give you lots of data, lists longer than three items and lengthy stories starting at the beginning and concluding with the punch line, they are probably a detail person.

- If they tend to reach for a pen and draw you a Mind Map, a model or a picture, or talk using metaphors and analogies, they are probably a big-picture person.

• Are they open and easy to get to know, or are they reserved and guarded?

- Either way, you need to establish some common ground. Look for shared interests, common background or places you have lived, kids of a similar age or at the same school/university, books you have both read – anything to show that you are on the same page of life.

- Use the same sort of language and the same level of detail when speaking or communicating by e-mail. Use their communication as a pattern for your own. When doing group communication, make sure that you cover the key points in the style most favoured by your boss.

• Do they ask you things, or tell you what to do?

- If they routinely give you detailed instructions on how to do a job, you need to work with them to reduce the detail. Ask them questions about purpose and desired outcome; ask them how they will assess the quality and relevance of what you produce. Ask if they think it would be appropriate if you tackled the task in a different way – suggest a brief plan of action to them and offer to work it up into a detailed plan for their approval.

- If they are very task oriented, they may well forget the people aspects of any situation or change – you could ask questions that show that you are alert to these potential issues and, in this way, your boss is likely to devolve some responsibility to you, so that they can get on with the, for them, more interesting work of planning tangible tasks and processes.

- If they ask for your opinion – give it, but couch it in terms of options, showing no real preference for which option is best – let them think about what you have offered and select a way forward. If you don't like the choice, ask questions that cause them to think through the implications in a little more depth.

• How intelligent are they? Really smart managers may be intolerant of people who don't pick things up as quickly as they do:

- If they are smart, you need to flatter their speed of thinking, but be subtle about it; don't fawn over them.

- If they are not so smart, you need to find ways of suggesting courses of action and supporting them. Make them look good in front of their peers and managers; never, never be critical of them in what you think are private conversations. You will soon find that nothing is truly private in an organisation. Be as supportive as is necessary, but guard against them becoming dependent on you, or they could be afraid of letting you go when the time comes.

• How stable are they? Can you predict from day to day how they will react in certain situations, or do they appear to be governed by the phases of the moon?

- There is a difference between temporary stress and permanent neurosis – help and support your boss at all times, but if they look like they have a tendency towards unpredictable or neurotic behaviour, you are best advised to leave them alone until they are in a better place.

As you start to find answers to all of these questions, you will be better able to understand their needs, and start to tailor your communication efforts to meet the way they like to receive and process information. Your aim is to make it easy for them to turn to you when they need help. Understanding how you can best support them is the first step towards building a successful relationship with them.

Further food for the curious

- Keller Johnson L. Are you delegating so it sticks? *Harvard Business Review*, Sept. 2007:

    - This short paper sets out five big ideas to help you become more effective in delegation.

- Delegation: Gaining time for yourself. Book chapter excerpted from *BR Essentials – Time Management*, May 2005:

    - This is a good primer that links the related arts of delegation and time management, and provides practical tips and advice.

Things for you to work on now

Key questions to ask yourself
<ul><li>What does my boss talk about most? What keeps them awake at night?</li><li>Is my boss a detail person or a big-picture person?</li><li>Is my boss primarily task focused or people focused?</li><li>How smart is my boss?</li><li>What customer-related problems keep on cropping up?</li><li>What does my boss's boss get most excited about? What could my boss do to make their boss happy?</li><li>What does my boss hate doing and why?</li><li>What things does my boss do that I think I could do, even though they are not connected with my current</li></ul>

job description?

- What skills knowledge do I have that my boss doesn't have?

- When my boss needs help, who do they turn to and why do I think they look to those people?

- What is my boss's biggest ambition and what can I do to help them achieve that?

Mini exercises you can try immediately

- Build a Mind Map of what is important to your boss. Include aspects of personal behaviour, likes and dislikes. Each time you interact with them, reflect on the interchange and update your Mind Map. Colour-code it – green for things they like, red for things that wind them up. Don't share this with anybody else and keep it safe and private.

- Watch how your boss interacts with your peers – how do they brief them, what level of detail do they give them? How do they react when people ask questions or don't seem to understand them? Make two lists: how they behave with you and how they behave with others. Which items on your list would you like to eliminate? Which items of the 'others' list do you wish were on yours?

- Review the results of your last exercise and make a new list that just has the behaviours you want your boss to show when dealing with you. Prioritise your list and work on your top priority. Think about how you might get them to adopt this behaviour.

Links to other questions

You may want to take a look at:

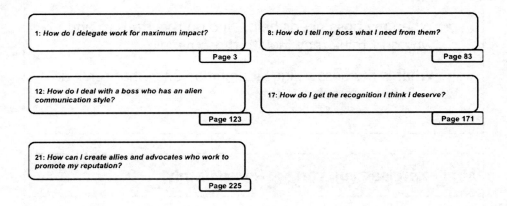

1: *How do I delegate work for maximum impact?*

Page 3

8: *How do I tell my boss what I need from them?*

Page 83

12: *How do I deal with a boss who has an alien communication style?*

Page 123

17: *How do I get the recognition I think I deserve?*

Page 171

21: *How can I create allies and advocates who work to promote my reputation?*

Page 225

8: HOW DO I TELL MY BOSS WHAT I NEED FROM THEM?

Why should I be asking this question?

After an individual or group meeting with your boss, do you ever feel a little lost and helpless? Maybe you are not sure about what you are supposed to be doing, or how to set about doing it. Most of us have these feelings at some time; what really hurts though is the knowledge that when our boss gave us the job and asked if we understood what was needed, we almost certainly said 'Sure thing, boss', when we were actually thinking 'Crikey, what have I got myself into?'. Now you feel that you can't go back and say help, and you just know that when you do take something back to them, it is going to be torn to shreds. What do you do? And how do you stop this situation happening again next time, if there is a next time?

The impact of the issue

We all perform best when we know what we are doing, know how to set about it and are confident that we have the skills and knowledge required to achieve the desired outcome. We feel good, and that feeling is apparent to our workmates – enthusiasm can be infectious and a team can get a real buzz from performing in the zone. Conversely, when we have little idea of what is expected of us, we work below our true potential and can become despondent and stressed. We communicate that stress to our co-workers and then we all spend more time talking about what we can't do than what we can do. The result is that time we should have spent performing well, we actually spend thinking about the probability of performing badly, our confidence takes a knock and we may start to develop a mild sense of grievance towards our boss. This is all bad news – but sadly the problem does not stop there. We tend to model the behaviour we see and, since we have been on the receiving end of poor briefings, we are more likely to repeat the crime and be equally poor when we brief others. And so a vicious cycle of miscommunication and confusion can become the norm in a team or organisation. Pretty soon a culture develops where poor performance is expected and tolerated, blame and finger-pointing abounds and everyone is busy protecting their own back. The consequence of this behaviour is that people can't find time to help their colleagues or provide great service to their customers.

Making sense of it all

So what do you do when you don't know what your boss wants you to do? The chances are that you will adopt one of the following three tactics:

- You search your past experience for a task that appears to be similar and then set about the new one in the same sort of way – possibly experimenting along the way in the hope that you can do a good enough job.

- You find someone else who you think might be able to do the task and then ask them how they would set about things. This might be a workable solution if you ask the right person, but often you end up asking someone you know rather than someone who knows about the task at hand.

- You put off dealing with the task and concentrate on things that you can do. This is a way of dodging the psychological stress of uncertainty and guilt.

The first two courses of action at least have the merit that you are trying to do something, but the reality is that what you are doing is conspiring with the powerless. You may hit upon a reasonably efficient course of action, but you will be operating without a clear insight of the purpose of the task and the desired outcomes. The only person who really knows what is required is your boss.

The only sensible thing to do is to stop this cycle before it starts. Get a proper and complete briefing at the outset; you will also need a good working relationship with your boss, so that you can get appropriate guidance and coaching as you go along. Sounds easy, but how do you do it?

Practical advice

Much of what passes for communication in our organisations isn't communication at all, it is just talking. We spend far too much time telling people things, rather than engaging in a dialogue that helps people to construct mutual understanding. So the first and most important thing to understand is that *you don't* just march in and tell your boss what you need from them. There are two really good reasons why this full-frontal approach is not a good strategy:

- You most probably don't know what you need from them.

- Even if you did know and you did tell them, they probably wouldn't hear and react because their brain is switched to transmit mode rather than receive mode.

You do need to open up the channels of communication and basically you have three tactics to achieve this:

- *Engage them in dialogue* – an open, two-way conversation that explores all aspects of a situation and results in both parties gaining deeper understanding.

- *Seek and give feedback* – this is an essential part of the process of dialogue and helps build personal understanding, trust and deeper relationships.

- *Seek coaching* – every time your boss gives you a new task, it is an opportunity to get some coaching. But don't just assume that it will happen, and don't assume that your boss has either the desire or the skills to diagnose what coaching you need and how to give it. You need to help them see and feel your needs.

Notice that none of the three tactics listed above are about overtly telling your boss what you need from them – they are all about ways of engaging with your boss, so that you help them to see what you need and take the necessary steps to fulfil your needs.

Tips for promoting dialogue

Dialogue is so much more than just a conversation; when you are in dialogue with someone you are engaged in a mutual search for purpose and insight, rather than trying to get your point across. It requires you to let go of your ego and opinions and listen without judging. When you participate in effective dialogue, you will:

- establish common ground;
- explore and challenge previously unexamined or unstated assumptions;
- explore new ideas and perspectives;
- learn to see the world through the eyes of someone else.

To achieve these things, you will need to listen at least as much as you talk. Value silence, pauses and thinking time in the process, and focus on building and maintaining empathy. This is a killer technique for having more productive meetings with your boss because, rather than you trying to tell them what you need, dialogue helps them to discover your needs and to discover something about themselves at the same time.

We are so used to talking at people and trying to get our point across that, at first, you are bound to find dialogue a tricky process. You cannot just wing it and hope that something useful will happen – you need to think and plan ahead, so that you can get a mental map of what you are trying to achieve and what you need to cover. Remember that as well as trying to promote dialogue, you are also trying subtly to coach your boss into dialogue, a structure that is, in all probability, alien to them. Make sure that you do the following:

- Start off with a focus on common interests and views rather than divisive or confrontational statements.

- Use concrete examples to illustrate general points or trends.

- Seek to examine the assumptions that might be used to explain or rationalise the trends. See if you have common assumptions – if not, look at the different aspects of the assumptions and the insight that produces.

- Challenge assumptions – use questions such as 'What makes you so sure that this is the natural consequence of that?' 'What might we be able to achieve if we were not bound by the idea that ...?'.

- If you are in a group meeting, look out for voices that are being marginalised. Don't assume that you know what they are trying to say, but, instead, ask questions to find out what the group is ignoring. Try question structures like 'We haven't heard how this might impact Ops – what are your thoughts on this proposal?' or 'I sense that you are uncomfortable with our conclusions – what are we missing here?'.

- When there is disagreement, make sure that the process is focused on conflict between value systems and assumptions, not on conflict between people or departments.

Be very clear that each meeting with your boss should have a purpose; don't confuse things by having multiple purposes jostling against each other and vying for supremacy. Specifically, don't confuse dialogue with decision making – each has a different purpose that requires a different mind-set. If you need a decision, come back later with a résumé of the understanding that was gained from the dialogue and a series of options and recommendations.

Dialogue is your way of building rapport, empathy and common thought processes with your boss. By doing so, they will start to trust you and, because they know how you think and work, they will naturally turn to you more and more when they need help or input. This is your way of helping them meet your needs – make dialogue a tool in your armoury.

Tips for getting feedback that helps you

A common complaint among workers is that they do not get enough feedback on their performance. Another is that the feedback they do get is of poor quality. The first step is to make sure that you get feedback, and the best way to achieve that is to ask, 'How am I doing?'.

When asking for feedback, the most important thing is to make the process as easy and painless as possible for your manager:

- Don't put them on the spot:
  - Keep it verbal not written.
  - Warn them in advance that you are going to ask, so that they can think seriously before they speak.
  - Have the discussion on their territory or neutral ground.
  - Make sure that you are in a positive frame of mind throughout.
  - Don't assume that it's reciprocal and that this is your opportunity to tell them what you think of them.
- Do the hard work yourself; prepare yourself, so that you can:
  - ask what they would like you to do more of, or start doing, and what they would like you to do less of, or

stop doing, rather than just asking them to judge you or 'rate' you;

– ask them how *you* can be of most value to *them*;

– offer some suggestions of your own about how you think you might improve and use them as a sounding board;

– act on the things you agree with, discuss the things you don't and keep an open mind – they might just have a point!

Once you are getting some feedback, you need to consider what you are going to do with it? This is 'pay-off' time in the world of feedback. You have learned something valuable about the impact you have in the world. Does it line up with what you intended? Does it match your own perception of your performance? If so, great. If not, *listen carefully* – avoid the temptation to defend yourself – that's only pride and it will get in the way. Remember, it may not be easy for your manager either (so don't make it more difficult for them!) Now is the time for you to help the giver say what they really want to say:

• Encourage them don't punish them:

– Listen quietly – no interruptions, no escaping into defensive strategy building – just concentrate on what is being said and mentally note questions or disagreements.

– Reflect back – summarise to check that you got the intended message and to show that you were listening. Their views are valid, even if you don't agree with them.

– Explore – you may, or may not, agree with what you hear, but ask questions to try to understand what is being said and why your manager sees it in this way. Stay calm, show interest and probe for specific details. Seek examples in those areas that are unclear or in which disagreement exists. Paraphrase again.

- Ask for more – more about this topic and, while we're at it, more about any other topic, too. Use phrases such as 'That's extremely helpful. Are there any other areas in which this is causing a problem?'

- Express your honest reactions – this includes feelings – 'I'm not really surprised, but I am disappointed ...'

Carefully evaluate what you have heard for accuracy and potential value. Make a summary statement of where you stand now. *Thank them* – you owe them that – but nothing else. Don't allow yourself to be manipulated into acting against your better judgement, or reciprocating by saying something nice (or nasty!) back.

Tips to help you seek coaching

One of the key things you need from your boss is coaching. They know stuff that you don't know, they have access to company information and resources that you don't, and they are called upon to do things of which you don't normally have visibility. You need them to induct you into some of these mysteries and to guide and support you as you step up to new challenges. But the chances are that they are neither skilled at coaching, or at diagnosing your coaching needs. So, rather than hope that they may be sent on a coaching course, you need to learn the structure and art of coaching, and then coach them on how to coach you. Naturally, you do not breeze into the boss's office and say 'OK boss, let me tell you how to coach me and no, that is not the way to go about things'.

One of the most common structures for coaching is the GROW model – goal, reality, options, wrap-up. If your boss has had any training in the art of coaching, they will most certainly have been introduced to this way of structuring a coaching session. Whether they are experienced or not, you need to be aware of the structure, so that you can help and encourage them to take you through this cycle:

- Goal – this is something that you should have thought of prior to meeting with your boss: what the topic is that you wish to work on and what your objective is. Be honest and specific with yourself and realistic: set one simple objective and think about how you can get your boss to work with you on this topic. It is a good idea to identify something that you are working on that needs this skill, and then take the materials with you that you are struggling with. Ask your boss if they have time to work with you to help you gain a better understanding of this area.

- Reality – this is where you need to engage in dialogue about what you can't do and what you need your boss to do so that you can do it. You will need to examine the assumptions that you both hold and work on a specific and relevant problem. Deflect any discussion of past performance; keep the conversation success based and future focused.

- Options – ask questions that start and maintain a discussion about potential options. Offer suggestions, but do it in a way that encourages your boss to probe your thinking and build on your ideas. Make sure that you agree on a mutual course of action before you move on, and agree who will make the next move and what it looks like.

- Wrap-up – summarise what you have learned and what you have agreed, but, most of all, be very clear about what you found most valuable in what your boss has just done. Talk frankly about what could get in the way of doing these things in the future – encourage your boss to think about how they can help you further on this and other matters.

If you become practised at engaging your boss in dialogue, seeking and giving honest feedback and looking for opportunities to be coached, you will find that you create a relationship with your boss where they just naturally seem to know what you need from them.

Further food for the curious

- Isaacs W. *Dialogue and the Art of Thinking Together: A Pioneering Approach to Communicating in Business and in Life*. Doubleday (1996):

  – A great introduction to the use of dialogue to transform the impact of face-to-face business communication.

- Ridings A. *Pause for Breath*. Live It Publishing (2011):

  – For those who want to go much deeper into the interpersonal aspects of establishing and maintaining effective dialogue.

- Clarke-Epstein C. Truth in Feedback. *Training and Development*, Nov. 2001, vol. 55 issue 11, pp. 78–80:

  – This short article captures the fundamental truths and misconceptions about the value and impact of the feedback process.

- Landsberg M. *The Tao of Coaching: Boost your Effectiveness at Work by Inspiring and Developing Others Around You*. Profile Books (2002):

  – A must-read for anyone about to become a coach, or seek coaching from a peer.

Things for you to work on now

Key questions to ask yourself
<ul><li>What is it about your work that you find most challenging?</li><li>What three things could your boss do that would transform the way you feel about your job?</li><li>What is it that winds everybody up, but your boss doesn't appear to notice? How would it help you and others if you could get them to notice and do</li></ul>

something about it? Identify three areas for action that relate to this problem.

- When you have a conversation with your boss, what is your most usual mode – speaking, listening, agreeing, disagreeing, challenging, accommodating, responding, or some other? What might the dialogue be like if you could adopt a different mode or different balance of modes?

- What do you feel is the most impressive aspect of the way your boss works? What would it take for you to develop that ability? How could you get your boss to pass on those skills to you?

Mini exercises you can try immediately

- Make a list of your skills and abilities. Narrow the list down to 10 things and put them in order with your best ability at number one. Now review the list and highlight those areas in which you believe you have developed most over the last 12 months. Pick the top two, and think about how you could develop those areas even further – what help would you need from your boss and how can you make that clear to them?

- Review your list again and, this time, focus on the two areas where you have made least progress or stood still. What would it take for you to get better at these things? If you had three wishes, what would you ask for to help you improve yourself in these areas?

- Think of an issue or problem that you feel you could make a contribution to solving – plan out a dialogue that you could have with your boss on this subject.

Focus on the questions you might ask your boss to bring their assumptions to the surface; you will also need to think about the background information and evidence you may need to support your dialogue.

Links to other questions

You may want to take a look at:

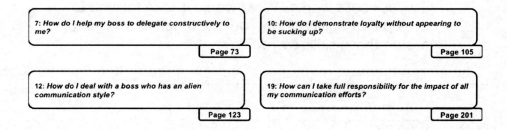

7: *How do I help my boss to delegate constructively to me?*

Page 73

10: *How do I demonstrate loyalty without appearing to be sucking up?*

Page 105

12: *How do I deal with a boss who has an alien communication style?*

Page 123

19: *How can I take full responsibility for the impact of all my communication efforts?*

Page 201

9: HOW DO I GIVE MY MANAGER FEEDBACK THAT HELPS ME AND BUILDS THEIR TRUST IN ME?

Why should I be asking this question?

Let's face it, most managers are pretty rubbish at the important things; you know, those things that generally make work a pleasure, help you develop and grow, and send you home feeling valued. The bad news is that they are unlikely to get any better because their managers are rubbish, too, and won't, or can't, spend the time needed to develop them to be better at managing you. Now you have two choices: you can hope that fate steps in and you get a better manager, one who cares about you and is skilled enough to develop you, or you can take action to improve your own position by learning to manage your manager.

Managing upwards is a key skill; your boss may, or may not, be skilled at their job, clear in their communication, or caring and compassionate, but one thing is for sure – they have more access to resources and more power than you, and they have a huge say in what you do now, what you will do in the future, what you get paid and how much visibility you get from above them.

If you want to get better, more interesting tasks, get promoted and get paid more, the most effective strategy is to learn to be good at managing your manager.

The impact of the issue

Making the effort to manage your manager is not 'brown nosing' or 'sucking up'. It is about communicating openly, learning to trust each other, succeeding together and helping each other to produce the best outcomes. Most people spend far too little time and effort on the art of upward management, often because they feel that:

- they don't like their boss;
- they don't want their friends to see them sucking up;
- they are frightened of their boss;
- they don't know enough about the job, or the organisation, to be able to suggest anything of value;
- they are in awe of management and/or don't have the confidence to engage in a dialogue about what needs to be done;
- they don't have any control over their boss or what work their boss gives them;
- senior management thinks their boss is useless and they don't want to be tarred with the same brush.

If you identify with some or all of the impressions above or some similar sentiment, we guarantee that you, your manager and your team are underperforming, that you often feel frustrated, are constantly beset by mistakes and rework, that you miss deadlines and there is constant fire-fighting and finger-pointing.

When you start to work positively with your manager, you start to take control of your own destiny and things are far less likely to spin out of control, to produce uncomfortable surprises or simply to sap your time in unnecessary rework or politicking.

Making sense of it all

The primary process that we use to monitor and regulate our behaviour is feedback. We take action, observe the results, reflect on why things turned out the way they did and then think about how we can modify our behaviour next time to get different, or better, results.

This is termed the 'learning loop' and was articulated neatly by David Kolb in 1984.

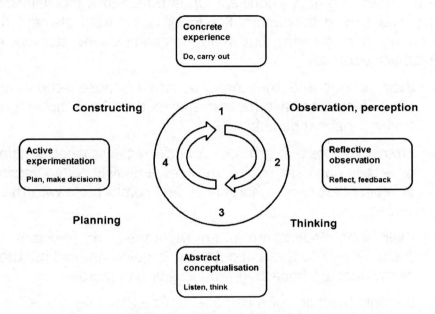

Figure 6: Learning loop[3]

Kolb's learning cycle suggests that it is not sufficient just to have an experience in order to learn – experience has to be backed up by reflection. This, in turn, allows us to make generalisations and formulate concepts, which can then be applied to new situations. Once we have this mental idea of how the world works, we are then able to test it out in new situations. The learner must make the link between the theory and action by planning, acting out, reflecting and relating it back to the theory.

---

[3] The learning loop is based on David Kolb's experiential learning cycle as set out in *Experiential Learning: Experience as the Source of Learning and Development*, published by Prentice Hall in 1984.

The thing that makes all of this work is *feedback* – information that we sense from the real world that gives us a sense of how things are playing out. This all sounds fine and does, indeed, appear to be a really good explanation of experiential learning – the snag is that, without appropriate feedback mechanisms, the whole thing falls apart. Feedback is a critical element for learning and growth, but many managers are starved of feedback because:

- their actions and the consequences of those actions are often separated in time and space; they have no way of seeing what happened;

- often their position provides a buffer against what is going on – they don't see reality, they see a heavily edited version of reality that their subordinates feel comfortable with them seeing;

- their subordinates are often frightened, or reluctant to speak openly to them about what is going on, or how their behaviours are impacting productivity and morale;

- the only feedback of a personal nature that they get is from their peers, and their peers don't have to work for them, so they again get an edited and distorted view of the world.

So we have a situation where managers need feedback because without it they cannot learn and develop. But their usual sources of feedback are largely closed off to them. And they may well feel embarrassed, or unable to ask subordinates for feedback for fear of looking weak or ineffectual. This is not good for them, but it is also not good for you; if they don't get appropriate feedback, they will not have a clue about how to develop you or how to become a more effective leader themselves.

Make it your goal to understand what your boss needs to know in order to develop both you and them; find a way of giving them the feedback they need to take both of you on your respective journeys.

Practical advice

The first step in establishing a working relationship with your boss is to tell them how you like to be managed, not because it is nice for you, or makes your life more pleasant, but because it will help you to perform better as a subordinate and them to perform better as your boss. Once they know that there is something in it for them, they are more likely to listen intently and try to use your skills more effectively. We will get on to specifics about how you might start to interact with your boss and how to get them to give you the help you need in a minute, but first you need to think about your relationship on three levels:

- How much inclusion do you want – do you like to know what is going on, to be invited to meetings, consulted on matters, etc. or do you just prefer to be left alone to get on with things?

- How much control do you want – do you like to know exactly what is expected of you and by when, a clear methodology and checkpoints, or would you prefer a blank sheet of paper and the freedom to do it your way?

- What degree of openness would you like with your boss – do you want to get to know them personally, share yourself with them, go for a drink after work, or do you prefer to keep your work and personal life totally separate?

Understanding your motives and desired outcomes will help you to think more clearly about how you need to shape the interactions that you have with your boss in order to get the direction and guidance that you need.

Giving feedback to your boss is similar to giving feedback to a subordinate, but with a little more ego massaging and deference. The most important thing to remember is that your focus is on how you can improve your relationship with your boss and what you can do to help you both to function well together. You are not necessarily trying to make them a better person – although that might be a positive side benefit!

When you are giving feedback to your boss, make sure that you have a plan of what you want to achieve with this particular interaction. Work on the principle of one objective, one meeting. The biggest single mistake that people make is to go into a meeting with a shopping list of things they want their boss to do. They are only human, so focus on one issue or behaviour, get that right and then move on to something else only when you are sure that your boss has got the message and is now performing to your entire satisfaction in relation to that issue or behaviour. Remember also that this is a relationship, so you need to be aware of what you say and do and how you say and do it. Have the following aims:

- Make your feedback easy to understand – not vague, not coded, but in context and 'owned' by you, not reported thirdhand from someone else.

- Make your feedback easy for them to accept – that means not passing judgement on them and not imposing your values. They are your boss and they may, quite rightly, be proud of their individuality, integrity and position. Ideally, try to phrase the feedback in such a way that the focus appears to be on you rather than them. Try something along the lines of:

  - 'Look, boss, I'm having real difficulty getting my head around how you want me to approach this task. I think the cause of my confusion may be that you think so much more quickly than me, so I am still trying to understand the why of what we are doing and you have moved on to giving me loads of great detail about the how. Could we just step back a minute and help me build a better picture of where we are heading?'

  - The advantage of this sort of strategy is that you have delivered a compliment about your boss's thinking, you have given your boss an ideal opening to give you some useful coaching and you have tactfully pointed out to your boss that they are a detail person and you need the bigger picture, so that you can understand and focus your efforts. This sort of triple whammy is a great way of building a productive relationship. When you are new to this technique, you are unlikely to think of this complexity of dialogue structure on the fly, so it is a good idea to think out how you can shape the dialogue before you start the meeting.

- Make your feedback easy to act upon – it needs to be immediate, relevant and about the way they behave. That way, it matters and allows them to improve. In the example above, we saw how a compliment opened up an opportunity for coaching. When you give your boss feedback, you are not trying to score points and provoke anger; you are trying to kick-start thinking and provoke action that helps you.

When the meeting/coaching session is over and you have given the feedback you planned, close out with efforts to maintain the rapport that you have built up and make your boss feel good about what they have done for you. Use the mnemonic WWW – EMEI (What Went Well – Even More Effective If) to give yourself a structure for this type of feedback session:

- What was particularly effective (specific examples and consequences)? This is your opportunity to train your boss to recognise how you need them to work with you – don't just hope that they recognised what they were doing, or that they have just done something different. Remind them.

- What was not so effective? Give specific examples of things they said, or did, and the consequences that those actions had for you. Depending upon the quality and depth of your relationship, you may be able to address feelings using structures like – 'When you said/did "x", it made me feel like ...'. There will have been times in the meeting when confusion was the order of the day and one, or both, of you appeared to be losing the will to live – put your finger on these areas of mutual frustration and explore together how you can avoid them in future. You might try asking questions along the lines of:

– 'Boss, there was a minute back there when we just seemed to hit a brick wall – then you said ... and we suddenly started to get it together. How did you know that was what we needed at that point to help us to see these new possibilities?'

– 'Boss, I was really confused until you grabbed the pen out of my hand and started to draw a diagram – I think I must be a very visual person and e-mail just misses that side of my brain. How can I get more of this sort of time with you without becoming a burden? It really does help me enormously and I get it so much more quickly this way.'

• Asking the sorts of questions we set out above helps your boss to recognise immediately what is really working for you, and also helps them to think about what they might consider doing differently next time.

• Check that they get the correct message – watch their body language. If appropriate, ask them to summarise and play back the things that really worked well for you. This way you are reinforcing their long-term memory, and leaving them on a high note of thinking that they just handled the meeting really well.

Further food for the curious

• Clarke-Epstein C. Truth in Feedback. *Training and Development*, Nov. 2001, vol. 55 issue 11, pp. 78–80:

– This short article captures the fundamental truths and misconceptions about the value and impact of the feedback process.

Things for you to work on now

Key questions to ask yourself

- What three things about the way my boss behaves and communicates have the biggest negative impact on our relationship or ability to understand each other?

- What three things about the way I behave and communicate have the biggest positive impact on my relationship with my boss?

- Which of my colleagues does the boss have the best relationship with – what are the interpersonal elements that appear to underpin the strength of this relationship? Is there anything that I could try to build into the way I interact with my boss?

- How do I feel when my boss tries to teach me something or coach me? What would have to change for me to feel better about this? Is the main area for change in me or in my boss?

Mini exercises you can try immediately

- Choose an aspect of your boss's behaviour, or manner, that gets in the way of you understanding them, or wanting to do your best for them. Relate this behaviour to how you are approaching an ongoing task, or project – think about how you can engage your boss in a dialogue about how the behaviour is getting in the way of you performing better. Think through some question structures that you might be able to use and identify one skill that you think your boss could coach you on.

- Think about a particularly successful meeting, or coaching session, that you had with your boss. What was it about that session that made it so productive? Make two lists – one that focuses on the things you did and the techniques you used, and another about the atmosphere and interpersonal relationship that you created. What would you need to do to recapture these feelings in another meeting?

Links to other questions

You may want to take a look at:

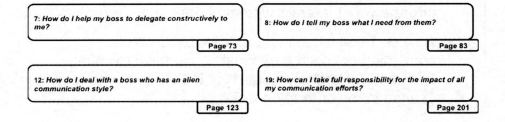

7: *How do I help my boss to delegate constructively to me?*

Page 73

8: *How do I tell my boss what I need from them?*

Page 83

12: *How do I deal with a boss who has an alien communication style?*

Page 123

19: *How can I take full responsibility for the impact of all my communication efforts?*

Page 201

10: HOW DO I DEMONSTRATE LOYALTY WITHOUT APPEARING TO BE SUCKING UP?

Why should I be asking this question?

Not so long ago, loyalty in an organisational sense meant blind allegiance to your boss, your organisation, or your professional body or trade association. Such unquestioning dedication and blind following led some people to sleepwalk into situations that became, at best, uncomfortable and, at worst, intolerable. Nowadays, loyalty is looked on in a different way – when we talk about loyalty we are talking about making a personal commitment to a set of personal and professional standards that characterise our behaviour towards our boss, our organisation and our profession. Loyalty and ethical behaviour go hand in hand, and you should never offer loyalty to someone, or something, that is at odds with your core principles and ethical beliefs.

We should also say at the outset that when we talk about loyalty to your boss, we are using the broadest definition of boss – if your immediate supervisor is a scheming rat who routinely disregards the values of the company and shows no sign of possessing a moral or ethical compass, then you need to look for someone else in whom to invest your loyalty.

Lots of people want to ride with you in the limo, but what you want is someone who will take the bus with you when the limo breaks down.

Oprah Winfrey

We all need to know who we can trust and who will remain loyal to us, especially in difficult times, and bosses are no different from anyone else. Loyal and trusted subordinates are likely to be the first to find out about things; they will be confided in, asked for their views and opinions on matters, and when times get tough, they will find shelter under their boss's organisational umbrella. Loyalty is a two-way street – when you demonstrate loyalty, it comes back in spades. Trust and loyalty are the foundations on which relationships are built; they are the key to becoming part of your boss's inner circle.

The impact of the issue

Whether you like it or not, feel it unfair or unjust, bosses tend to have favourites. Everyone will know who the favourite is and may well view them as 'teacher's pet'. If, however, everyone understands why someone is the favourite and that this favouritism is justly deserved, they will probably be OK with it. Favourites tend to have a history with the boss; this may have been built over the long term, or it may have been forged in a recent and intense situation or crisis. Whichever is the case, you can be sure that when your boss had their back to the wall, someone stepped forward and provided support, and that someone now enjoys returned loyalty that to outsiders looks like favouritism.

All organisations have their own 'folklore': stories and legends about the deeds of their leaders; these stories are told and retold, and live on long after the consequences of the deeds have been forgotten. The folklore shapes people's beliefs about the organisation in general and its leaders in particular – in many respects, the stories are the culture of the organisation. You need to understand where your boss fits into these stories; do they have a lead role, or are they part of the chorus? Are they about to write a new chapter of the story, or are they a fading star? Understanding your boss's place in the company narrative will help you assess their need for support and the sort of acts of loyalty that will be quickly noticed. It's difficult to predict ahead of time what sort of acts are destined to become part of company legend, but one thing is for sure: it is never routine or ordinary. So when you see your boss going out on a limb, or doing something that every sane person thinks is ethical but foolhardy, rather than running away, so that none of the resultant mess sticks to you, this is the very time to step forward and lend your support. You, too, may become part of the folklore, but you will certainly become part of your boss's loyal network and that loyalty will be repaid.

Making sense of it all

Managers are always on show, and their personal credibility is the sum of all their decisions, actions and reactions, and how they relate to people and the respect they accord to others. Consistent behaviour builds a collective view of your character, and this picture precedes you into every meeting and interaction. Like it or not, you carry with you a product description that everyone can read, but you can't write – what is says on the outside of your tin is the result of who you are, not who you would like to be, or how you would describe yourself if you could.

When we first get to know someone, our initial judgements are based on what everyone sees on the outside of the tin. Many never look any deeper; they take at face value the collective view and, in doing so, they reinforce the stereotype for others.

Before you pledge your loyalty to someone, you have to get to know them. This means peeling off the outside veneer, looking past what everyone else sees and getting a feel of the real person. This is never easy; extroverts don't show their real self because they are playing a role. Conversely, introverts are difficult to fathom because they guard their privacy and are introspective by nature. You need to get past external behaviours to get a sense of what is really important to your boss, what their hopes and fears are, their visions and their dreams, what excites them and what gives them the cold shivers. You also need to allow your boss to see the real you. Loyalty is a two-way street; you have to mirror the qualities that you admire. If you extend these qualities to all you deal with, you will not be perceived as someone sucking up to their boss, but as someone with admirable qualities who is respected and admired as having an unwavering moral compass.

Building trust takes time and effort because it can only be based on a deep personal relationship. Put simply, you have to care about people and be there for them when they need you most, rather than when it's convenient for you. When you have a caring relationship with someone, it is not difficult to know what to do in any particular set of circumstances – but knowing what to do and doing it are sometimes not so easy because we have multiple loyalties, and sometimes these loyalties come into conflict.

We often see managers in agonies of indecision, torn between a course of action they know to be right and a conflicting loyalty to someone, or something, else. This sort of conflict arises when a superficial loyalty is in conflict with a deeper, subconscious loyalty, and it is that deeper loyalty that defines the 'rightness' of an action. These hidden loyalties are always anchored in your core values, the things that define you as a person – never act against these core values. Personal loyalty is important, but always stay true to who you are and your core ethical beliefs.

Practical advice

Being loyal to your boss, or your organisation, is about looking out for them, making sure that they do the right thing, and protecting their back when others waiver in their commitment to a course of action that they know to be right, but don't have the stamina, focus or energy to follow through on. Loyalty involves being supportive and helpful and, above all, not being critical, gossiping or saying and doing anything that might undermine your boss or your organisation. In public you always speak well of your boss and, if need be, you defend their actions. In private it is your job and your duty to give them feedback to challenge the ethical and moral grounds of their actions and decisions and to help them reflect on the outcomes of their actions, so that they can develop into a better boss and a more effective business leader.

In your dealings with your boss and other senior leaders in your organisation:

- Accept that they have power by virtue of their position, network and experience. If you want to have influence, you need access to their support and resources, and you are not going to get this unless they trust you and have a relationship with you. When you take actions that build trust, you are making a deposit in your loyalty bank.

- Don't expect perfection from your leaders – but do expect and demand ethical behaviour. Watch the little unthinking behaviours; they are the real clue to someone's deep-seated values. We can all take on a persona for a while, but it is the little things that point to the real character.

- Study your boss's management style; how do they deal with their bosses, how do they deal with their subordinates, the security guard, the cleaners, etc? All bosses have something they can teach you, whether it be positive or negative; you just need to look for it.

- Try to make your boss look good. Or, if you can't do this, at least make sure that you don't say or do anything that makes them look bad. Never try to score points, or belittle your boss in public or in private. Watch how you treat others – never put anyone down. It is not gracious and, although people may smile at the time, they are making a mental note that you are not to be trusted.

- Never complain about your boss to others – if they are doing something that harms you, go and sort it out with them (*see 'How do I give my manager feedback that helps me and builds their trust in me'*).

- Give your boss a sincere compliment from time to time – we are not talking about birthday presents or gifts, we are talking about the gift of recognition. You know how great you feel when someone recognises that you have done something great – your boss is human, too, but because of their position, people are less likely to overtly recognise the little things they do for them.

- Remember that your boss is part of a food chain, that your main loyalty is to the continued success of the organisation, and that your boss is just the vehicle that gives you access to a wider and more senior network. Get to know your boss's boss and look for ways to show loyalty in a way that they notice.

- Ask yourself what keeps your boss awake at nights and whether you have it in your power to make them rest more easily.

Further food for the curious

- Knippen JT and Green JTB. Coping with one's boss: showing loyalty to your boss. *Managerial Auditing Journal*, 1996, pp. 42–44:

  - A short three-page article that covers some interesting points.

Things for you to work on now

Key questions to ask yourself
• What are your core values and principles? The things that govern who you are, how you react and how you make decisions. Core values are very different from personal preferences – values are things like ethical

behaviour, telling the truth, loyalty, integrity, helping other people, public service, meaningful work, etc.

- What are the behaviours and values that you find most appealing in other people – why do you think this is?

- What are the little clues you can look for that give you confidence that someone shares your value system?

- What would it take to challenge one of your core values?

Mini exercises you can try immediately

- Think about your boss – how much do you care about them? Make a list of anyone, or anything, that could take precedence over them if you were to find yourself with a conflict of loyalties.

- Think about the three or four values that are most important to you, and then look at all the people you have felt loyalty towards over the years and see how many of these values they shared.

- Make a list of the words, actions and behaviours that give you a clue that others share your core values. Look for examples of these words, actions and behaviours in your boss. When you find them, use affirming statements to show that you are on the same wavelength.

- When one of your peers needs help, give it graciously, with no expectation that it will be repaid in kind.

Links to other questions

You may want to take a look at:

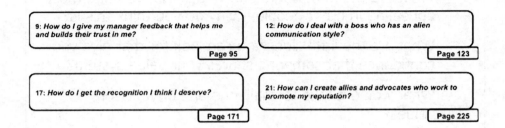

9: *How do I give my manager feedback that helps me and builds their trust in me?*

Page 95

12: *How do I deal with a boss who has an alien communication style?*

Page 123

17: *How do I get the recognition I think I deserve?*

Page 171

21: *How can I create allies and advocates who work to promote my reputation?*

Page 225

11: MY BOSS IS A BULLY, WHAT CAN I DO, HOW DO I COPE?

Why should I be asking this question?

If it is happening to you, you are not alone. A recent US study of bullying in the workplace revealed that 13% of US employees are currently bullied, 24% have been bullied in the past and 12% have witnessed workplace bullying.

If you feel bullied, then this is an issue and you shouldn't let others belittle or make light of your feelings. However, you also need to look at the situation from your boss's perspective and through their value and belief systems. Their behaviour may stem from frustration, rather than malice. For example, some managers believe that if you are not aiming to progress up through the ranks of an organisation, you have given up and are on a slippery slope of decline. Their subordinate, on the other hand, may be the type of person who is happy where they are, and not pushing for promotion to the next level. The perceived bulling behaviour of the boss may, therefore, be born out of frustration that their subordinate is not achieving what the boss feels they are capable of.

Remember that, although the problem may lie with the bully, the solution is in the hands of those experiencing the bullying behaviour.

The impact of the issue

Bullying is incredibly destructive; it leaves a person feeling powerless, confused, upset, angry and exhausted. It can destroy your self-esteem and totally undermine your ability to achieve anything positive. Productivity and self-confidence suffer, impacting on both the individual and the organisation alike.

Making sense of it all

Just because you feel bullied, or perceive your boss to be a bully, it does not necessarily mean that this is either your boss's intent, or that they are an inherently bad person. Your boss may be suffering from frustration, lack of self-esteem, abuse, ineptitude, or suchlike, themselves. A clash of styles, or value systems, can also result in the perception of being bullied.

Malevolent intent is a core component of deep-seated bullying. This intent may be conscious or unconscious. Genuine bullies can be extremely destructive, but are, fortunately, quite rare. In order to help us deal with them, it helps to categorise them according to their degree of cleverness and also their degree of self-control, as illustrated in Figure 7.

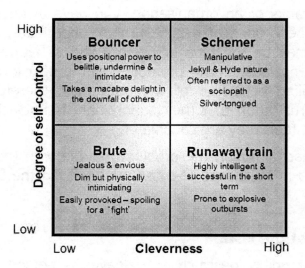

Figure 7: Types of bully

Let's explore the four types in a little greater depth.

The brutes – these are the easiest to spot. Their lack of self-control means that they are prone to sudden and uncontrolled outbursts, which can be physically intimidating. Because they are not too clever, they do not think through the consequences of their actions for others or, indeed, for themselves.

The bouncers – in some ways these are like brutes, but either through training, or because of their position, they have learned to control their emotions. However, under stress, they still tend to rely on physical or emotional pressure to get their own way. They are seldom overtly aggressive, but they know how to apply pressure and they can be relentless in doing so in order to get what they want.

Runaway trains – these people are clever, so they know how to manipulate people in order to get what they want. However, their lack of self-control means that they are totally unpredictable and their attention is likely to wander. These are difficult bullies to deal with, as you can never be quite clear about what might tip them over the edge.

The schemers – these are the most dangerous of all and also the most difficult type of bully to deal with. They are both clever and in control and, therefore, extremely difficult to expose. They are silver-tongued and most people would view them as wonderful people. The 'Jekyll' side of their character would only be revealed to an unfortunate few. Bullies in this category are commonly referred to as 'sociopaths'.

Practical advice

The first step is to determine whether malice is intended, or not? Is your boss a true bully, or simply someone with issues that are negatively impacting on their behaviour towards you? Once you have made this decision, refer to the relevant category below.

No malice is intended – with this type of boss you will need to understand why you feel bullied – the root cause of this perception. Make a list of the situations and circumstances that result in you feeling bullied. What did your boss do or not do, say or not say? What led up to this event? What type of person is your boss, what is their communication style, how does it compare with your own? What is important to them, what are their core values, what keeps them up at night? What pressures are they currently under that could explain their behaviour?

- Make a judgement as to the motives behind their behaviour. Are they frustrated with you because they feel that:

    - you are not driving as hard as they are towards a particular goal?

    - you are giving them too much or too little detail?

    - you won't make a decision without all the facts?

    - you leap to conclusions before you have all the facts?

- Are they themselves being bullied and mirroring this behaviour because it makes them feel better or more in control?

- Are they suffering from stress, or lacking in self-confidence or self-esteem?

- Are they struggling in their role and out of their depth?

- Do they have personal issues?

Once you have a handle on what is driving their behaviour, you will need to consider your strategy for dealing with the situation. Your tactics may include the following:

- Make them feel good about themselves:

    - Help them to develop their skills and to shine at something.

- Build on their suggestions – use the words 'yes and ...' to steer them rather than 'yes, but ...'.
- Offer them the 'limelight'.
- Massage their ego and praise their intellect.
- Get them to talk about themselves – remember this is most people's favourite subject. This will have the added benefit of getting to know your 'enemy'.

- Make them feel comfortable about you:
  - Help them to understand you – your values and drivers.
  - Be truthful and transparent.

- Don't give them any ammunition:
  - Be firm and strong.
  - Don't be sloppy or slapdash.
  - Keep your cool.

- Protect yourself:
  - Cultivate your friends – we all need a shoulder to cry on from time to time.
  - Cultivate allies – this will limit the bully's sphere of influence.
  - Keep positive about yourself and your own abilities.

Malice intended – these are the real bullies. They are capable of destroying their victims' self-esteem and making their lives a misery. First we will offer some general advice and then move on to consider more specifically how to deal with each of the different types.

General advice

Keep a factual log of every instance that you feel bullied. Keep copies of any documents that refer to you, or your work, in a negative light. Many incidents may appear trivial in isolation, so it is important to establish a pattern over a period of time.

You will need this factual evidence when you confront your boss, ask for help, or, indeed, if you make a formal complaint. In addition, writing things down often helps put the situation into perspective, and can often make you feel better and more positive.

Get some help; consult your HR department, your union representative or your safety representative. They may accompany you when you speak to the bully, or see them on your behalf. They can also put you in touch with support groups and help you with a formal complaint if it goes that far. If the bullying is affecting your health, visit your GP.

Keep positive, stay calm and be strong. Remember that criticism and personal remarks are not connected to your abilities. They reflect the bully's own weaknesses, and are meant to intimidate and control you.

Now consider which category of bully your boss falls into. How clever are they? How much self-control are they able to exercise? Refer to the model in the previous section and then, according to their classification, consider the more targeted advice below.

Dealing with the brutes – time alone will often expose this type of bully and show them up for what they are. Your best approach is to marginalise them, to cultivate relationships around them, and wait for the day when they reveal their true colours for all to see.

Dealing with the bouncers – speak to them, tell them that their behaviour is unacceptable and ask them to stop. This type of bully will not like to be confronted, particularly by someone who also has the ability to remain calm and civilised. Stick to the facts, but explain the impact of their behaviour and how it makes you feel. Help them to succeed, to develop their skills and to shine at something. Offer them the limelight.

Dealing with the runaway trains – praise their intellect, build on their suggestions and generally make them feel good about themselves. This will hopefully reduce their volatility. Make them feel comfortable with you by helping them to understand you. Be truthful, but also firm. Never be sloppy or slapdash.

Dealing with the schemers – with this type of bully, the majority of the bullying behaviour goes on behind closed doors. Find out if they are doing the same thing to others; you may well find that you are not alone. Even if you are alone, the more people that know what your boss is doing to you, the more difficult it is for them to flourish. Do your homework on them; as they say, 'get to know your enemy'. When you understand their 'hot buttons', make yourself useful, help them out, make them look good and massage their ego. In the meantime, cultivate your network and engage the support of your allies and advocates.

Further food for the curious

- Kakabadse A. Facing Up to the Dark Side of Leadership. *Think: Cranfield*, Nov. 2010:

    - An interesting insight into leadership when it goes wrong and the motives and drivers that can lead to 'bad leadership'.

Things for you to work on now

Key questions to ask yourself
<ul><li>Is my boss a true bully, i.e. do they have malicious intent?</li><li>If you answer yes to the above question – which category do they fall into?</li><li>If you answer no to the above question – what do they</li></ul>

do that causes you to feel bullied and what are the motives behind their behaviour?

- Does my boss bully anyone else, or have they done so in the past? Is it just me?

- If your boss has a history of bullying behaviour, how have/do others dealt/deal with the situation?

- Are there any patterns or triggers to your boss's bullying behaviour?

- How have you dealt with your boss's behaviour to date and what were the outcomes?

Mini exercises you can try immediately

- Compile a list of all the instances when you felt bullied – be factual and specific. Note dates and times, circumstances, your feelings and reactions. Now look for any patterns or triggers, e.g. if the behaviour always manifests itself in the afternoon and your boss goes out for lunch, it could be drink related.

- Share your notes with a trusted friend or colleague – ask them how they would deal with your boss in such situations – you may get some fresh insights and you will definitely feel better for getting things off your chest.

- Keep telling yourself 'I'm OK' – remember the problem is with them, not you.

- Try a little ego massaging and watch their response.

Links to other questions

You may want to take a look at:

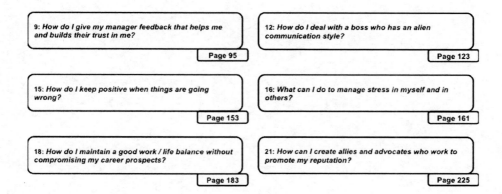

9: *How do I give my manager feedback that helps me and builds their trust in me?*

Page 95

12: *How do I deal with a boss who has an alien communication style?*

Page 123

15: *How do I keep positive when things are going wrong?*

Page 153

16: *What can I do to manage stress in myself and in others?*

Page 161

18: *How do I maintain a good work / life balance without compromising my career prospects?*

Page 183

21: *How can I create allies and advocates who work to promote my reputation?*

Page 225

12: HOW DO I DEAL WITH A BOSS WHO HAS AN ALIEN COMMUNICATION STYLE?

Why should I be asking this question?

In the words of George Bernard Shaw, 'The biggest problem with communication is the illusion that it has been accomplished'.

Effective communication between boss and subordinate is essential. If you and your boss are not communicating effectively, you will be wasting a lot of time attempting to deliver what you 'think' your boss wants, inevitably to find your assumptions are fundamentally flawed.

One of the things we hear most from managers when coaching them is:

> Often when I come out of a meeting with my boss, I realise that I have no idea what they want me to do. Yet when they asked me if I understood, I said yes! Sometimes after the meeting, I have asked others who were at the meeting if they know what we are supposed to be doing, and they shake their heads and say that they have no idea.

The consequences of this sort of miscommunication will be annoyance and disappointment on behalf of your boss and resentment and frustration on your side. Both of you will lose credibility in the eyes of each other, relationships will become strained and both of your reputations will suffer.

The impact of the issue

When a subordinate is perceived not to understand what is expected of them, the typical reaction from the boss is to place the blame firmly at the door of their subordinate. The boss assumes that the problem is the subordinate's fault, and, therefore, the subordinate's responsibility – we often hear sentiments such as 'When is this turkey going to get it?' or 'Why can't people just do what I ask of them?'.

It is very easy to confuse competence with style. We tend to view our way of approaching a task to be the best way, our way of communicating to be the most effective, etc. and if we see others doing it differently, it is very easy to dismiss them as being 'incompetent' or, worse still, 'stupid'. We all think and process information in different ways, depending upon our psychological predisposition. Also, the way we think tends to determine our approach to problem solving. This difference in thinking and problem-solving styles gives rise to two areas of confusion and breakdown when bosses brief us on new tasks:

- They may use language and logic structures that are different from our own and we, therefore, have difficulty following their line of thought. If it becomes obvious to them that we don't understand their language, they may think that we are 'thick'.

- They approach problem solving differently than we do, so when they try to give us a specific briefing on what they want us to do, it makes little sense to us because we wouldn't naturally approach a problem in this way. If it becomes obvious to them that we don't understand their approach to the problem, they may think that we are 'incompetent'.

Although these two have their roots in the same issue, namely our preferences for dealing with and processing information, each area of confusion needs to be approached in a slightly different way if we are to build better communication with our boss.

Making sense of it all

The following analysis is based on Carl Jung's theory of psychological type. This theory describes two dimensions which are of fundamental importance in relation to communication style:

- *Level of detail* – some people like lots of detail, while others just want the big picture or 'headline'.

- *Basis for decision making* – some people base their decision making on objective logic, while others base their decision making on subjective values and the impact of their decisions on the person/people concerned.

These two dimensions are used to generate the matrix in Figure 8, which describes the four resulting 'types' of people, each with their own style and needs.

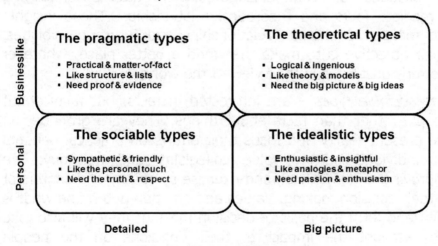

Figure 8: People types

The pragmatic types – like facts and are cautious not to go beyond the facts. They rely upon their five senses to guide them and favour literal interpretation of that data. They make decisions through logical analysis of the data and other empirical evidence, evaluating the pros and cons of all the

125

possible options. Their objective is to reach fair, reasoned and rational conclusions.

The theoretical types – like ideas, theories and concepts. They read between the lines and value the interpretation of such insights. They need to have an answer to the big 'WHY' question. They rely upon gut instinct and sixth sense in their decision making, intuitively knowing the answer or way forward. They pursue their chosen course of action with confidence and certainty. Their objective is to make sense of the world by making connections and building mental models; they seek to find ways of helping others to see, to bring clarity from disorder.

The idealistic types – like the figurative and the symbolic. They are ingenious and creative and are interested in the complexities of communication, the patterns underlying immediate facts and theoretical relationships. These insights are focused on human relationships and future possibilities. Their objective is to make the world a better place, whatever 'better' constitutes in their view of the world.

The sociable types – are interested in facts, but facts about people rather than facts about things. They are grounded in the present reality and focus their efforts on practical benefits for individuals. They value collegiality and harmony, are approving and uncritical, and exercise sympathy and sentiment in their decision making. Values and emotion determine what is right and form the basis of decision making; they will also take into account the impact of their decisions on the people concerned. Their objective is to make the world a nicer place.

Communication is not a one-size fits all approach; what works for you is not necessarily what works for your boss. If your boss is a theoretical type and you are a social type, it may well feel like you speak French and your boss speaks Mandarin Chinese. As you can see, different types think and process information in different ways – different things seem important to them and this governs what they say and how they say it. If you can learn to tailor your communication and speak your boss's language, you are far more likely to engage them and ensure your message is received as you intended. If you can't find a way to speak their language then you have to find a way to help them to realise when they need to restructure their communication, so that you get the message in an unambiguous way. You cannot take an interpreter into every meeting, so you need to find ways of working that help you both to simultaneously translate for each other.

Practical advice

If you and your boss have different personality types, you will benefit greatly from adapting your communication style to that of your boss. So what will you need to do?

A pragmatic boss will need honesty and clarity, and specific and relevant facts. They will appreciate a pragmatic, common-sense approach. Use a sequential, step-by-step approach when explaining a situation or event. Give specifics: the what, why, who, when and a clear plan of action. If possible, offer proof and evidence that it has worked for others; focus on the tried and tested approach, rather than the novel or the unusual. Make sure all the numbers add up; be accurate and precise and give *all* but *only* relevant information in support of your case. Keep it businesslike; don't get too personal or over-evangelical. Focus on the hard facts, rather than the effect on the people and their feelings about it. Conclude with the impact on the 'bottom line'

A theoretical boss will want you to be businesslike, concise and to the point and focus on the big picture. They will need you to answer the big question '*Why?*'. Start with your idea, proposal or conclusion, remove most of the detail and back up with a few key high-level facts. Keep lists short; theoretical types think in threes – three key facts, three reasons why, etc. Focus on models and theories, rather than pictures and images.

Focus on results and objectives, rather than on the effect on the people and their feelings about it. Be direct and to the point, don't hesitate or waffle, and radiate confidence.

An idealistic boss will want unique treatment, for you to listen carefully and show an interest in their ideas. Try to inject passion and humour into your conversation, demonstrate that you truly believe in what you are saying and make it sound exciting. Focus on the idea or concept, not the detail as to how you arrived at it. Use imagery and metaphor, rather than fact or theory to impart your message. Ask your idealistic type for their input – remember they have ideas, too, and also feelings. Talk about the 'greater good', 'making a difference' to humanity at large – rather than individual people; remember, in the mind of the idealistic type, individuals are expendable for the good of the masses.

A sociable boss will want to build a personal connection with you. They will want you to demonstrate empathy and practicality, to tell the truth, the whole truth and nothing but the truth. Give facts and details, but facts and details about real people. Avoid generalisations, or impersonal language such as 'downsizing' or 'rightsizing'; talk instead about the effects on Fred, Joe and Harry. Demonstrate caring and empathy towards individual people. Ask open questions and probe gently, actively listen and encourage them to do most of the talking; don't patronise them or talk at them. Avoid big intuitive leaps or off-the-wall ideas; focus on the practical realities of today.

How do I know my boss's type?

- A pragmatic boss will:
    - be interested in facts, use precise language and learn from experience;
    - give you lots of information and long lists, i.e. more than three items, when asked a question;

- make decisions on facts utilising impersonal and logical analysis from cause to effect, from premise to conclusion;

- use a step-by-step, sequential approach to describe a situation;

- use the words 'thinking' or 'thought' rather than 'feeling' or 'felt'.

- A theoretical boss will:

  - be interested in possibilities, theoretical relationships and abstract concepts;

  - give you impressions, rather than detail, and short lists, three items or fewer, when asked a question;

  - be quick in their decision making, using intuition coupled with impersonal objectivity; they are confident individuals with a strong sense of self-worth;

  - use analogies and anecdotes to illustrate a situation and leave you with impressions, rather than details;

  - use the words 'thinking' or 'thought', rather than 'feeling' or 'felt'.

- An idealistic boss will:

  - be interested in possibilities, symbolic meanings, things that have never happened but might be made to happen, or truths that are not yet known but might be;

  - give you impressions rather than detail and lists no longer than three items when asked a question;

  - make decisions based on their own personal values and the impact of those decisions on others; their aim will be to make the world a better place, whatever 'better' is in their book;

  - use analogies and anecdotes to illustrate a situation and leave you with impressions rather than details;

- use the words 'feeling' or 'felt', rather than 'thinking' or 'thought'.

- A sociable boss will:
  - be interested in facts, but facts about real people and true stories about what has helped these real people;
  - give information and stories about real people and their experiences and lists longer than three items when asked a question;
  - make decisions based on facts with personal warmth, weighing how much things matter to them and others;
  - use the words 'feeling' or 'felt', rather than 'thinking' or 'thought'.

Further food for the curious

- Dunning D. *Introduction to Type and Communication*. Consulting Psychologists Press (2003):
  - This short, practical booklet examines how knowledge of our own and others' personality type can lead to more effective communication.

Things for you to work on now

Key questions to ask yourself
<ul><li>Do I get frustrated with my boss because they don't get to the point, or do I get frustrated with my boss because they are vague and not interested in the practical realities?</li><li>Do I consider my boss to be cool and uncaring, or indecisive and sentimental?</li><li>How do I think and process information – what is my personality type and what is my natural style?</li></ul>

- How does my boss think and process information – what is my boss's personality type and what is their natural style?

- How adept am I at modifying my natural style to communicate more effectively with my boss?

- Consider the e-mails your boss sends you – how long are they?

- What tone does my boss take with me?

Mini exercises you can try immediately

- Think of a meeting that you had with your boss that left you wondering what you were supposed to do, or how you were supposed to present the results of your work. Identify two or three points in the meeting where you felt most lost; make a list of the steps you could take next time you find yourself feeling similarly lost. Put your plan into action.

- Next time you have a confusing encounter with your boss in a team meeting, look carefully at the other members of the meeting, and pick out someone who looks lost and confused. Talk to them afterwards and ask them why they are confused. See if you can use your new understanding of personality types and the way we process information to help them understand why their communication is breaking down. In helping them, you will learn to better understand your own communication issues.

- Analyse an e-mail trail between you and your boss. How do they lay out their logic? How do they give you information and evidence? Do they talk in metaphors, concepts, or just lists of facts? Try to match the length and style of your response to fit better with the way your boss writes and thinks. Monitor your success by looking carefully at the way your interaction develops.

- Next time your boss verbally briefs you on a task, write a half-page summary of what you think you have been asked to do and write it in the style they usually adopt in their e-mails to you. Take the summary to your boss, and ask them if they could look over it and confirm what they want you to do. If your boss starts to rewrite your summary, you know that you have not fully understood how they think and you need to use this encounter to refine your approach to them. Keep trying this strategy until you start to get positive responses like an enthusiastic 'Yes, that's exactly what I want'.

Links to other questions

You may want to take a look at:

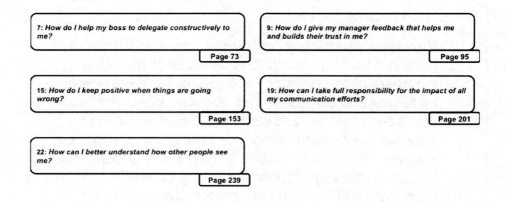

7: *How do I help my boss to delegate constructively to me?*

Page 73

9: *How do I give my manager feedback that helps me and builds their trust in me?*

Page 95

15: *How do I keep positive when things are going wrong?*

Page 153

19: *How can I take full responsibility for the impact of all my communication efforts?*

Page 201

22: *How can I better understand how other people see me?*

Page 239

HOW DO I MANAGE MYSELF?

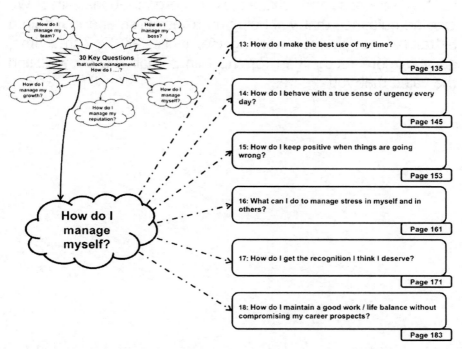

One of our favourite daydreams is to imagine how we will spend the £8.7 million that we are going to win on the lottery – notice that we are quite specific about the amount involved. It is a harmless-enough fantasy, but ultimately pointless, especially as neither of us have ever actually bought a lottery ticket in our lives!

When it comes to managing aspirations, anxieties and emotions at work, most people take the same approach as our lottery-winnings spending plan; they engage in wishful thinking and, just as with our lottery dreams, wishful thinking never got anyone anywhere. But it doesn't need to be like that – just as you put time and effort into managing other people, you can also put time and effort into managing yourself – with potentially surprising results.

In this section, we explore *six* key questions that open the door to you being more productive, more focused and more resilient to the stresses and challenges of organisational life. We provide guidance that will help you to establish and maintain a better balance in your working life, while, at the same time, gaining more recognition for the things that you do well and the value that you create.

13: HOW DO I MAKE THE BEST USE OF MY TIME?

Why should I be asking this question?

Our time is a precious and limited commodity. We buy other people's time to do things we don't want to do, or can't do, and our time is bought by whomever we work for. Most people don't analyse where their time goes – a similar attitude to money is called reckless spending. Here are some thought-provoking quotes on the subject of time:

> *How we spend our days is, of course, how we spend our lives.*

> *The good people are already busy.*

> *Work always expands to fill the time available.*

The impact of the issue

We never seem to have enough time to do all the things we want to do, or think we ought to do. Modern life cajoles us into spending a significant proportion of our time in reactive mode, responding to e-mails, paper mail and telephone calls, attending meetings, dealing with people that turn up on our doorstep, etc.

We often waste time agonising over priorities, swapping between activities because we can't decide which is the most important and searching for things we have lost because we are too busy to organise ourselves.

Many managers feel overstretched and, as a consequence, are constantly battling to fit everything in, while, at the same time, striving to meet unrealistic deadlines. They find themselves constantly playing catch-up and invariably start to come to the office early, leave late and work evenings and weekends. The answer is to delegate, but delegation takes time, time that we do not have, so we decide it is quicker to do it ourselves. Doing it ourselves leads to even more work out of office hours and, of course, you cannot delegate to anyone when you are working from home at the weekend.

Making sense of it all

Our aim is to be effective in what we do and efficient in the way we do it. However, we often confuse efficiency with effectiveness; for example, you may scrub floors efficiently, but if this is not what you are paid to do, it is not an effective use of your time:

- Efficiency is time related; it is about doing things the right way.

- Effectiveness is goal related; it is about doing the right things.

Effectiveness is about doing those things that are important, the tasks, activities and decision making that will help you to achieve your purpose and help build the business, i.e. it is about doing the job you are employed to do and what you get paid for doing.

It is relatively straightforward to plan our time based on the urgency of a task; however, we often forget to take into account the importance of a task. These two measures are mutually independent; just because a task is urgent, it does not necessarily follow that it is important, or vice versa. Based on these two measures, tasks, therefore, fall into one of four categories as shown in the matrix in Figure 9 adapted from Covey's *The 7 Habits of Effective Managers*.

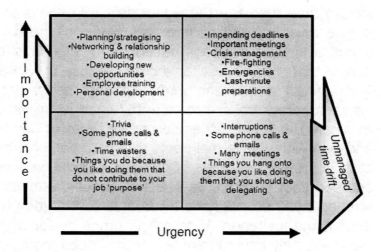

Figure 9 Priority matrix[4]

If we don't actively manage our time, it tends to get swallowed up by activities that fall into the bottom-right quadrant; this is nearly always at the expense of activities in the top-left quadrant. The consequences of insufficient time in the top-left quadrant are rework, fire-fighting and crisis management, which, in turn, leave even less time for planning and strategising; a vicious circle sets in and we cease to become effective.

Practical advice

In order to turn this vicious circle into a virtuous one, we need to ensure we spend sufficient time in the top-left quadrant and minimise the time we spend in the other three. The following pointers will help you achieve this:

---

[4] US President Eisenhower is quoted as saying, 'What is important is seldom urgent and what is urgent is seldom important'. This idea was brought into management mainstream thinking by Stephen Covey in his business classic *The 7 Habits of Highly Effective People*, first published in the UK by Simon and Schuster in 1989.

- *Banish time thieves* – these include junk e-mails or e-mails people have copied you into that you don't need to know about, irrelevant meetings, meetings for meetings' sake, or people that stop by just for a chat because they are bored. Turn off all e-mail and mobile phone alerts. Set e-mail filters to draw your attention to what is important and eliminate the spam. Schedule certain times of day to check and deal with your e-mail; only deal with personal texts and calls out of office hours. Don't have social network sites open on your desktop. Be selective about the meetings you attend; if you do not have a valuable contribution to make, decline the invitation. If someone drops by for a chat, tell them you only have a minute – if they need more, schedule them in at lunchtime or the end of the day.

- *Concentrate* – get to know your own body clock. If you are most productive in the morning, do those tasks that require more brain power then; leave those phone calls that don't require a lot of thought until the afternoon when your energy levels are dwindling:

  - Take mini beaks – a simple five-minute walk to the coffee machine can do wonders to recharge your batteries.

  - Remember to eat – we need fuel to maintain our energy levels and the right type of fuel. Avoid heavy meals that take energy to digest and sugary snacks that cause your blood-sugar levels to yo-yo; instead, go for complex carbohydrates and small amounts of protein that provide you with a slow and sustained release of energy.

  - Do one thing at a time – you can only concentrate effectively on one thing; therefore, only have one task in front of you at any one time. If you must multitask, put files to one side when you are not looking at them.

- *Delegate* – we delegate tasks to grow our subordinates and to create space in our diaries for other activities. Effective delegation is not easy; the principal challenges are:

  - The initial overhead when we delegate a task for the first time – it is probably true that, in the short term, we could do the task more quickly and better ourselves, but the consequences are that our subordinates never learn to do new things and that we run out of time while they run out of work.

  - Letting go of jobs that we like doing – this is called growing up.

  - Learning to trust and overcoming the fear of losing control.

  - Taking back jobs when our subordinates ask for help – subordinates are very good at upward delegation, so make sure the ball stays in their court; always remember, you can delegate responsibility and authority but you cannot delegate accountability!

- *Use the 80:20 rule* – some things do need to be perfect, but more often than not, 80% is good enough. We all have a tendency to over-engineer and strive for perfection in all that we do. Ask yourself 'Is it fit for purpose? Will it do the job?' If the answer to these questions is yes then stop. Always have the Pareto Principle in the back of your mind, that 20% of the effort will give you 80% of the benefit.

- *Eliminate wasted time* :

  - Plan your time, schedule those important, but not urgent tasks and also plan time to deal with all the day-to-day stuff that lands on your desk. Plan time during the day when you will deal with your e-mail, rather than reacting to each and every alert.

  - Utilise dead time – use travelling time and waiting time to catch up on your reading or e-mails. Have a folder of reading material ready to grab as you leave the office.

- Avoid procrastinating over those things that you don't feel like doing because they are difficult, unpleasant or uncomfortable. Do them first – you will be amazed at how much better you feel, and how much more productive you will be without the weight of an unpleasant task hanging over you.

- Be decisive – most of us waste plenty of time dithering over fairly trivial decisions; any decision is often better than no decision. If a course of action is taking you in the right direction then carry on; if it is not, remember you can always change course. Apply the 80:20 rule to information gathering; gather enough, rather than striving for all that is available.

- *Get organised*:

  - Be realistic about what you can achieve in any one day; ensure you leave time to get yourself organised, delegate effectively, deal with the day-to-day stuff, eat and have a little 'me' time in order to switch off and relax.

  - Operate a one-book system – have a notebook that you write everything down in. If you need to refer back to who said what in a meeting or find a phone number, it will be there. It gets rid of the clutter and you will stop losing information.

  - Chunk tasks – group similar tasks together and do them as a batch.

  - Don't get distracted – if you think of something else you need to do while in the middle of another task, make a note so you won't forget it, but complete the task you are currently working on first.

- Develop a filing system that works for you and use it. You will need to allocate a little time each day to keep it under control.

- Don't let other people's lack of planning throw you off course. As one fiery secretary we know would say: 'Your lack of planning doesn't make it my emergency!'.

- *Learn how to say 'no'*:

  - The vital thing to bear in mind is that you cannot possible say 'yes' to everybody all of the time. It is far better to be honest and learn to say 'no' rather than 'maybe', 'if I can fit it in', 'possibly', or suchlike. Don't give people false hope. Be firm, be fair, be honest, be consistent and be polite. If it is your boss who is demanding your time, set out what you have to do and ask them to prioritise – make sure they understand the potential consequences of any compromise they suggest – write it down.

A word about e-mail

In today's high-tech world, we spend less and less time talking to people and more and more time sending e-mails, leaving voicemails and playing telephone tag. The middle managers we work with typically say they spend 30 to 40% of their time on non-human interactions. This is both frustrating and monotonous and saps our energy reserves. Learn to use e-mail appropriately. When messages are simple and straightforward, nothing can beat e-mail; however, complex or ambiguous issues are always best dealt with face to face, or, at least, over the telephone. Use the copy facility wisely and frugally and teach others, in particular your subordinates, to do the same. Make the subject line meaningful and, again, teach others to do the same; set an example. If you do get copied in on things that you don't need to know about, either delete them without reading beyond the subject line, or file them in a 'just in case' file. If your e-mail takes more than 30 minutes a day then something is wrong; go back and reread this advice.

Further food for the curious

- Oncken W and Wass D. Management Time: Who's got the Monkey? *Harvard Business Review*, Nov./Dec. 1974:
    - One of the most impactful articles we have come across on the subject; the authors use a monkey analogy to highlight the issues of time management.

- Hallowell E. The Human Moment at Work. *Harvard Business Review*, Jan./Feb. 1999:
    - A very interesting article discussing the pros and cons of e-mail communication, when to use it and when not to use it.

- Covey SR. *The 7 Habits of Highly Effective People – Powerful Lessons in Personal Change*. Simon & Schuster (2004):
    - More on the time management matrix which Covey popularised in 1996 in his book *First Things First*.

Things for you to work on now

Key questions to ask yourself
▪ Who controls how you spend your time – you or events?
▪ If you feel that you are at the mercy of events – what steps can you take now to regain some control over your life?
▪ How organised do you currently feel?
▪ How efficient are you at completing tasks?

- What sort of things do you always put off doing? What is it about them that you don't like? What would have to change for you to start to feel differently?

- How effective are you, i.e. are you doing the right tasks?

- If you had more time, what would you do with it?

Mini exercises you can try immediately

- Establish your priorities:

  - Summarise your purpose in one sentence – remember this is what you are employed for, not what you necessarily do.

  - Compile a list of all your current tasks.

  - Against each task, identify its importance, and then quite separately, its urgency.

  - Now plot your tasks on the priority matrix.

- Analyse how you spend your time:

  - For a period of two weeks, keep a log of your activities, noting how long they take and which quadrant of the priority matrix they fall into.

  - Analyse what percentage of your time you have spent in each quadrant.

  - Ask yourself how you feel about this.

- Then consider what you are going to do about it.

Links to other questions

You may want to take a look at:

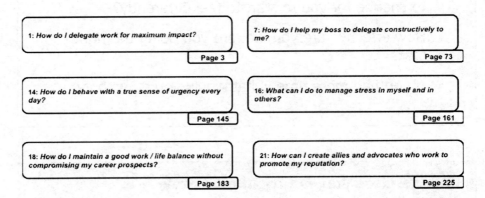

1: *How do I delegate work for maximum impact?*

Page 3

7: *How do I help my boss to delegate constructively to me?*

Page 73

14: *How do I behave with a true sense of urgency every day?*

Page 145

16: *What can I do to manage stress in myself and in others?*

Page 161

18: *How do I maintain a good work / life balance without compromising my career prospects?*

Page 183

21: *How can I create allies and advocates who work to promote my reputation?*

Page 225

14: HOW DO I BEHAVE WITH A TRUE SENSE OF URGENCY EVERY DAY?

Why should I be asking this question?

We live in a world where we can have pretty much instant access to anything we want 24 x 7. Our society seems to crave instant gratification; we want success and we want it now. Against this background and an ever-increasing pace of life, it is easy to believe that when we respond very quickly, we are behaving with urgency and that to strive for an even quicker speed of reaction is the right thing to do. The reality is that urgency and speed of reaction are not the same thing. Urgency is not about speed; it is about focus and energy – focusing relentlessly on what is important for survival, for growth and for change and to do it now, not sometime in the future when you have time in your busy schedule.

Most managers believe that they have created urgency when they see lots of people running around doing lots of things. Paradoxically, in order to have the time to behave with urgency, it is often necessary to do less – i.e. to create the space needed to be able to take action when action is needed, to make commitments and follow them through. At a time when we seem to be constantly running faster just to stay in the same place, when our diaries are crowded with back-to-back meetings from 8 am to 7 pm, clearing the space to be able to devote time to take focused, urgent and energetic action may appear to be an impossible task, but it is essential and we must find a way of achieving it.

The impact of the issue

Managers are not paid to do the routine to keep the wheels turning – that is the role of team leaders and supervisors. Most day-to-day operations can take care of themselves without much attention, or oversight, from a manager. What the manager is paid to do is to make the wheels go around more effectively.

Better still, they are there to envisage and create an organisation that doesn't run on wheels, but rather has some sort of frictionless superdrive that costs less to run and produces more output with greater quality and customer satisfaction.

In short, managers are paid to achieve the extraordinary, rather than the ordinary.

You can't achieve extraordinary things when you are bogged down with other people's trivia and noise, which they should be dealing with themselves. Most managers either feel that they are powerless to achieve anything other than maintain the status quo, or they feel afraid to try anything different in case it fails; sometimes they may really have the desire, but they just can't find the time, or the energy, because they are so busy doing the less important stuff.

Making sense of it all

A sense of urgency is not to be confused with frantic activity focused on meeting upon meeting, fire-fighting, back protecting, or the pursuit of the trivial or the unimportant. Urgency is about focusing on a few key things and then making the time and finding the energy to see those key things through to completion. In their article 'Beware the Busy Manager', Bruch and Ghoshal report on their findings from 10 years spent studying senior managers in organisations around the world. They suggest that, in their experience, as many as 90% of all managers squander their time on all sorts of ineffective activity. They call it 'active non-action', a great expression that neatly describes the sort of frantic posturing that we see from many managers. The big question is what do you have to do to be a part of the 10% of managers who are apparently focused enough to make a difference.

Bruch and Ghoshal identify four types of behaviour associated with how a manager approaches their job: the disengaged, the procrastinator, the distracted and the purposeful. We will look specifically at the purposeful manager, as that is the model to which we should all aspire.

Perhaps the thing that most distinguishes the purposeful manager is the way they define themselves with respect to their work and their autonomy for action. Most managers appear to be content to sit in a box defined by others – by their peers, their job description, the business environment and what other people think will work, or is appropriate. They operate only within the confines of how their box has been defined.

Purposeful managers are not constrained by the hand that life deals them – they don't play the cards, even when they know they hold a losing hand. What they do is trade in the cards to get a better hand. They use their network to access required resources, they cultivate relationships with influential people, and they build and acquire competencies with the sole aim of increasing their freedom to act.

So acting with urgency and purpose is about proactively managing your environment to increase your choice and freedom to act, and then acting with focus on one or two key initiatives to the exclusion of all else, and maintaining energy throughout until your goal is achieved.

Practical advice

We have suggested that the purposeful manager is one who understands the value of focus and applied energy, and also appreciates that these are the two qualities that technology and the modern organisational structure appear to be set up to steal from you. So the first rule of acting with urgency and purpose is to actively manage your time – if you allow yourself to be swept along at the pace of others you will lose focus and deplete your reserves of energy. Here are some basic rules for you to try:

- Set aside specific times of day to deal with e-mail, phone calls and visitors. The most purposeful managers are rigorous about protecting their time:

  - Turn off all alerts on your phone and PC – you are not its servant; it is yours. If you start to respond to everything as it hits you, there is no way that you can prioritise. The only way to prioritise is to wait until you have a bunch of e-mails/tasks and then decide calmly, using the urgency/importance grid, which to tackle and which to ignore (*see 'How do I make best use of my time?'*).

  - When deciding on urgency, your prime measure should be 'does this task contribute to the one or two primary change initiatives that I have set myself, or accepted from the leadership team?'

  - Increasingly, managers don't have personal assistants to protect them and they have open electronic diaries that everyone can see. This may be very egalitarian and the modern equivalent of saying 'my door is always open', but it is certainly a sure-fire way of letting other people fill your day with stuff that is important to them, but may be irrelevant to you. Get into the habit of blocking out at least 40% of your time each week – use the software functionality to show the time as busy and private. Make a rule that the only people who can steal this time from you are people well above your pay grade.

148

- Build in time to reflect on what is happening and what your priorities are. For instance, if you have a one-hour commute to work by car; it may be an idea to designate the morning commute as your reflection time and have your mobile phone turned off. The evening commute, by contrast, may become known to your staff as the time to run things past you, or to give you catch-up status reports. Encourage them to talk to you rather than e-mail you. If you need an audit trail, you could ask them for a short confirmation e-mail – in all other cases, verbal communication should be the order of the day.

- As well as creating time to focus, you also need to find ways of reducing stress and topping up your energy levels. This is an individual and personal need that is likely to be fulfilled outside the work environment by:

  - engaging in an absorbing hobby;

  - doing sport, exercise or meditation;

  - giving something back to your local community – strangely, sometimes the more energy you expend, the more you seem to have.

Once you have got hold of your time and you have found the wellsprings of energy you need for the journey, you must focus all your attention on the journey itself. This requires you to address a meaningful challenge, something that is bigger than your immediate department. It should be of importance to the continued growth and sustainability of your organisation, you should have choice in the way you approach the challenge and you need to enlist the support of your network to gain broad organisational acceptance that finding a solution to this challenge will produce lasting value for the organisation.

Once you have found such a challenge, it is easy to see what needs to be focused upon and how you will recognise when you have been successful. It has to be something that you are prepared to make a very visible personal commitment to and also something that you are prepared to bet your reputation on.

Without such a challenge, urgency can only be maintained for very short periods. It is the difference between the 200-metre sprint and the marathon. Urgency is about the long game and finding the reserves of energy and commitment that can carry you through the 26 miles of the marathon to the finishing line.

Further food for the curious

- Bruch H and Sumantra G. Beware the Busy Manager, *Harvard Business Review*, Feb. 2002:

    - This is an insightful article that opens the box on what managers really do and how they fritter away their time. The stunning conclusion is that fully 90% of managers squander their time on ineffective activities. The good news is that the paper identifies the characteristics of different management behaviours and provides useful pointers on how to become more purposeful.

- Kotter JP. *A Sense of Urgency*. Harvard Business Press (2008):

    - This short and engaging book provides an explanation of the tactics that have been found to be effective in creating urgency during change initiatives.

Things for you to work on now

Key questions to ask yourself

- What is important to me – how do I want to make a contribution to this organisation and why am I uniquely placed to make that contribution?

- What does the organisation need to achieve in order to survive and prosper – what is my part in this journey?

- What have I done this week to increase my circle of influence and thus gain more freedom of action?

- What do I need to concentrate on in the next three months in order to increase my freedom of action even further?

Mini exercises you can try immediately

- Do an audit of your diary for the last two weeks – how much of your time was focused on bringing about something new for your organisation? Don't count talking-shops or project-update meetings – we are interested in tangible actions that you took that could bring something new to fruition.

- Look at your diary for the next two weeks – purge the time bandits, get rid of the stuff that just spins wheels. Block out some 'me' time, so that you can reflect upon why you are a manager and what you are going to achieve that is different in the next 12 months.

Links to other questions

You may want to take a look at:

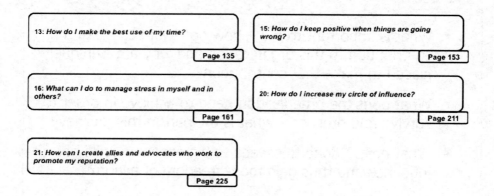

13: *How do I make the best use of my time?*

Page 135

15: *How do I keep positive when things are going wrong?*

Page 153

16: *What can I do to manage stress in myself and in others?*

Page 161

20: *How do I increase my circle of influence?*

Page 211

21: *How can I create allies and advocates who work to promote my reputation?*

Page 225

15: HOW DO I KEEP POSITIVE WHEN THINGS ARE GOING WRONG?

Why should I be asking this question?

We constantly have to deal with incompetence, stupidity, insensitivity, rudeness, indifference, and those who simply can't be bothered; the list goes on and on. Events conspire to mess up our carefully laid plans: things that don't turn up when they should have, a key player who goes off sick at exactly the wrong time, our car won't start just as we are about to leave for a crucial meeting; as they say, life can suck, bad things happen! When they do, keeping positive in the face of adversity can be challenging. In the right frame of mind, you may easily ride the waves. However, on another day, it could be a very different story; when events conspire against us, they drain us of our physical and mental energies.

The impact of the issue

We all have to deal with problems, issues and things that just don't go right. We get stuck in traffic jams and in endless queues, receive the wrong or damaged goods, drop and break our iPhone, miss a flight, take the wrong turn, have to pick up the pieces when a member of our team messes up – the list goes on.

Letting things get to us is not good for us; our well-being, our productivity and our creativity will all suffer, our energy reserves are depleted and our motivation dwindles. Indeed, a recent study, published in *Nature Neuroscience*, substantiated that pessimism was not good for our health. A study on nearly 100,000 people showed the optimists among the group to have a lower risk of heart disease and lower death rate in comparison to the pessimists.

Just as enthusiasm is infectious, so negativism is contagious; a negative attitude will spread like wildfire and have a knock-on effect to all of those around us.

Making sense of it all

The real test of a positive nature comes in the face of adversity. When things start to go wrong, it is not so easy to stay positive. The test is how quickly you bounce back. You may find you have a moment or two when it all gets on top of you; you lose control, your composure slips and you feel the onset of despair. But when the moment is over, your fighting spirit comes back, your sense of humour recovers and you start to see the funny side; you make the best of the situation and take the proverbial bull by the horns.

When things are going wrong, some people try to ignore the situation – 'sticking your head in the sand' and ignoring the problem is not going to help it go away. The longer problems remain unaddressed, usually the worse they become. Problems need to be embraced, not ignored. If handled properly, problems can be the catalyst that helps us to see differently and adopt new thinking patterns. They are a powerful learning opportunity.

The question 'Did things go wrong, or just not as planned?' is always a good one to have at the back of our minds. When you double-book yourself, your flight gets cancelled, or a supplier delivers the wrong product, these are simply examples of LIFE itself. You can't live a life in which everything goes according to plan. It's the ups and downs, the unexpected twists, the moments of serendipity that keep us on our toes and provide us with those special moments and instances of inspiration. It is good to remember that *perfection isn't living and living isn't perfection*. Life does not play out like some perfectly constructed script, it is about finding value in times of disillusionment, accepting that things won't always go as planned and using unexpected life experiences as opportunities; opportunities to get creative, to learn, to grow and to build bridges.

It is relatively easy to recover from minor glitches in our lives. However, the challenge comes when something really bad happens, such as someone close to us becoming seriously ill or losing our job; these are the real tests that mark out our ability to remain positive.

Having a positive attitude is vital for your well-being in life and for your success in business – as they say, 'it is your attitude, not your aptitude, that determines your altitude'.

Practical advice

There are many things you can do to help stay positive and prevent those negative thoughts from taking root. Next time events conspire against you and your positivity is put to the test, try some of the following:

- Don't be frightened or too proud to ask for help – it is very easy to get so close to a problem that we can't see the 'wood for the trees'. In such cases, someone else may be able to take a different perspective, to see a way through that is not obvious to us.

- Talk things through – when we articulate our fears, worries or concerns out loud, often they don't sound so bad. When we get things off our chest, it can make it easier to move on. Psychologists point to the importance of 'change talk' – the idea that before people can move on, they have to articulate the things that are getting in their way.

- When things go wrong (or not as planned), put the situation in perspective by asking yourself the following questions:

- Is the world going to stand still because of this?
- Can I have another go?
- Can it be mended?
- Can I buy a new one?
- How much will this matter in one, five, 10 years' time?
- What are the alternatives?
- What lessons can I learn?
- Will I be remembered for this at my funeral?

These questions help us to see that about 90% of the things that we get worked up about are really rather trivial and, in the grand scheme of things, are not worth ruining our day over. We all have bad-hair days – don't blow them out of proportion, get over it and move on.

- Take time out – forget about your problems for a day; just go out and do something fun. Go to a movie, go for a ride on your bike or have a game of golf, anything that is completely different, that you enjoy and that fully absorbs your attention. Readdress the problem another day when you are re-energised and in a better place.

- Re-evaluate, not just the situation, but also your outlook on the situation. Instead of complaining about the plan that is not working out, make a new plan. Instead of griping about a procedure that failed to deliver the required outcome, analyse the reason why and develop a new and better procedure. Take action to create the best possible outcome, rather than stressing over outcomes that are unattainable. Remember, we are either the master, or the victim, of our attitudes.

- Focus on what you can control, or influence, rather than what you can't. It is a pointless waste of energy and mental capacity fretting and worrying about things that you can't change; focus on what you can achieve, rather than what you can't. Don't let what you cannot do interfere with what you can do.

- Look on the funny side – humour and attitude are closely related. Instead of focusing on the loss in a robbery, someone with a good sense of humour may say to a friend 'We finally got rid of that awful figurine that my aunt bought us'.

- Don't give up – just because something went wrong once, or failed, it is no reason to give up, or not to try again. Remember Thomas Edison's famous saying, 'I did not fail: I just succeeded in finding 100 ways not to make a light bulb'.

Don't just wait for things to go wrong before you take action. The following everyday advice will help you to remain positive and look on the brighter side of life:

- Plan your day – this will help to improve your focus and prevent that overwhelmed feeling, provided that you are neither too ambitious nor too rigid. Ensure there is a little slack to enjoy some moments of relaxation, and delight in the serendipity of those chance encounters. Don't expect everything in life to go as planned; if you do, you will be quickly disappointed.

- Focus on the good, the positive. Life tends to be a self-fulfilling prophecy – positive thoughts produce positive outcomes just as negative thoughts produce negative outcomes; we tend to get what we expect.

- Nurture positive relationships and surround yourself with positive people, who will give you energy and make you more positive, rather than negative people who drain you of energy and depress the mood.

- Read inspiring and motivational books; listen to inspiring podcasts or music – by focusing on something positive, it will help you to keep positive.

- Look after your physical well-being – exercise, eating well and getting enough sleep can all contribute to a positive attitude:

  - Exercise is good for both mind and body; those endorphins improve our mood and provide us with that feel-good factor.

  - Nutrition – as they say, 'an army marches on its stomach'; if you are not getting the right fuel in sufficient quantities, you will find it more difficult to find the energy to keep positive when things are going wrong; indeed, the 'B' vitamins are particularly important for our mental well-being.

  - Sleep – we all need sufficient sleep, and the right amount for us. If you have problems getting to sleep, try some relaxation techniques just before you go to bed.

  - Relaxation – we all need to unwind from our busy lives. Try listening to your favourite music, reading a novel, watching a 'soap', taking the dog for a walk, meditation or other relaxation techniques such as tai chi.

- Inject some 'me' time into your life – no matter who you are or what you do, everyone needs a little 'me' time each day to recharge those emotional batteries. This is one of the single most important things that you can do for yourself, so start today.

- If you feel persistently sad, unmotivated, anxious, hopeless or fearful, it may be time to seek professional help.

On a final note, may we all remember to lighten up, to let go, and to live life to the full. Remember, our time on this planet is limited and finite; life is not a dress rehearsal!

Further food for the curious

- Sharot T, Korn CW and Dolan RJ. How unrealistic optimism is maintained in the face of reality. *Nature Neuroscience*, June 2011:

    - An insight into the neuroscience behind optimism and the health benefits of retaining a positive world view. The negative aspect of underestimating the risks is also discussed.

Things for you to work on now

Key questions to ask yourself
<ul><li>Am I a glass half full person or a glass half empty person?</li><li>Do I let the little things that go wrong in my life get to me?</li><li>How quickly do I bounce back when things do go wrong?</li><li>What was my reaction, or my attitude, the last time something went wrong in my life?</li><li>How prepared am I to ask for help?</li><li>How willing am I to talk things through with others?</li><li>What do I do to relax, to unwind?</li><li>Do I get sufficient sleep and exercise?</li><li>How good is my diet?</li><li>Am I able to see the funny side of things?</li></ul>

Mini exercises you can try immediately

- Practise a few relaxation techniques and see how they make you feel.

- Plan a little 'me' time into your life. Start with small steps, e.g. aim to read a novel on that plane or train journey to work, rather than do your e-mail.

- For a period of two weeks, try to eat only healthy foods, minimise your caffeine and alcohol intake, get at least seven hours' sleep per night and take at least 20 minutes' exercise each day. Monitor how you feel and your ability to cope with life's ups and downs.

- Make a list of all the people you could turn to for emotional support, to unburden or to provide a little TLC.

Links to other questions

You may want to take a look at:

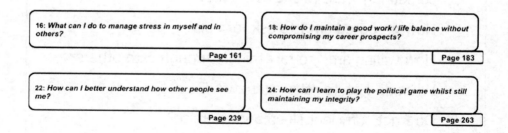

16: *What can I do to manage stress in myself and in others?*

Page 161

18: *How do I maintain a good work / life balance without compromising my career prospects?*

Page 183

22: *How can I better understand how other people see me?*

Page 239

24: *How can I learn to play the political game whilst still maintaining my integrity?*

Page 263

16: WHAT CAN I DO TO MANAGE STRESS IN MYSELF AND IN OTHERS?

Why should I be asking this question?

Stress is now the biggest cause of sickness and absenteeism in the UK, costing the economy billions of pounds a year. Statistically, it has overtaken backache. According to the Health and Safety Commission, 41% of the workdays lost due to illness last year were attributed to stress. The Trades Union Congress (TUC) estimates that work-related stress costs the economy up to seven billion pounds per annum.

The impact of the issue

Chronic stress is not good for us and can make us seriously ill; it can contribute to heart disease and memory loss, and suppress our immune response, making us more vulnerable to viral infections and more susceptible to developing certain cancers.

Studies have shown that people with certain personality traits are more prone to stress than others. If some, or all, of the following apply to you, you will be statistically more likely to suffer from stress at work:

- If you have an intolerance of ambiguity – finding it hard to deal with situations where there are multiple views or irresolvable differences and no single 'right answer'.

- If you are apt to focus on a rigid, single approach – seeking perfection in answers to questions or ways of doing things.

- If you only see short-term perspectives – preferring to deal with the here and now, to 'fire-fight', to focus upon the immediate issues of the day.

- If you can't see nuances and complexities in situations – taking things literally and failing to read between the lines, or see the subtleties of situations.

- If you are unable to make fine distinctions in judgement – overlooking the subtle alternative viewpoints which, if taken into consideration, could alter the judgements we make.

- If you avoid consultation – making decisions and dealing with issues on your own; withdrawing into yourself and failing to talk things through.

- If you have a tendency to rely on old, inappropriate habits – following processes and procedures simply because 'we have always done it this way' and failing to see when methods and practices become outdated, or are no longer appropriate.

- If you are less creative – utilising the narrow focus of logic and analytics to find more and more ingenious ways of streamlining processes or perfecting techniques, rather than the genuine lateral creativity of the intuition and imagination.

People with the personality traits listed above tend to get attracted to certain professions. These include IT, accountancy, dentistry, engineering, and such like. It is interesting to note that these are the very professions commonly cited as being the most stressful. This poses the question, 'Is it the profession that is stressful, or is it more to do with the type of person that is attracted to that profession?' – a chicken or egg dilemma.

Making sense of it all

First we need to understand the difference between stress and pressure. When under pressure, our bodies produce adrenaline; this is good because adrenaline gives us the drive and energy to do stuff. Without adrenaline coursing around our veins, we would be sorely tempted to stay in bed and have a 'duvet day'. So pressure enhances our performance, but only up to a certain point. If we exceed our limit, and pressure continues to be applied, we get stressed and our performance starts to decline, as shown in Figure 10.

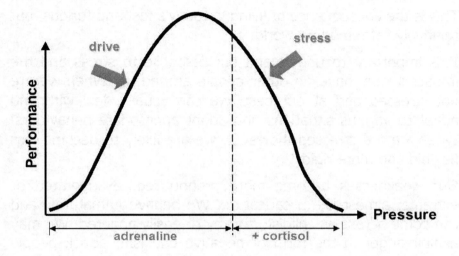

Figure 10: Effects of stress on performance

When we are stressed, our bodies start producing a second hormone called cortisol. Cortisol is the hormone designed to keep us safe, to put us in the best physical state to deal with the fight and flight reaction. Consequently it was very useful to our ancient ancestors who had the daily need to fight for their lives and flee from oncoming lions and the like. These days, however, few of us have a daily need to fight for our lives, or encounter lions on the loose.

Today, we get stressed in business meetings, by political issues, by people being late, by things we can't control or not going to plan, sitting in our cars in traffic jams to name but a few. In such situations, we do not make use of the cortisol rampaging around our blood vessels as we were designed to, i.e. in the form of extreme physical exertion; instead, it breaks down into harmful chemicals within our bodies which:

- cause damage to the walls of the heart;

- shrink the hippocampus, the part of the brain which turns experiences into memory;

- suppress our immune response, making us more susceptible to picking up bugs and developing cancers.

This is the consequence of living in today's fast and furious, but relatively safe, modern world.

It is important to understand our response to stress and the impact it may have on other people around us. When we are not stressed and at our best, we can usually deal with and adapt to various situations and adopt appropriate behaviours. When we are stressed, however, we are likely to become less flexible and more rigid.

Our weaknesses become more pronounced, exaggerated or extreme, almost like a caricature. We behave immaturely and can come across as childish, touchy or easily angered. We may exhibit anger in the form of negative criticism, attack people for being illogical, focus our anger on isolated facts and details, or become angry with people who are ignoring future impending disasters. We develop tunnel vision and perceive the world as black and white, all or none; we lose the ability to make fine judgements, or appreciate others' attempts to suggest alternative ways of looking at things or solving problems.

As a direct consequence of this loss of perspective, we also lose our sense of humour; to see the humour in anything requires the broad perspective that includes nuances and shades of grey.

Practical advice

Now let's consider what measures we can take to reduce the negative impacts of stress on both ourselves and others.

First there are some universal de-stressors like exercise, for example. However, don't be fooled into thinking that this will solve the cortisol problem. Exercise needs to be done at the moment the cortisol is produced. Going to the gym in the evening after a bad day in the office will do you good generally, but by that time the cortisol will have done its damage.

The only way to resolve the cortisol issue is to either avoid its build up in the first place, or engage in some form of strenuous activity at the moment of its production, such as going for a run around the block, or beating the hell out of a punchbag.

Second, go and do something completely different from your day job and something that exercises a different part of your brain. For example, if your job requires a lot of intellectual thought and theorising, try gardening or cooking. If your job involves a lot of human interaction and negotiation, take the dog for a walk, or sit down with a good book or crossword puzzle.

Finally, we need to consider the impact of personality. What may be one person's stressor may be another person's remedy, and vice versa. Consider the list of potential remedies below and reflect on what would work for you; they will not all work for you, so you need to be choosy. If you find it difficult to make a choice now, just try one of the suggestions listed below and see how it makes you feel. If you feel better as a result, carry on; if it isn't working for you, then try something else:

- Take time out to:
  - schedule in unscheduled time;
  - engage in fun activities;
  - engage in relaxing activities;
  - pursue hobbies and recreational activities;
  - find time for family and friends.

- Talk through your issue with an appropriate person – a close friend, or an uninvolved person, for example. This can help you to:

  – confront and reframe the problem;

  – receive reassurance or confirmation about a course of action;

  – rebuild self-esteem or confidence to validate competence or worth;

  – receive TLC (tender loving care) from them;

  – decide on priorities, or saying no selectively.

- Have some time alone to recover, regroup, or regain control.

- Ask for/accept help:

  – in identifying possibilities or options;

  – to share the burden, or help with the task.

- Engage in physical activity/exercise.

- Engage in a distracting activity.

- Refocus on the positive – what will work, what can be done – rather than on the negative – what won't work, or can't be done.

If you are dealing with other people under stress, the following pointers may help.

Table 3: Dealing with people under stress

Do	Don't
▪ Encourage them to articulate their concerns and try to identify any connections.	▪ Try to reason with them. ▪ Contradict them.

▪ Acknowledge their feelings and empathise with them.	▪ Tell them what to do.
▪ Ask them what it is about certain situations that makes them particularly stressful. Try to identify the triggers.	▪ Minimise, or dismiss, the concerns they have expressed.
	▪ Make fun of anything.
▪ Ask them what would need to change for them not to feel this way if, and when, that trigger event happens again.	▪ Apply even more pressure.
▪ Get them to talk through their feelings and, in doing so, to identify a way forward.	
▪ Offer to support them in any appropriate and practical way.	

Further food for the curious

- Quenk N. *In the Grip; Understanding Type, Stress and the Inferior Function*. OPP Ltd, Oxford (2000):

  – A short, yet comprehensive, book that deals with the relationship between stress and personality type.

- *www.nhs.uk/Conditions/Stress/Pages/Introduction.aspx*:

  – Basic, but useful, advice.

Things for you to work on now

Key questions to ask yourself

- How clear are you about your role at work and what is expected of you?

- How much control do you have over the way you work?

- How much involvement do you have in relation to changes at work?

- How well do you get on with your boss? How easy do you find it to talk to your boss? Does your boss support you?

- How well do you get on with your colleagues? Do they support you?

- Do different people at work place you in a position where you have conflicting priorities or demands?

- Are you given unachievable deadlines?

- Do you have to work very intensely and find it difficult to take sufficient breaks?

- Do you feel pressured to work long hours?

- Are there any arguments, friction or strained relationships at work?

- Are you suffering from harassment or bullying at work?

Mini exercises you can try immediately

- Make a list of the things that give you stress. Now think of some instances when you have been under stress and describe your behaviour. Finally note down what you do to reduce stress.

- Share your notes with a trusted friend or colleague – ask them if they have anything to add. Which and how many of the remedies listed above did you employ? Now plan your strategy for next time you are under stress or undue pressure.

- Tell the people close to you, and whom you can trust, what stresses you and what helps you return to equilibrium – that way they will know what to avoid doing to reduce the likelihood of you getting stressed in the first place and, if it does happen, what they can do to help you return to a positive state.

- Get control of your diary and learn to say 'no' when appropriate. Believe it or not, how we spend our time is the one thing we do have control of – just think what you would do if you had a phone call from a close friend or family member who was in serious difficulty and needed your help right now. Wouldn't you just drop everything and go running?

Links to other questions

You may want to take a look at:

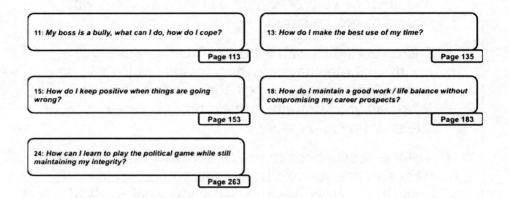

11: *My boss is a bully, what can I do, how do I cope?*

Page 113

13: *How do I make the best use of my time?*

Page 135

15: *How do I keep positive when things are going wrong?*

Page 153

18: *How do I maintain a good work / life balance without compromising my career prospects?*

Page 183

24: *How can I learn to play the political game while still maintaining my integrity?*

Page 263

17: HOW DO I GET THE RECOGNITION I THINK I DESERVE?

Why should I be asking this question?

Many years ago, a friend of mine went along to the head of HR of a large organisation and said:

> Look, every year lots of people get promoted to a higher grade and better job, and there is always at least one promotion that nobody can understand. Everyone in the whole organisation shouts, 'How did that idiot get promoted?' This year could I please be that idiot?

The fact is that we all like to think that we are doing a great job and we all at some time wonder why other people above us can't see how good we are. We feel we should receive greater recognition, our partners think we should, and our friends sympathise with us that we were unlucky not to be recognised this time, but that we are sure to be promoted next time. Other people always appear to get the best jobs, people who are just not as good as we are — it's just not fair.

Now we don't want to be controversial, but the fact is that it probably is fair. The reason that it is fair is that in the global history of corporate life, nobody ever got promoted because they could do their job well. The reason you got the job in the first place was because you were expected to do it well. Doing your job well, or even excellently, is just your way of buying an entry ticket for the promotion lottery. In fact, if you can do your job much better than everyone else, there is a real disincentive for your boss to promote you because they then have a real problem of how to fill your shoes.

You get promoted because you find a way to convince the people that matter that you are capable and ready to do the next job, not that you are ace at doing the one you are currently in. In most cases, you will be require to act, think and behave in ways that are simply not required in your current role – so you can never demonstrate that you are ready for these things by doing what you are doing, no matter how well you do it.

The impact of the issue

Our organisations are full of people who feel that their talents are not sufficiently recognised and this leads to frustration, low levels of motivation, friction and, in extreme cases, ill health and absenteeism. Once you start to get the feeling that you are undervalued, stress increases and every little slight is taken as further evidence that the world is against you. The harder you work to show your value, the more stressed you become. Personal relationships start to break down, friction and organisational factions emerge, and team and individual performance suffers.

Just how people react depends on their personality type and the impact that they can have depends on their circle of influence. Here are some broad categories of reaction – see if you recognise some of the behaviours:

- Extroverted types will moan and groan to everybody and anybody that will listen, thereby disrupting others around them and consequently spreading an atmosphere of gloom and despondency. By contrast, introverts may retreat into their shell and become uncommunicative and, in extreme cases, take on a victim mentality.

- Some may waste loads of time trying to rationalise the situation. This can be introspective, or it could involve endless circular discussions with anyone who will listen, as they analyse every nuance of every event of their immediate past life. Others may throw their toys out of the pram and sulk. Alternatively, the reaction may be an emotional one: depression, gloom and despondency or weeping.

- Some may use their planning skills in an attempt to outwit the system, while others may simply break the rules and buck the system.

Once people start to feel that others are gaining credit they don't deserve, or preferential treatment, respect for management and the system will erode and chaos can ensue.

Making sense of it all

Have you ever been at a meeting where someone contributed an idea, not just any old idea but a truly great idea? Nobody supported it, but 10 days later, you find that someone else who was at the meeting has stolen the idea and is running with it. To make matters worse, they are getting lots of praise and attention. Ever seen this happen? Has it happened to you? How did you feel? It's probable that, like most people, you were annoyed, frustrated, demoralised, determined to get even – any, or all, of the above. You probably complained indignantly to anyone who would listen that it was your idea and that you could have achieved what they have.

We could all do things – but the reality is that most of us don't; we may have lots of good ideas, but how many do we act upon?

The way to get recognition is to stop being someone who thinks about doing things and start being someone who actually does things. You need to recognise that good ideas are worthless. Good ideas plus action are what gets people noticed. So instead of getting negative and hurt, take some positive action – find out what this other person did that enabled them to turn an idea into a viable proposition. Find out how they did it and then start to see how you can do it yourself next time you get another good idea.

Maybe you look around your organisation and see that people a lot less competent than you appear to get more than their fair share of management attention. Maybe some people, who to you appear to be in a constant state of chaos and random action, get praised for fixing things; things that anyone with half a brain could see that they broke in the first place. Does the squeaky wheel appear to be getting all the grease? Well the squeaky wheel may get attention, but it is good for us to remember that attention is not the same thing as respect.

Understand and use the power of the voice of the customer. Marketing people talk about this all the time – they are usually trying to get an insight on unmet, or unstated, consumer needs. We all have customers – you need to look along the value chain to your boss, their boss and the eventual recipient of your goods and services – what can you do to make all their lives easier and how can you get them to feed back down the food chain that they value your efforts on their behalf? Nothing speaks so loud as unsolicited positive feedback from outside the organisation. That is why there are now so many websites that provide personal recommendations – Trust a Trader, TripAdvisor, LinkedIn – they are all trying to tap into the power of the personal recommendation. If you are on LinkedIn, you probably have 30 or more connections for every one personal recommendation; that is because it is easy for someone to accept an invitation from you, but it is quite a different matter to take the time and risk their own reputation in recommending you. Think of LinkedIn as a metaphor for your face-to-face interactions – what would it take for someone you routinely interact with to take the trouble to send your boss an e-mail saying how much you have helped them? What can you do to make that more likely to happen?

Consider the story of two admirals. In their book on corporate cultures, authors Deal and Kennedy tell the story of the power of mutual recognition. Two junior officers in the Dutch Navy made an agreement that on every social occasion they found themselves at, each would sing the praises of the other. They appeared to have no ulterior motive for speaking well of the other and this had a significant effect, revealed only when they were both made admirals – the two youngest admirals ever appointed in the Dutch Navy.

Practical advice

Recognition comes when you are noticed and respected by those who matter. Here are some tips to increase the chances of getting the positive attention that you desire:

- *Treat every meeting with upper management like a job interview* – generally, the only time we think about our abilities, our successes and our hopes and aspirations is when we are applying for a job. If we behaved with our boss the way we behave with prospective bosses at interview then maybe we would not need to be at an interview in the first place. Give your current boss the same courtesy and attention that you would if you were pitching for a job:

  - Never miss an opportunity to sell yourself. Relying on telepathy is not a great strategy – if you hope your boss might notice something, bring it to their attention, even hit them around the head with it.

  - When your boss starts to talk about a potential new initiative, think about what you can bring to the table and pitch for a place on the team. Remind them of your talents and successes and set out why you think you are the one for the job. Follow it up later with a brief e-mail that includes good ideas that were not discussed in the meeting.

  - Be generous with your praise of others, but make sure that some of the stardust also falls on you. You could use a structure along the lines of: 'It's really great what Joe, in finance, has done. His team have shown a 15% reduction in debtor days in the last two months. It creates a real buzz of excitement to see this sort of progress; you will remember with your guidance I implemented a similar programme in the first quarter and we are still seeing the benefits of that in our numbers.'

- *Don't waste anybody's time* :

  - Don't be late for meetings.

  - Turn your phone off before you enter the meeting, not when it rings during the meeting.

  - When someone asks you to do something, don't give them a list of excuses – just do it graciously and do it on time.

  - Always be prepared to go the extra mile for people; it is a good investment in your deposit account of respect.

  - Be honest if you can't do something, or haven't got the time; don't leave people dangling, or give them false hope.

  - Be prepared to admit mistakes, or errors of judgement, early in the process; minor problems grow into major issues when left unaddressed.

- *Give praise and recognition to others* :

  - Don't look for praise for something that your team did – look for praise because you inspired them to do it in a way that others could not have done.

  - Ensure the team takes the credit for what they have done; however, if things do go wrong, it is your responsibility, so take the blame on the chin. You will be respected for this.

-   When someone external to your team or organisation praises one of your people, make sure everyone knows about it. Spread a little joy.

-   Never miss an opportunity to draw your boss's attention to the good things that your people do. Also praise your peers when they have done something worthy of praise.

• *Learn the art of upwards management* :

-   Find out how your boss measures success – what matters to them – then, when you report progress on an issue, talk in terms of the things that matter to them and how what you have done contributes to their goals.

-   Ask your boss what you can do to make their life easier, or to help them get the recognition they deserve. Show them that you are happy to bust a gut to help make them look good.

-   Congratulate your boss when they do something good for the organisation – you would be amazed at the effect. Just as you feel undervalued, the chances are that your boss feels the same way, and you may be the only person who voiced praise for what they have just done. What goes around comes around – praise is never wasted.

• *Listen to everyone* – we mean really listen and show that you value what they have to say:

-   When you are looking upwards and outwards, ask questions that help you to offer suggestions as to what you can do to make their successes bigger, better and faster.

-   When you are looking downwards at the people who work for you, ask questions that help you to understand how you can remove obstacles and roadblocks that give them hassle, or make their lives unnecessarily complicated.

– When looking to your peers, ask questions that give you insight on what they are currently doing that could be of benefit to your boss, your team, or someone else higher in the food chain, and see if there is anything you can do to magnify that effect or smooth the path.

• *Don't take problems to your boss – take solutions.* Better still, take a range of evidence, analysis and alternate solutions and present them in a way that lets your boss naturally jump on the solution you think is best. Then agree with them by saying something like, 'I thought that may be the best idea, but I wasn't sure that I had seen all the angles. How can I help you make this work?' This way you gain several advantages:

– You are seen as a fixer, rather than a moaner.

– You show your boss that you think the way they do; it's just that they think more quickly, which is why they are the boss. They feel good, you get praise; they will inevitably look to you next time they need something fixed.

• *If you have an official job description, shred it.* Like we said earlier, you don't get promoted for doing your job – so you need to take every possible opportunity to do things that would not appear in your job description in a million years. Your aim is to be noticed and appreciated by senior people who you would not, under normal circumstances, get to interact with. Here are some good ways of doing this:

– Find out what major change initiatives are planned and get yourself onto the pilot or project team.

– Get involved with customers, site visits and fact-finding and liaison work.

- Offer to mentor, or coach, one of the fast-track graduate intake.

- Suggest that you could coach someone who has been identified in the talent pool.

- Join professional networking groups and user groups – offer to present papers and write articles for their magazines. Put yourself forward to speak at conferences.

- Carve out a name for yourself in your professional community – become someone that the trade press looks towards for comment and wise counsel.

- Cosy up to your communications and marketing department – ask if they get asked to contribute to magazines, etc. and see what it would take to get you on to their list of names they put forward.

- Enquire about getting media training, so that if the company needs a spokesperson, you are in the frame.

• Think beyond the confines of the job. A great way to get noticed is to become the person who makes social things happen and/or gets positive press coverage. Try some of the following:

- Get on the organising committee for the Christmas party.

- Create a relationship with a local charity, get your organisation to become a sponsor, organise events and get press coverage. Your boss will just love to see their picture in the local press.

- Set up a golf society, or yoga group, or anything that lets you build a wider network in the organisation.

- Organise theatre trips, or other similar cultural events – trips to the football, or the dog track, that turn into 'jolly boys' outings' don't carry the same positive, upper-management feel, so if you want to do these, keep them low key.

– Find out what would really make your boss's partner happy and try to find a way of making that happen. If your boss's partner loves fast cars, organise a track experience day. If your boss's partner loves Take That, organise a trip with VIP access. Or better still, invite Gary Barlow to open your next charity event – you never know, he may say yes, in which case you are suddenly known and loved by everyone in the organisation.

Further food for the curious

- Runion M and Fenner S. *Perfect Phrases for Office Professionals: Hundreds of Ready-to-use Phrases for Getting Respect, Recognition and Results in Today's Workplace*. McGraw Hill (2011):

  – This is a simple-to-read book that you can dip into and use as a memory jogger when you are stuck for words, or can't think of a suitable way of blowing your own trumpet.

- Deal TE and Kennedy AA. *Corporate Cultures: Rights and Rituals of Corporate Life*. Perseus books (1984):

  – Although this book has been around for a while, it provides a good insight into the power of corporate culture and why some norms of behaviour and rituals are easily seen and recognised.

Things for you to work on now

Key questions to ask yourself

- What do you actually want? Is it just a pat on the back, a bonus, to get voted employee of the month or be given a special project for example? Unless you can define what is important to you, it is difficult to set about increasing your chances of getting it.

- What steps have you taken to gain the recognition you want – how did they work out?

- When did you last give recognition to one of your team or peers? How was it received? How has your relationship with that person developed as a result of your actions?

- Does your ultimate customer know who you are? If they did, would they care?

- When did you last do something to make your boss look good?

Mini exercises you can try immediately

- Write or update your CV – make sure that you capture all your recent successes. Put the focus on what you have achieved and the impact it had on key measures of organisational performance, rather than what you know, or what you have learned.

- Review your new CV and pick out your two biggest successes of the last 12 months, and the two or three key personal attributes you think contributed to your success. Write several elevator speeches (30-second sound bites) that highlight your abilities and your achievements.

- Scan the organisation and identify the three or four people that are obviously on the way up – it won't be difficult to see them, as they will be very visible! Make it your business to be seen with these people and spoken of in the same breath.

Links to other questions

You may want to take a look at:

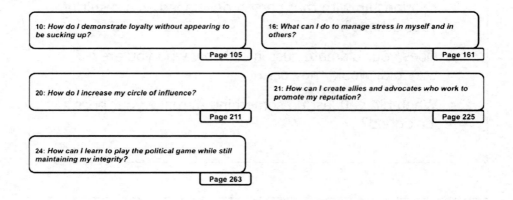

10: *How do I demonstrate loyalty without appearing to be sucking up?*

Page 105

16: *What can I do to manage stress in myself and in others?*

Page 161

20: *How do I increase my circle of influence?*

Page 211

21: *How can I create allies and advocates who work to promote my reputation?*

Page 225

24: *How can I learn to play the political game while still maintaining my integrity?*

Page 263

18: HOW DO I MAINTAIN A GOOD WORK/LIFE BALANCE WITHOUT COMPROMISING MY CAREER PROSPECTS?

Why should I be asking this question?

Pick up any newspaper or magazine and you will see that 'work/family balance is fast becoming the hot career issue of the decade'.

One lunchtime, while on holiday, Robina and her husband were sitting in a lovely restaurant with an idyllic view overlooking the sea. Opposite was a family of four, also having lunch. Robina observed them with curiosity over a two-hour period. The mother sat at one end of an oblong table chatting and laughing with her two children, whom she guessed were in their early teens, while the father sat at the opposite end of the table with his attention firmly focused on his BlackBerry. The father did not raise his head to either converse with his family, or take in the stunning view for even a moment!

This caused Robina to reflect back on her first job at a shipyard. It was in the early 1980s, before the advent of e-mail or mobile phones. When you left work, you left work. When you went on holiday, you went on holiday. In those days, the entire shipyard closed for a fortnight; therefore, on your return from holiday, you just picked things back up as you had left them two weeks previously; no last-minute rush before you departed, or frantic catch-up on your return.

However, life today is very different. What is it about the nature of our organisations and our society that make us so reluctant to be out of contact, to let go and have any 'me' time?

The impact of the issue

We recently discovered a new word in a psychology magazine, *weisure*, used to describe the time you spend when you are not at work, but you are still working. Activities that fall into this category include reading your e-mail, rather than a newspaper or a novel on your train journey home, or talking about that afternoon's meeting at after-work drinks.

If you want evidence of this phenomenon, look no further that the annual e-mail-addiction survey run by AOL. Some of the results are truly startling and, perhaps worryingly, most of us will probably confess to having done at least some of these things ourselves at some time:

- 62% of people check work e-mails at weekends.
- 59% of people check e-mail from the bathroom.
- 19% of people choose vacation spots with access to e-mail.

Indeed, *ITV Tonight* recently commissioned a survey asking 2,000 full-time employees about their working lives. The results revealed a nation feeling the pressure of juggling work and home:

- 70% said they were spending most of their lives working.
- Over 50% said they worked more hours than they were paid for.
- 32% felt that working too hard had made them ill.
- 74% believed that they suffered work-related stress.
- One in five admitted to spending only 20 minutes a day with their children.

We're all guilty of this gradual drift towards a reluctance, or inability, to switch off from work. It might seem like a good use of 'dead time', but too much *weisure* time means you don't switch off enough, which is bad for your mind and your body. Consider the following quote:

> *In early life, people give up their health to gain wealth. Then in later life, they give up wealth to regain their health.*

Now genuinely answer the following question:

> *Do you work to live or live to work?*

Making sense of it all

With the advent of modern technology, we literally have the ability to work any time, any place and anywhere. We are bombarded with information and requests for a few moments of our time at every corner; it is down to us to sort the wheat from the chaff, the useful from the junk. It was estimated that 40 exabytes (4.0 x 10 to the power of 19) of unique new information was generated worldwide in 2008. One exabyte is about 100,000 times the information contained within the National Library of Congress. Just imagine what number this has grown to today and what it will grow to by next year.

Research shows us that the way we work in the 21st century makes us, paradoxically, less effective than ever. Taking e-mail as one source of inefficiency, researcher Christina Cavanagh from the University of Toronto found as much as 12% of payroll costs are spent on ineffective use of e-mail that drains an organisation's time and energy. Research also shows that interruptions over multiple information channels sap our cognitive ability and reduce our effectiveness. E-mail can become quite addictive; we just *have* to respond when we hear or see that e-mail alert.

The frenzied use of smart phones leads to a culture of 'virtual presenteeism', with consequences for the quality of both our working and personal lives.

Social media can be even more addictive and time-consuming. Did you know that the number of text messages sent and received every day exceeds the total population of the planet?

It doesn't even stop there; with the advent of blogs and wikis, the pressure is on us to keep up to date with, and contribute to, the knowledge base of the business community as a whole and society at large.

Are we becoming less secure, more dependent? Indeed, are we becoming hive creatures who cannot exist, or function, without an umbilical to the mother creature, the social hub?

Our families also expect more of us – they demand 'quality time', a more exhilarating day out than the time before, a better holiday, a more upmarket restaurant, the latest trainers, etc. Schools expect parents to contribute more to their children's educational experience in terms of both time and money, while their teachers' training days seem to be on the increase. Society drives us to 'keep up with the Joneses'. In addition, we have more laws to abide by, more speed cameras to avoid, more forms to fill in and more passwords and PINs to remember with every passing day.

In essence, we all have more balls to juggle with at any one time and more choices to make about our scarce resources of time and money than ever before – life has become, and is becoming, tougher!

Most of the literature in relation to work–life balance advises you to improve your time management; to become better at prioritising and delegating; to turn off new e-mail alerts and tackle your e-mail in focused bouts; in essence, to work smarter rather than harder. We believe that solving issues around work–life balance has to go deeper than simply getting better at time management – yes, that is an important first step, but you also need to give serious attention to the issue of fulfilment.

Better time management on its own simply helps us to do more of the same, to be more focused and effective on a particular aspect of our life. Adjustments to work–life balance require a change in attitude and priorities and a shift of mind-set.

Let us reflect for a moment on Maslow's classic Hierarchy of Needs that was developed in the 1940s.

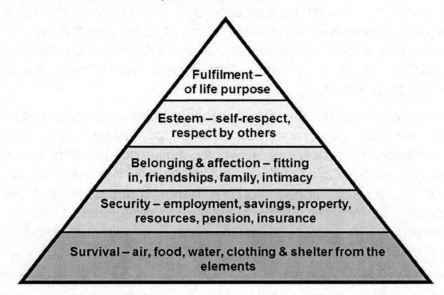

Figure 11: Maslow's Hierarchy of Needs[5]

How much of our time and mental energies are focused on 'fulfilment'? How many of us could readily articulate our life's purpose if asked to?

Do modern society and the work ethic of today encourage us to focus more of our efforts on certain levels of the Hierarchy and fewer on others?

In today's world, survival and security are inextricably linked by the psychological pressure to acquire and maintain a certain lifestyle. Although western society will ensure that few of us are likely to starve to death, the psychological pressures to ensure our future security are probably greater than those encountered by the previous generation. We can no longer expect the luxury of a job for life or an index-linked pension.

---

[5] Maslow's Hierarchy of Needs is based on the work of Abraham Maslow and his theory as first proposed in his 1943 paper 'A theory of human motivation', *Psychological Review*, 1943, 50(4): pp. 370–96.

Our children require greater and greater financial support as the cost of university education increases by leaps and bounds; in addition, we can no longer expect our children to find a deposit themselves for their first mortgage. Comfort in our retirement is looking less certain, as the interest on our savings struggles to keep up with inflation and our pension funds continue to wither.

With the advent of LinkedIn, Facebook, blogs and wikis, and so on, we are encouraged to belong to, interact with and contribute to society as a whole; not just the people we interact with on a daily basis, but potentially the whole world. Our presence is global, along with our reputations and the opportunity for international prestige and recognition. Does the modern world encourage us to trade more survival, security and esteem for less belonging, affection and fulfilment?

Human beings are social creatures; therefore, it is important for us to feel a sense of belonging and acceptance; to give and receive love and affection. In the absence of these, we become susceptible to loneliness, social anxiety and, ultimately, clinical depression.

A sense of belonging may be fulfilled by club membership, the office environment, professional organisations, sports teams, religious groups, or social connections with friends, family members, close colleagues, etc. A sense of belonging is not, however, achieved on the Internet; it requires both physical presence and emotional connection. Technology and modern society encourage us to spend less and less time interacting with people face to face.

Scientists warn us that this is at our peril, since studies into brain chemistry have demonstrated that positive human-to-human contact affects our hormone balance; it increases the levels of positive hormones that make us feel good and promote trust and bonding, and reduces the level of stress hormones that ultimately make us ill.

Consider the adaptation of the classic project management triangle in Figure 12. We must work out how to live our lives, given the constraint of only 24 hours in any one day. There are three key factors that we need to address in relation to our work–life balance; spending less time on one will allow more flexibility in the other two areas; however, we must consciously consider and be prepared to accept the consequences. In an ideal working day, we may spend approximately eight hours on personal care, eight hours on leisure and eight hours working. If we spend more time working, we spend less time on leisure and/or personal care. The potential consequences are exhaustion, both physically and mentally. In the long term, our health and well-being are likely to suffer.

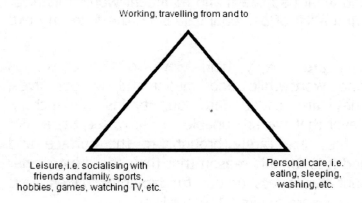

Figure 12: Work–life balance triangle

According to the Organisation for Economic Co-operation and Development (OECD), the Danes top the bill for the country with the best work–life balance. Their findings revealed that Danes devote 68% of their day, i.e. 16.3 hours, to personal care and leisure, the ideal mix! Only 0.02% of Danes work more than 50 hours a week. Also, 78% of Danish mothers go back to work once their children are in school. In the study, the UK failed to feature anywhere in the top 10.

Practical advice

The top level of Maslow's Hierarchy of Needs symbolises a state of being in which the highest levels of fulfilment and individual happiness are achieved. For each individual this will be different. One person, for example, may have a strong desire to become an ideal parent; another may wish to be a top athlete; while a third may find fulfilment in painting and the arts. We may also take pleasure and find fulfilment from helping others, or in silence and tranquillity, for example.

What is your 'life purpose'; what would make you look back in your old age and say 'I have had a happy and fulfilling life with no regrets'? The following exercise will help you articulate your life purpose and what happiness and fulfilment would mean for you. You will find a list of personal values on the following two pages.

Personal values are deeply held views of what we, as individuals, find worthwhile and meaningful in our lives. Sometimes they are coded into our brains at such a fundamental level that we are unable to easily see them. For many of us, they are rarely brought to the surface and questioned, and it is for this reason that they can create inner conflict. Without awareness of our fundamental values, it is difficult for us to ensure fulfilment in our lives.

Step one: 'What do I value most?' From the list of values (both work and personal), select the 10 that are the most important to you – as guides for how to behave, or as components of a valued way of life. If appropriate, add values of your own to the list.

Table 4: List of behaviour values

Things you value most		
Advancement and promotion	Fortune and material wealth	Personal growth
Adventure	Fun	Physical challenge
Arts	Having a family	Power and authority
Being home	Having a 'soulmate'	Privacy
Beating my personal best	Helping other people	Public service
Challenging complex problems	Helping society	Quality of what I take part in
Change and variety	Independence	Religion
Competence	Influencing others	Recognition
Competition	Inner harmony	Reputation
Creativity	Integrity	Responsibility and accountability
Decisiveness	Intellectual status	Search for truth
Ecological awareness	Job tranquillity	Security
Economic security	Knowledge	Self-achievement
Effectiveness	Leadership	Self-respect

Efficiency	Love of country	Sharing affection with others
Ethical practice	Loyalty	Stability
Excellence	Meaningful work	Status
Excitement	Membership of the community	Telling the truth
Fame	Money	Tolerance
Fast living	Order (tranquillity, stability, conformity)	Wisdom
Fast-paced work	Personal challenge	Work under pressure
Freedom	Personal development	

Step two: 'From 10 to three' – having identified 10 values, imagine you are only permitted to have five:

- Cross out the five you would give up.

- Now cross out one more so that you are down to four values.

- And finally cross out another to bring you down to three values.

Now you have the three values you care most about.

Step three: 'Articulation' – take a look at these three values:

- What specifically do they mean for you? What do you expect from yourself as a result of these values – even in bad times?

- How would your life be different if those values were even more prominent and practised?

- What would an organisation be like which encouraged employees to live up to your values?

Does your lifestyle (working and social life) permit you to 'live out' your values and gain happiness and fulfilment? Use the work–life balance triangle (Figure 12) to help you with this one – how much time do you spend at each point of the triangle; does this split work for you? Is any aspect suffering at the expense of the others? What gives when the pressure is on?

Step four: 'Rebalancing' – assuming this split does not work for you (or why else would you be reading this question?), you need to make changes in your life. This will require a mind-set shift, otherwise your plans will remain good intentions that you will start tomorrow, or when you are less busy; the only problem is that tomorrow will never come. Remember, work always expands to fill the time available. Here are a few examples of things you may consider doing:

- Sleep – make sure you get enough for you; most of us need around seven to eight hours per night. Without a good night's sleep, you will not function either efficiently or effectively. Tasks will take twice as long as they should do and the results will be substandard.

- Exercise – make sure you get a little every day, even if it is only walking from the car park to your office, or taking the stairs, rather than the lift.

- Eat properly – we cannot function without fuel, so make sure you get a well-balanced diet, avoid sugary foods and eat your greens.

- Get some 'me' time – everyone needs a little 'me' time each day to recharge those emotional batteries; read a fiction book or newspaper on plane and train journeys, rather than do that report or check your e-mail.

- Get some leisure/family time – leave your briefcase in the office apart from in exceptional circumstances, switch off your work phone in the evenings and at weekends – if it's really urgent, they will phone you on your personal number.

- Spend quality time with your family – arrange to do things, go for a walk in the park, visit friends, etc.

- Model yourself on the Danes – restrict your working hours to no more than 40 hours per week. You will be surprised at how much more effective you will be when you are fresh, relaxed and energised. If you work in the type of organisation that values physical presence over output, don't follow the herd; instead, become a role model for others. Work fewer hours than the norm, but, within those hours, make a truly significant and high-quality contribution that gets you noticed. Ultimately, you will find that by spending more quality time with your family, by injecting slack into your schedule and allowing yourself 'me' time, you will have more energy to be super-inspirational and super-productive when you are at work.

Further food for the curious

- Caproni P. Work/Life Balance: You Can't Get There From Here. *The Journal of Applied Behavioural Science*, June 2004; 40, 2:
  - An insightful and fascinating article, written from the heart, offering a new perspective on the issue and illustrated with many personal examples.

- Price I. *The Activity Illusion*. Matador (2010):
  - An insight into why we work the way we do in the 21st century; why we live to work, rather than work to live, and what we can do to resolve the situation for the good of both ourselves and the organisations we work for.

- Hallowell E. The Human Moment at Work. *Harvard Business Review*, Jan.–Feb. 1999:

  - An enlightening paper providing insight into the brain chemistry behind face-to-face human interaction and how the absence of 'human moments' can wreak havoc in organisations.

Things for you to work on now

Key questions to ask yourself

- What motivated me to read this chapter? What do I feel needs to change in my life?

- On the three-point triangular model, what does the balance look like today? How would I wish it to be?

- How big is the journey? When will I start? What is likely to get in the way?

- Am I sufficiently motivated to bring about change in my work–life balance? Have I bought into the process, both intellectually and emotionally? Is my heart truly in it?

Mini exercises you can try immediately

- Complete all four steps of the exercise outlined above.

- Plan your strategy – target dates, milestones and measures; i.e. how you will know when you have achieved each goal.

- Share with a friend or trusted colleague, someone who can challenge your assumptions, who can act as a confidante and who will provide a 'sanity check'.

Links to other questions

You may want to take a look at:

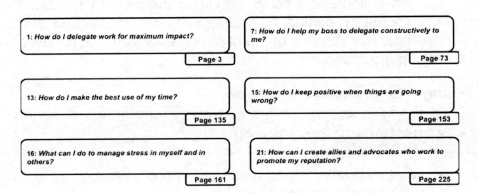

1: *How do I delegate work for maximum impact?*

Page 3

7: *How do I help my boss to delegate constructively to me?*

Page 73

13: *How do I make the best use of my time?*

Page 135

15: *How do I keep positive when things are going wrong?*

Page 153

16: *What can I do to manage stress in myself and in others?*

Page 161

21: *How can I create allies and advocates who work to promote my reputation?*

Page 225

HOW DO I MANAGE MY REPUTATION?

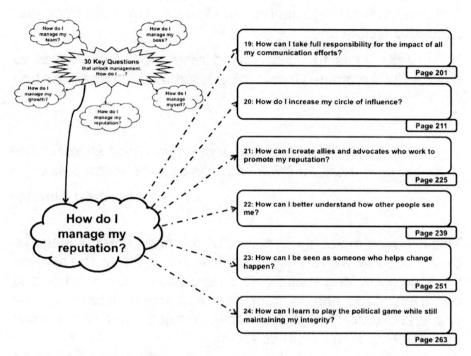

19: How can I take full responsibility for the impact of all my communication efforts?

Page 201

20: How do I increase my circle of influence?

Page 211

21: How can I create allies and advocates who work to promote my reputation?

Page 225

22: How can I better understand how other people see me?

Page 239

23: How can I be seen as someone who helps change happen?

Page 251

24: How can I learn to play the political game while still maintaining my integrity?

Page 263

Perception is everything – it is not what you are, but what others perceive you to be, that is important. What they see first is your reputation; it is the cumulative effect of all your deeds and how others perceive and interpret those deeds. It will also be coloured by the stereotypical images held about the professional and social groups to which you belong.

Your reputation tends to precede you – others form opinions about you before they even meet you. They will have already formed an impression of what you may be like based upon their stereotypical image of people in your profession, or from your walk of life. When they do meet you, they will at first pick up on any indicators that reinforce the stereotypical image that they have already formed.

Once you get past the initial barrier, you now have to contend with their unspoken interpretation of what they have heard about you from others. Again, they will look first for things that support your reputation from what they have heard about you, and they will tend to ignore, or dismiss, any indicators that contradict that image.

It can take years to build a good reputation and seconds to destroy it. Abraham Lincoln nicely summed up the situation when he said:

> *Character is like a tree and reputation like a shadow. The shadow is what we think of it; the tree is the real thing.*
>
> **Abraham Lincoln**

This is a nice metaphor because, all too often, people judge us by the shadow we cast and when the sun is low in the sky, we tend to cast a long shadow. Our reputation is our shadow and our every deed and interpersonal interaction determines the shape and density of that shadow. A much wiser person than us, Socrates, is on record as saying:

> *The way to gain a good reputation is to endeavour to be what you desire to appear.*
>
> **Socrates**

In this section, we answer *six* key questions that point to ways in which you can set about trying to be what you desire to be. We point to tangible steps that you can take to start to build your reputation. This is an area that most people leave to chance; they do not actively try to manage the impressions that they create.

Unless you take responsibility for managing your own reputation, you will wake up one morning to find that you have a reputation that is solely based on the impressions and imaginings of others. Others, who may not know much about you as a person, may not understand your values and drivers and may feel no sense of responsibility for the impressions they create when they talk about you.

Make a personal commitment to yourself today to take a close look at the shadow you cast – and if you don't like what you see, take some of the steps that we suggest in order to take control of your own reputation.

19: HOW CAN I TAKE FULL RESPONSIBILITY FOR THE IMPACT OF ALL MY COMMUNICATION EFFORTS?

Why should I be asking this question?

Just because you have communicated a message, it does not necessarily mean it has been received and understood at the other end.

We have all heard the 'Chinese whispers' story, reputedly from the first World War, that a message was sent back from the battle front saying 'Send reinforcements, we're going to advance'. The message was passed from one trench to another and after multiple face-to-face, phone and radio operator communications, the message that reached headquarters was 'Send three and fourpence, we're going to a dance'.

This story may be amusing, but it has serious and profound consequences – what we say and what other people hear are not always the same thing. In an organisational context, we communicate because we wish to achieve specific outcomes, outcomes that we are held accountable for. It is, therefore, incumbent on us to take responsibility for what people hear, rather than for what we say.

The impact of the issue

Communication is the lifeblood of any organisation.

If we take the analogy of our own human physiology a step further, we see that without effective communication, nerves don't communicate with musculature, our heart doesn't know to pump faster during physical exertion, and so on and so forth.

It is the same with organisational life. Without effective communication, people become demotivated because they don't see the results of their efforts, they don't know what is expected of them or understand their purpose within the greater context of the organisation as a whole. Silos develop; departments work at best in isolation and at worst in competition; the whole thing becomes disjointed and productivity suffers.

On an individual basis, poor communication leads to misunderstanding, wasted effort and ultimately distrust. People start to focus their energies towards speculating about the potential motives that may underpin the message, rather than the content of the message and what they are required to do with it. When we are the one doing the communicating and others don't seem to get our meaning, we tend to blame them and simply repeat the same message in the same way, but louder; both parties end up feeling resentful and frustrated.

Making sense of it all

Communicating is not about talking. We communicate for a purpose; we have intent. We also expect that, if we communicate our intent or purpose to others, we can, through co-ordinated action, produce certain outcomes. So, when we communicate, we need to be really clear about:

- our intention – what purpose are we trying to achieve;
- the outcomes we wish to produce.

A communication event is made up of three parts:

- the sender;
- the communication medium;
- the receiver.

This gives us three potential points of failure:

- The sender:
    - There is a lack of clarity about the intent.
    - There is a lack of content – we assume that people know as much as we do and, therefore, we don't need to tell them things.
    - There is a lack of clarity about the outcome.
    - There is a poor choice of words, or lack of congruence between our words and corresponding actions.

- The communication medium:
    - It is the wrong medium.
    - There is noise in the medium.
    - There is interference from other, apparently supportive, initiatives that actually dilutes our message, rather than adding to it.
    - There is garbled transmission – this is particularly true when we use a cascade process of management briefings – each manager puts their own spin on the message and the result is chaos and confusion.

- The receiver:
    - There is a lack of understanding of intent – they have not been adequately prepared for this initiative, so they think it relates to something or someone else.
    - There is wilful misunderstanding of intent – the receiver perceives that they may lose something as a result of this communication, so they put a poor spin on it when passing it on.
    - There is inadequate or confusing content – most written communication lacks a cohesive governing thought – verbal communication can be even more confusing.

—   There is a lack of understanding of the outcome we are trying to produce.

For information to be received as it was intended, we need to communicate clearly and in the right way, i.e. the right time, the right place, the right medium and the right context.

The right time — if someone is rushing off to an important meeting, just about to catch a plane, or focused on a key issue, then wrestling with trying to communicate with them on a totally unrelated subject is probably not a good idea; their attention will be focused on the subject/task in hand and your message will simply wash over them. You will either get an ill-considered response, or none at all; any information you convey will, in all probability, be instantly forgotten.

The right place — noisy, public areas may not be the best environments for some discussions. Sometimes it may be best to converse on neutral territory. Lifts, corridors, car parks and bathrooms may, again, not be the right environment for many discussions. On the other hand, a less formal environment, such as a wine bar or coffee bar, may be the best place for tricky discussions or negotiations about an interpersonal issue with a colleague or peer.

The right medium — some people prefer written communication, while others prefer verbal. Some messages are simple to convey, while others are complex. Some may be contentious, or touch on sensitivities. We have all heard the stories of people being fired by text message. Indeed, we have even witnessed instances of people being dumped by a partner via a 'post-it note' attached to the screen of their PC.

The right context — you need to be clear in your own mind about the intention of your communication and the outcome(s) you would like to elicit. If you are not clear then, sure as eggs are eggs, your receiver certainly won't be. The content of your messages needs to be clear, unambiguous, relevant and appropriate to the outcome you wish to produce. Consider the following mini case.

> *A manager we know was unhappy with the way one of their subordinates produced reports; they felt they were too long, too wordy and slow to get to the point. Having tolerated the situation for some time, they eventually told their subordinate that they were unhappy with the way they produced reports and told them to buck their ideas up. The subordinate reflected for a moment and then interpreted the situation as 'they need more detail'. If intention is not communicated clearly, the desired outcome gets lost and it is left to guesswork or chance.*

Practical advice

Consider time, place, medium and context. Take into account both the message you wish to convey and the person/people you need to convey it to. Choose wisely and appropriately. Be prepared to exercise both patience and pragmatism.

The right time – ensure that neither the receiver nor you are rushed. You may wish to help prime them by sending some pre-reading material; if you do this, keep it short and very clear. Ensure you are both in the right frame of mind to discuss the subject in hand.

The right place – does the subject under discussion lend itself to a formal or informal environment? Where would be quiet and free of interruptions? What resources and or facilities may you need?

The right medium – what would be most appropriate: face to face, telephone, e-mail, letter, text, etc? How does the receiver like to be communicated with? Extroverts tend to prefer face-to-face or telephone communication and introverts prefer written. What is practical, given the constraints of time and geography?

The right context – don't just tell; reach out and check for understanding. Be open and honest, even if the truth is uncomfortable. Speak from the heart and give real examples to back up, or illustrate, your point.

A word about e-mail communication – when communicating via e-mail, a few simple rules will significantly enhance the effectiveness of your messages:

- Ask yourself 'Is this the most effective method of communication for this particular message?' – consider the sensitivity of your message, the receivers' communication preferences and their physical proximity.

- Get the length right – extroverts write and prefer short conversational-style e-mails, whereas introverts write and prefer longer and more comprehensive e-mails. Extroverts may only read an e-mail until the point they think they know what you are writing about; they will stop there and take whatever action they think appropriate. Therefore, it is wise to restrict your e-mails to one question only when dealing with extroverts, as any subsequent questions will go unread.

- Use an effective tone – this is even more important than with face-to-face communication, as you haven't got body language to soften a blow or harsh word. Tone is the personal touch that compels a reader to react positively, or negatively. An effective tone will encourage co-operation and consideration. An ineffective tone will do exactly the opposite. Consider the following examples:

  - I am mailing you to remind you about our follow-up meeting scheduled for tomorrow at 11 am. Last time we met you kept me waiting for 20 minutes; I do not expect to be kept waiting this time.

  - I just wanted to check that we are still OK for tomorrow at 11 am. I appreciate that you are very busy and wish to thank you for your time. I understand

206

that you have many back-to-back meetings, so please let me know if you need to adjust the time of our follow-up.

How would you respond if you received either of the above messages in an e-mail?

A word about report writing – the most important part of any report is the executive summary. However, most of us primarily focus our efforts on the body of a report, with the executive summary becoming a last-minute afterthought. Most executives will only ever read the executive summary and, if inspired, skim through a little of the body of the report. If the executive summary doesn't hit the spot, all the effort dedicated towards the body of the report will have been wasted.

The executive summary must be a genuine summary of the whole of the report; it must be sufficient for a busy executive to grasp the issue and make a decision. The executive summary is not an alternative term for an *introduction*. Executive summaries should:

- establish the purpose of the report and why it is important or of interest;

- summarise the current status in relation to the topic of discussion;

- explain precisely your key message and/or findings;

- state what you want to happen and what actions you want taken, by whom and by when;

- assume you're writing for someone who is very busy, and very impatient;

- assume they will be asking 'What's the point? What do I do with this information?', so apply the 'So what?' test to everything you write.

If excited by the executive summary, your reader may dip into the body of the report. Make it easy for them, make it inviting;

use space, structure, bullet points, bold type, numbering, short sentences, paragraphs, etc. Text that is too dense is the quickest and easiest way to switch a reader off. Take the opportunity to put key messages in section headings.

Further food for the curious

- Hallowell E. The Human Moment at Work. *Harvard Business Review*, Jan.–Feb. 1999:

    – An insightful paper which reviews the pros and cons of e-mail communication and the benefits of face-to-face contact.

Things for you to work on now

Key questions to ask yourself

- Do you end up talking at cross purposes from time to time?

- When faced with difficulties in getting your message across, have you ever repeated the same message in the same way but louder?

- Do other people either tell you to get to the point or accuse you of being vague and imprecise?

- How long are your e-mails?

Mini exercises you can try immediately

- Review your e-mail inbox. Who do you like getting e-mails from? Who do you hate getting e-mails from? Compare the style and layout of each type of e-mail – which elements of the communication make you feel energised and aligned to the proposed course of action?

- Take a look at a report you have written recently: is your executive summary a genuine summary of the whole report? Does it provide pointers to the issue and key findings?

- Consider your own style of communication and your interactions with others. What is your approach to selecting the appropriate time, place, medium and context?

- Pick a key stakeholder with whom you don't easily connect. Determine their preferred communication style; make a list of the steps you can take now to improve communication with this individual. Put your plan into action.

- Consider what you have learned from this activity and extend this approach to your other key stakeholders.

- Ask people for feedback on your communication approach and amend your style in line with that feedback.

Links to other questions

You may want to take a look at:

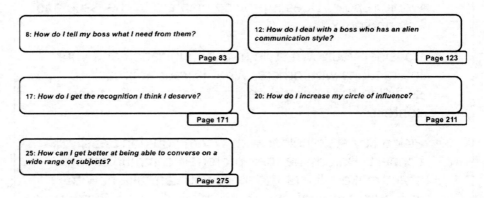

8: *How do I tell my boss what I need from them?*

Page 83

12: *How do I deal with a boss who has an alien communication style?*

Page 123

17: *How do I get the recognition I think I deserve?*

Page 171

20: *How do I increase my circle of influence?*

Page 211

25: *How can I get better at being able to converse on a wide range of subjects?*

Page 275

20: HOW DO I INCREASE MY CIRCLE OF INFLUENCE?

Why should I be asking this question?

People tend to do business with, and refer people to, people they know, like and trust. The more people who know and trust you, the more referrals you will get. This is obviously important if you are in sales or marketing, but it is also equally important in every organisational setting.

Cast your mind back to that excruciating experience at school when you all stood in a line, while two sporting stars picked their teams. They didn't pick the best players, they picked the people they knew, liked and trusted. If you were new and unknown, you were left until last and nobody wanted you.

It is just the same in organisations. The people who get the interdepartmental transfers, the special courses, the places on the cross-functional action teams, the select places on the company away day – these are the people who are known, trusted and respected far beyond their work team or department.

If you want to get on, you need to raise your visibility and start working on your sphere of influence.

Some would call this networking. Now when we talk about networking, we are not talking about the use of social networking tools, such as Facebook or LinkedIn. While they are both fine tools and very useful, they lack the key element, the 'ingredient X' – a sense of how much you *trust* someone. You don't come to trust somebody by clicking on a web page; you can become inquisitive about someone, you can even develop the beginnings of a sense of liking, but trust can only be built through face-to-face interaction over a significant period of time.

So when we talk of networking, we are talking about a purposeful social interaction that builds a trusting relationship and results in someone being willing to risk their own reputation by recommending you.

The impact of the issue

We illustrate the importance of building your circle of influence and how this can strengthen your personal reputation, and the trust that people are prepared to invest in you, by setting out the story of Robina's early organisational life and subsequent professional development.

My career commenced within the shipbuilding industry. It was the early 1980s and I joined a shipyard along with nine other engineering graduates. I spent the first two years on the shop floor as a 'fitter's mate', in order to complete my training to become a chartered engineer. During this time, I learned little about engineering, but a lot about people, industrial relations and shop-floor survival tactics.

Following my stint on the shop floor, I went into the planning department and quickly became involved with the very first roll-out of computers onto the shop floor.

I was appointed to manage two major projects: the first was a manufacturing control system that I affectionately named COMICS (computer-oriented manufacturing information and control system) and the second an access-control system, whereby entry to, or exit from, the shipyard could only be gained via a bank of 20 computer-controlled turnstiles.

At this point in my life and career, I was naïvely unaware of the potential human and social problems that we now know are a characteristic of any project that seeks to change long-established and cherished ways of working.

I was also unaware of the stages a computing project should go through, the development life cycle or the existence of development methodologies; I, therefore, operated purely on instinct, gut feeling and basic common sense.

And yet, both projects were a huge success. I cannot claim they went in on time, to budget, or as specified, since there was no budget, plan, or detailed specification. The systems, however, worked: they fulfilled business imperatives, the workforce liked them and the unions were content. Over the period of time covered by these projects, I was promoted three times, my salary doubled and I became the youngest manager in the history of the shipyard.

As my career progressed, I learned how to manage projects and develop systems 'properly'; it was at this point in my career that things started to go downhill. Don't get me wrong, I never did a bad job, but I could never recapture my early successes. The question is why?

As I look back over this time, my analysis of the situation is as follows. As my career progressed, I had moved away from engineering and become a fully fledged member of the IT community and, in doing so, I had also moved to the finance sector where money was more plentiful and business was booming. I was sent on training courses; I learned about methodologies, process and procedures and project management. I watched my peers and bosses, learned from them and tried to emulate their behaviour. However, somehow along the way I forgot what came naturally to me – the people side, networking and building relationships!

During the early part of my career I had naturally (for me that is) focused on building relationships with people. I did this throughout my two-year stint on the shop floor. Later, when I talked to the people on the shop floor and to the unions, I was not viewed as an outsider.

I was one of them and trusted because we had a common experience and understood each other's values. When I told them that the implementation of the IT systems wouldn't threaten their jobs, but would ease some of the more mundane aspects, they believed me and willingly helped my projects happen.

During the middle years of my career, I learned to consider the time I had spent on relationship building as a luxury, rather than as a necessity. I, therefore, stopped doing it because I didn't feel I had the time; I felt that I should be concentrating on 'work'. Lunch breaks became a snatched sandwich, while catching up with my e-mails, rather than dining with, talking to and getting to know the people who would be impacted by my endeavours: my stakeholders and business peers.

I have now retrained as a psychologist and had a chance to reflect on where I went wrong; I understand how I ignored a natural, and oh, so important, talent of mine – that of relationship building. I have recently embarked on a major study of IT professionals who have progressed beyond the ranks of IT and made it to the position of CEO. Such individuals told me that they spent 50% of their time networking and relationship building, while in that top IT role. As one of the CEOs in my study so succinctly put it, 'IT leadership is about getting the best out of people and not about building processes and procedures'.

If only I could have my time again, I would make sure that I never lost sight of the importance of relationships!

Dr Robina Chatham

In organisations as in life – who you know, how they think about you and their willingness to put their reputation on the line to help you have a far bigger influence on what you can achieve than anything you can do on your own. Your circle of influence is key to your success – make it your business to build and expand it, so that when you are faced with a daunting task, you look up for help and find that you are surrounded by willing hands who have your best interests at heart.

Making sense of it all

When some people talk of a circle of influence, they do so in an attempt to give you a focus for your attention. In his book *The 7 Habits of Highly Effective People*, Stephen R. Covey distinguishes between:

- *Our circle of concern* – all the things that might interest us on which we can focus our energy. Our circle of concern may be made up of things like our family, our mortgage, our job, the economy, global warming, heart disease, educational inequality, the state of the health service, and so on. Although these may all be noble causes, some clearly lie outside our ability to have a direct influence.

- *Our inner circle of influence* – this is a smaller subset of the circle of concern and is made up only of those things that we can actually do something about.

Covey argues that by learning to focus on those things that you can do something about, that you do have some control over, you can become more proactive, productive and energised. Wasting your time and energy worrying about things over which you really have no control is counter-productive. He goes further in suggesting that if you focus too much on the wider circle of concern, the things that you have no control over, the effect can be to increase feelings of negativity, which, in turn, can have the effect of reducing your circle of influence.

There is no doubt that where you focus your attention and energy is important, and there is considerable merit in the idea that you should prioritise those areas where your skills, knowledge, experience and mental and emotional connection allow you to make the biggest difference. However, when we talk about circle of influence, we are talking about building relationships with people; how you can build deeper, more trust-based relationships, and techniques that you can use to dramatically increase the number of people that you know and who trust you.

Trust is the key word because people do business with, and refer people to, people they know, like and trust. It's as simple as that.

But trust is such an ephemeral quality – how often do you see someone briefly in a TV programme and think, 'I wouldn't trust them'? Perhaps you look at someone in the street, or in a shop, and think 'I wouldn't trust them'. We all have a tendency to make initial assessments of trust on pretty tenuous information. Maybe this is because learning to trust someone takes time and effort. We risk having our trust abused and, if this happens, we become even more reluctant to make the effort again.

So one of the key factors in our willingness to make the effort to trust someone may be our assessment of how useful we feel that person may be to us in the future. If we feel that they may be helpful, we are more inclined to make an effort to get to know them.

Once we start to engage with someone, we may find that they can indeed be helpful to us, in which case we are likely to invest even more time and effort to maintain our acquaintance. If they then go on to be helpful, we invest our trust in them and we feel an obligation to be helpful in return.

Put bluntly – trust is the way we measure someone's ability to help us get what we want.

So if you make an effort to help someone get what they want, and you do it in an ethical and honest manner, you will increase their level of trust in you and, in return, you build a bond of obligation that you can call upon at a later date.

This leads us nicely to our central question, which is – How can I create opportunities to interact with more people in a way that encourages them to like me and trust me?

The obvious answer is that you need to network more. But before you rush off to meet more people, let's take a moment to understand what networking is:

- Networking *is* a purposeful human interaction with the sole aim of building trust. You do this by focusing on the other person, their needs and what you can do to help them fulfil their needs.

- Networking *is not* selling, either yourself or your product; it is certainly not an opportunity to boast of your achievements or prowess. It is not small talk, because that has no purpose, or useful outcome, other than passing time; nor is it an opportunity to practise amateur psychoanalysis, or run a self-help clinic.

Networking as a means of marketing yourself is a skill that needs to be understood and practised. It is much more than just meeting people and, despite the hype of technology-enabled professional networking tools, it is also much more than just getting connected online.

In his 1999 article, 'The Human Moment', Edward M. Hallowell set out the two conditions that must be simultaneously present for a human moment to happen – the same is true for your networking efforts because, when you network, you are creating a human moment. The two building blocks on which you build trust are:

- physical presence;

- emotional and intellectual engagement.

As your purpose is to build liking and trust, it also follows that your focus should be firmly on the person you are engaged with, their needs and how you may fit into fulfilling those needs. By doing so, you can demonstrate your value to them by helping them to achieve their goals.

Set your own goals aside; there will be time enough to get around to those once you have built the trusting relationship.

Practical advice

We have seen that if you want to increase your circle of influence, you have to get out there and network; that means you build relationships with everybody and anybody you come into contact with who could be of value to you in the future.

You may feel a little daunted by this prospect because you can't assess people's potential value to you, unless you take the trouble to get to know them, and you don't have the time to get to know everyone you bump into. So you need to establish a strategy on how to target and prioritise your networking efforts.

We suggest that you work on the following groups in this order:

- Inside your organisation: make it your business to find out who the key players are in each department, who is sponsoring each major project or programme, who is managing each project on behalf of the sponsor and who reports directly to board members. These are all people who should be in your circle of influence – you need to make opportunities to interact with these people and find out what you can do for them, even if it is something as simple as introducing them to someone else. Make it your business to do something for them and show them they can rely upon you.

- Outside your organisation, but inside your professional discipline: you already have something in common – your area of expertise. Now look for a way to leverage that – you may be able to help them solve a problem, access a resource that is unknown to them, or introduce them to like-minded people. This may be a longer-term pay-off, but it is time well spent. Look for opportunities to engage with people in communities, such as:

  - your customer community – the people who use and care about the goods and services that you provide;

  - specialist groups under the banner of your professional body;

  - journalists (both retained and freelance) who write on your subject;

  - conference organisers and speakers.

- Outside your professional discipline, but working in the same sector as you: this is playing the long game, but it does have two big advantages:

  - It helps you understand the needs and drivers of people who face different problems than you, and gives you valuable practice at building relationships where you don't have a common bond of professional knowledge.

  - It can give you new insights that you would never pick up by interacting with like-minded people – this sort of boundary spanning is a key skill and makes you a valued asset on cross-functional teams.

OK, so now we have narrowed down the universe to a handful of 15 to 25 people that you will target in order to expand your circle of influence.

In addition, make it your mission to give a little to the people you come across each day who are generally ignored by the masses, such as security guards, car-park attendants, cleaners, drivers, receptionists, etc. Acknowledge their existence, engage in a little small talk and look for an opportunity to compliment or thank them. We all like to feel valued for who we are and what we do, and people in such professions are vital, but rarely noticed or acknowledged. They also have their own network and pretty soon word will get around – 'that one is OK', 'he's not stuck up like the rest', 'she made my day'. Remember that value can come out of the most unlikely acquaintanceships.

To do this you will have to be generous with yourself and your time because you never know what you might need from someone in the future. As they say, 'be nice to people on your way up because you might meet them on your way down'.

Now for some general advice on sensible tactics to follow when engaging with someone you want to influence. This is a long list, and we suggest that you start by choosing one or two ideas and building them into the way you do things. Once these have become embedded as good habits, revisit the list and choose two more areas to work on:

- Always speak well of others; never slag anyone off behind their back. If you say something bad about someone to someone else, how does that someone else know that you are not doing the same to them behind their back?

- Take an interest in other people and their activities and interests. For most people, their favourite topic is either themselves, or the achievements of members of their family. Listen carefully; this is how you get to know someone and find out about their values and what is important to them.

- Develop the ability to converse on a wide range of subjects – your aim is to show that you know just enough about what they are saying to recognise that they are making a really valuable contribution and to be able to ask meaningful questions that give them the opportunity to impress you some more. Resist the temptation to show them how much you know on the topic.

- Look for common interests – these will always provide an easy, non-threatening ice-breaker on any occasion.

- Actively listen to others and accept that they have a valid point of view, even if you don't agree with it. If you can learn how they see the world and why they see it like they do, you will be better placed to assess how you can help each other.

- Praise, rather than criticise, and never, ever argue with someone. You cannot win an argument – if you lose, you have lost and if you win, you have lost because you have just created a grievance in the mind of the other person, and potentially destroyed any chance of that person ever trusting you.

- Demonstrate empathy and sensitivity to the moods and feelings of others. You need to engage emotionally as well as intellectually.

- Respect and value people for who they are without trying to change them.

- Demonstrate modesty and humility and be prepared to admit your mistakes, or that you are wrong. Develop your sense of humour and ability to laugh at yourself.

- Put yourself out to help others without expecting anything in return.

Finally, try to end every interaction with an enquiry that gets to the heart of how you can help them. This is your trump card because it demonstrates that you have been listening and that you care about them, and it gives you an opportunity to start another interaction with them at a later date. But you need to be a little subtle about how you do it. Here are some ideas that you can adapt and adopt to your own situations:

- If you are building rapport with someone inside your business, but outside your discipline, try something like:

  - Wow, I had no idea what your programme was trying to achieve, it sounds really exciting. But from what you've said, your biggest issue seems to be that you are lacking a skilled 'x' – can you tell me more about what you need from this person, so that I can keep my eyes out for someone who might fit the bill?

- If you are building your business and looking for prospects for yourself, don't ask outright; use reverse psychology, show you want to help them find prospects and you can be sure that when you do, they will return the favour. Try something like:

  - How would I recognise someone who would be a good prospect for you?

Notice with both the examples above that you are feeding back to them that you have intellectually engaged with their issue and you are on their emotional wavelength with regard to their immediate needs. Also, by asking them for a pen picture of what they need to solve their issues, you have left them with a lasting impression that you are actively engaged with them to solve their problem. Even if you don't actually help them this time, they will remember your interest and willingness to go out of your way for them. You have started to build trust and obligation.

Further food for the curious

- Hallowell EM. The Human Moment at Work. *Harvard Business Review*, Jan.–Feb. 1999:

  - A classic *HBR* (*Harvard Business Review*) article that makes the social and psychological case for ensuring that we create the time and space to have meaningful human interaction and points to the potentially dire consequences when we don't make the effort.

- Yemm G. Influencing Others — a key skill for all. *Management Services*, Summer 2008:

  - A short, four-page article that introduces and expands on influencing strategies and tactics.

- Covey SR. *The 7 habits of highly effective people — powerful lessons in personal change.* Simon & Schuster (2004):

  - Lots of useful self-improvement guidance based on identified winning habits; needs deep study to get the best out of it.

Things for you to work on now

Key questions to ask yourself
• What do you hope to achieve in the next 12 months and who could help you achieve it?   • What have you done in the last two weeks to build a new relationship with someone in your organisation?   • Last time you went to a conference or professional gathering, how many new people did you get to know and how many of them did you subsequently help in any way?   • What are you currently doing to build professional links with people outside your organisation?

Mini exercises you can try immediately

- Make a list of the 10 most influential people in your company – now plot them on a diagram, showing their relationships to the board and to each other. How many of these people know who you are, trust you and would ask for you if they were staffing up an important project?

- Look at the relationship map that you created in the previous exercise. Prioritise three people that you want to work on to build greater trust and understanding. Devise a strategy to make it happen and commit yourself to three actions that you will complete in the next 10 days.

Links to other questions

You may want to take a look at:

13: *How do I make the best use of my time?*
Page 135

17: *How do I get the recognition I think I deserve?*
Page 171

21: *How can I create allies and advocates who work to promote my reputation?*
Page 225

24: *How can I learn to play the political game while still maintaining my integrity?*
Page 263

25: *How can I get better at being able to converse on a wide range of subjects?*
Page 275

21: HOW CAN I CREATE ALLIES AND ADVOCATES WHO WORK TO PROMOTE MY REPUTATION?

Why should I be asking this question?

'No man is an island' (John Donne, 1572–1631); we need the support of others to flourish both socially and organisationally. Another way of looking at this is to think about loyalty and what it means for you. You may, for instance, be a loyal fan of Apple – you may own the latest iPhone, iPad, etc. If you do, we think that it is a safe bet that you also take every opportunity to tell your friends about the features of your latest iPhone and how good Apple products are in general. Who needs advertising when you have zillions of loyal customers who never miss an opportunity to do your advertising for you by telling the world how amazing your products are? What works for products also works for people.

Loyalty can be defined as – the willingness of someone, a customer, an employee or a friend, to make a personal sacrifice in order to strengthen their relationship with you. This is gold dust because, when someone recommends you, they are putting their own reputation on the line. The amazing thing is that if you can engender true loyalty in people, they will willingly and repeatedly put their reputation on the line for you. When people make overt displays of loyalty to you, they are saying something very positive and very powerful about you; it is the aggregated effect of all these little displays of loyalty that builds your reputation and your personal brand.

In the case of people, loyalty tends to be a reciprocal arrangement – so if you want others to work actively to promote your reputation and your personal brand, then you need to be working equally actively to promote theirs whenever the opportunity arises.

The impact of the issue

Many very competent people go unnoticed in organisations because they are buried deep within their specialist departments and nobody, especially themselves, is working to proactively advertise their talents to a wider audience. It's not enough to be good; you have to be seen to be good. That means that you have to find a way of getting into the spotlight while you are strutting your stuff. Now some people achieve personal advertising by announcing themselves with a loud fanfare blown on their own trumpet – but it is so much more effective if other people draw attention to you, and they do so because they genuinely admire you and want to see you do well.

The easiest way to accelerate career progression is to foster a strong network of personal advocates, people who spontaneously sing your praises in the right ears at the right time and work tirelessly to get you noticed and your talents recognised and rewarded. They sell your reputation and, in doing so, they establish a 'brand' that is you and an expectation and promise about what your brand can deliver.

When the CEO asks who you are, you do not want the answer to be 'That's Joe from IT' or 'Jane from HR'. Your brand has to be very different from your role if you want to stand out from the crowd. So the sort of response you are aiming for is something along the lines of, 'That's Joe; if you want a project organised right and brought in on time you need Joe on the case', or 'That's Jane; I don't know how we would have gained agreement on the new pension terms without her skilful and sensitive negotiation skills'. These are both examples of a personal brand shaping how people see your past actions and successes, and how they project your capabilities in a way that implies your ability to produce future successes.

Making sense of it all

You are just one person and you can only be in one place at a time, but reputation and professional identity can exist simultaneously in many minds at the same time, and can be working on your behalf without your knowledge or awareness.

So the questions you should now be asking yourself are how you can successfully market yourself, so that you create a positive professional image in the minds of the people you meet and how you can make each and every interaction powerful and persuasive, so that, in effect, you become your very own advertising agency, selling your personal reputation and brand.

As we explore this idea further, we deal with two different, but related, topics, namely:

- your curriculum vitae or CV for short;
- your personal brand.

For most of us, marketing ourselves is not something we give much attention to, unless we are looking for a new job – then, typically, we dust off the CV, and spend some time thinking and writing about ourselves and our capabilities and qualities.

We have seen hundreds, no thousands, of CVs and we would have to say that, generally, most people are pretty poor at talking or writing about themselves. The problem we find with CVs is that they tend to be past focused and descriptive in nature – that is, they concentrate on previous roles and the areas of responsibility within those roles; they read very much like a job description and say little about the person fulfilling the role, the capabilities of that person and what they, as a unique individual, achieved that no one else could have done in the same situation.

However, a prospective employer is only interested in the past as a predictor of the future. They want to know if you have ever done anything surprising and if you are likely to do something even more surprising for them if they hire you. What the prospective employer needs is a CV that is future focused and success based – they need to see what you made happen that wouldn't have happened without you.

So we could all get a bit better at writing CVs, and you should always keep your CV updated because it is good discipline and a vehicle to make you think about your own marketability.

But the CV is what you write about yourself and is only a small part of the story; your reputation is governed by what other people think and say about you and that is a story built upon thousands of interactions over a period of time that they individually interpret and make sense of. You should not leave those interpretations to chance; it is your reputation, so take some responsibility for it.

The way you shape people's interpretations and, hence, your reputation is to establish for yourself a 'personal brand'.

We are all familiar with the idea of a 'brand' and instantly recognise brand names and their related products such as Apple, Persil, Coca-Cola and BMW.

These are all brands that carry with them innate attributes that you then associate with their individual products; attributes such as innovative, reliable, environmentally friendly, refreshing, healthy or safe – these are all psychological keys that are triggered when we engage with a brand.

The brand has at its core a simple essence – the key message or governing thought (example – kills 99% of household germs); the essence is then rounded out by considerations of:

- benefits – the way the brand can solve your problems;
- values – what the brand stands for;

- reason to believe – evidence of efficacy, expert endorsements and demonstrations of effectiveness;
- consumer discriminator – the single most compelling reason to choose the brand.

A brand has an identity, but it also carries with it a promise to deliver. Great brands carry a mental and emotional connection, and have the power to shape how we will look at and accept a product even before we see it.

We believe that the way to manage your reputation and build loyal advocates who work to enhance your reputation is to think of yourself as a product and work to create a personal brand.

Your personal brand has the ability to shape people's impressions of you in a way that will then colour how they interpret your deeds and achievements, and how they talk about them to other people.

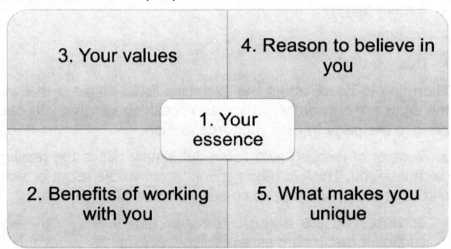

Figure 13: Personal brand key[6]

---

[6] Our depiction of a personal brand key is based on some of the elements of the corporate brand key developed by Dr Robert Passikoff.

We suggest that you start to think about your brand by using a similar structure to that of the marketing professionals.

Let's look more closely at the five elements of the personal brand model.

1. *Your essence* – what do you want your brand to say about you? What is your essence and what are the phrases that you would like to spontaneously spring to mind when people think about you? Are you:

- a problem solver?
- a completer/finisher?
- a tough, but fair, negotiator?
- a boundary spanner?
- business focused?
- an innovative thinker?
- a team player?
- friendly?
- trustworthy?

The thing to notice about the examples listed above is that all the items are outwardly focused and speak about what you can bring to the party to help your organisation.

2. *Benefits of working with you* – put simply this is the reason to choose you. Think in terms of your most visible talent or skill and what that gives your customer. For example:

- Because you are a great communicator – they can feel confident that their message will get across.
- Because you are a Six Sigma black belt – they know you will eliminate waste.
- Because you are an experienced planner and have led high-profile projects – they can be assured of getting easy-to-

understand red, amber, green (RAG) progress status reports.

- Because you are an experienced contract negotiator – they know that you will negotiate a contract that produces high levels of value.

3. *Your values* – This is a combination of what you stand for and also what your reputation says about you. In terms of your values you may wish to be known for your:

- honesty;

- sense of fair play;

- commitment to environmental sustainability.

Your reputation is how other people interpret your every deed. It is important that what you say about yourself and what your reputation says about you are in full alignment.

4. *Reason to believe in you* – this is about tangible evidence of why you are better than the alternatives. It is likely to be based upon the following:

- Personal testimonials – these are from other people you have worked for.

- Expert endorsement – these may be from people in your field, but from external bodies.

- Awards and professional achievements – maybe you have been recognised as a fellow of your professional body, or you have published journals articles or books, or spoken at conferences. Maybe you have won a prestigious award from one of your clients, or have been nominated '...of the year'.

- Case studies or demonstrations – nothing speaks quite so loudly as a winning implementation. Can you point to something that you created that is currently producing organisational benefit? For example:

  - You created the sales-forecasting system.

- You designed the new office layout.

- You installed the new test plant.

- You authored the latest company brochure.

5. *What makes you unique* – based on all the elements of your brand key, this single sentence should be memorable and mark you out as different. For example:

- You are the only person in the company who has led a successful post-merger integration.

- You have successful turned around three failing projects.

- You led the company's most successful marketing campaign.

We cannot overstate the importance to you of taking control of your own 'brand'. If you don't know what image you are trying to project to the outside world, how can you begin to hope that anyone else will be able to project a consistent and positive image on your behalf?

Practical advice

So how do you go about shaping and communicating your brand? First ask yourself, 'What am I doing to win loyal personal advocates?' and 'What am I doing to demonstrate my level of loyalty in return?'.

We suggest that you sit down and use the *personal brand* template shown in Figure 13 to work out and document what you want your own brand to be.

Spend some time looking at magazine and TV adverts to see how they have a governing thought, supportive evidence and claims that are then projected forward in terms of a benefit that you can accrue by using the product.

On one side of A4 paper, start to build your personal brand statement. Begin with 'your essence', a governing thought about what you can do for the organisation; look at the following examples and then construct a simple future-focused statement (ideally no more than eight to 12 words) that encapsulates what you want to be known for. For example:

- Cuts through red tape to improve the bottom line.
- Drives innovation to produce top-line growth.
- Turns around failing projects.
- Writes great proposals that win bids.
- Brings teams together and improves performance.

Once you have constructed a governing thought, start to surround it with:

- the benefits of working with you;
- your values and personality;
- the reasons to believe in you;
- what makes you unique.

Once you have your personal brand in place, start to imagine some stories that capture your essence, and weave many of the other attributes into the narrative. Make sure that you can tell each of your stories in less than 30 seconds. Build six to 10 stories about yourself, using your personal brand description, and check that they are conveying a consistent and simple-to-understand message.

Now we are not suggesting that you start to tell your own stories – no, the point is that these are the sorts of stories that other people naturally and subconsciously build to rationalise, explain and understand who you are. They interpret your everyday actions in ways that support their mental story of you. And it is through their interpretations that your reputation is built.

So once you have your stories, you keep them to yourself, but you use them to check the consistency of your own behaviour, actions, reactions, and moral and ethical positions. Each time you interact with someone, you should be asking yourself, 'Are my actions and words consistent with the story of myself and my essence?'. By starting to live your own story, you will start to manage the reputation you create in the minds of others.

What we have described may appear to be a little strange because it is an alien way of thinking. But imagine for a moment an actor: they get a script that describes a situation and gives them words to say, the emphasis to place on those words and directions about how to interact with the other players. But it is as if the character suddenly appeared from outer space – without a life history, the actor has no way of knowing what motivates their character, or how they might react on saying or hearing any of the words. So the actor's first task is to create a backstory, a full picture of their character as a real, living, breathing being – only by doing this can they hope to convey to their audience the real identity and reputation of their character. The result is that, at the end of the show, you go away not having just listened to a load of words, but having engaged with, and come to know, some real characters. When an actor gets it right, you come away feeling that you have actually met that person and have a sense of what makes them tick – this is not just an outcome of good script writing, it is the actor's ability to convey, in a very short space of time, the essence of the character they are portraying.

We have a great advantage over actors because we know our own backstory. The problem is that we never think constructively about our backstory and how it can be used to shape people's impression of us.

We suggest that you use the tools we have given you to construct your own story and to start to use that story in a consistent way that is capable of shaping how people think and feel about you. Once they buy into your reputation and who you are, they are far more likely to actively work for your benefit.

So just to summarise:

- Understand and live your own brand values.

- Keep your message simple – you want others to be able to see it and then articulate it spontaneously, so you need to connect with their heart, as well as their head.

- Be relevant – your brand is only of value if it has the capacity to make a difference to other people's lives. Focus your stories on what you can help people achieve.

- Be consistent – you have hundreds of interactions each day and you have to make sure that everyone, and we mean everyone, sees the same essence of you every time.

- Be seen – you cannot achieve effective personal branding by hiding behind your role or staying in your box – you need to get out and take the risk of exposing yourself.

- Be heard – once you are out and being seen, you also have to make sure that you are heard. Remember that what you say is only 10% of the equation – the other 90% is how you say it, how your actions are in congruence with what you say and how you follow through on your words and actions.

Further food for the curious

- Sills J. 'Becoming Your Own Brand'. *Psychology Today*, Jan.–Feb. 2008:

  - A very short and punchy article that introduces the idea of managing your reputation as a personal brand.

- Reichheld FF. The one number you need to grow. *Harvard Business Review*, Nov.–Dec. 2003:

  - An interesting paper that suggests that a single customer survey question can act as the best predictor of growth. It appears that it is all about loyalty, a customer's willingness to recommend your product or service to a friend. We say what works for companies also works for individual loyalty and personal growth.

Things for you to work on now

Key questions to ask yourself

- What is your personal brand? What are the key selling points that mark you out as someone to know and rely upon?

- What have you achieved in the last year that is so noteworthy that even people who don't know you will have been impacted by what you did? What could you do to ensure that when people tell this story, they also mention your name?

- What is it about the way you relate to people that would cause a mere acquaintance to recommend you and your work to someone in their inner network?

- What things can you do that might be of value to a senior manager in another part of your company – what would it take for that manager to know who you are and want to use your talents?

- When was the last time you updated your CV?

Mini exercises you can try immediately

- On one page of A4, build your 'brand key'. At the centre of the page, write one sentence (eight to 12 words) that captures how you would want people to describe you. Surround this sentence with the attributes in the brand key.

- Watch some TV adverts – analyse the format, the simplicity of the message and the way it is reinforced. Now spend some time writing a 30-second TV advert for yourself. When you are happy with it, think of three things you can start doing today that might cause people to spontaneously think and feel that way about the 'you' that you have envisaged.

- Revise your CV – at the top of it put the sentence from your personal brand key. Now instead of saying what you have done or what you are responsible for, pick out five things you have achieved in the last 18 months and write a paragraph on each. Make sure that each paragraph highlights one or more of the aspects in your brand key. End each paragraph with a statement of the outcome of your actions in measurable terms.

- Revise your CV each year before your annual performance review.

Links to other questions

You may want to take a look at:

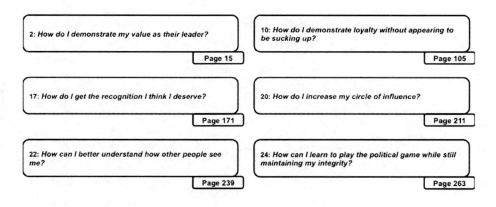

2: *How do I demonstrate my value as their leader?*
Page 15

10: *How do I demonstrate loyalty without appearing to be sucking up?*
Page 105

17: *How do I get the recognition I think I deserve?*
Page 171

20: *How do I increase my circle of influence?*
Page 211

22: *How can I better understand how other people see me?*
Page 239

24: *How can I learn to play the political game while still maintaining my integrity?*
Page 263

238

22: HOW CAN I BETTER UNDERSTAND HOW OTHER PEOPLE SEE ME?

Why should I be asking this question?

Reputations and first impressions have a huge impact on how people behave towards us: whether they view us as trustworthy or not, whether they want to deal with us or not, whether they answer our calls or try to avoid us. Perhaps the most potentially damaging aspect is how they speak about us when talking to our peers because this, in turn, colours how yet more people see us.

Both reputations and first impressions tend to be based on very minimal information and coloured by the opinions, perceptions, interpretations, beliefs, biases and prejudices that we all carry with us. What other people think about us often reveals more about their values and beliefs that about our own. For example, if we rushed to break up a fight across the street, one person may view our behaviour as *brave*, while another person may view the same behaviour as *foolhardy*.

By understanding how reputations are formed and first impressions are made, we are better placed to understand how we can impact on them for the better.

The impact of the issue

Over the years, we have researched the stereotypical images of a variety of professions. We have listed a few below. You will note that these images tend to focus on the negative aspects rather than the positive – this, unfortunately, is human nature. If we have touched on your profession, please don't take offence or blame us; remember, we are merely the messenger:

239

- The IT stereotype:
  - is comfortable with logic, facts and data;
  - is uncomfortable with ambiguity and unpredictability – they like to follow clear and unambiguous rules;
  - lives in a world of black and white where there are no shades of grey – there is a right way to build a system and a wrong way to build a system;
  - is politically naïve and lacking in business awareness;
  - is cautious, conservative and risk-averse;
  - is good at deconstructing problems, but poor at synthesis, i.e. understanding in the context of the greater whole;
  - lacks interpersonal skills and a sense of humour;
  - adopts a victim mentality – can't win, so won't fight;
  - is poor at accepting criticism – often rationalising it away.
- The librarian stereotype:
  - is earnest;
  - is rigid;
  - is fearsomely protective of their domain;
  - is self-effacing;
  - wears sensible shoes, tweed suit, droopy sweater;
  - has spectacles on a chain;
  - is dull, probably with no social life;
  - says 'Shush!' a lot.
- The accountancy stereotype:
  - is introverted;
  - is dull and boring;

  – is rigid and inflexible;

  – is risk-averse;

  – is precise and pedantic;

  – has an eye for detail;

  – is structured and rule-oriented;

  – is accurate and good with numbers;

  – is conventional and conservative;

  – is truthful and reliable;

  – is rational and objective;

  – is unbending;

  – is frequently summed up with the phrase 'bean counter'.

- The sales stereotype:

  – is short-term focused – only interested in the current deal;

  – leaves things unfinished – is off to win the next one;

  – tells you what you want to hear;

  – promises the earth, delivers the minimum;

  – is unstructured;

  – breaks the rules;

  – is flash and arrogant;

  – believes they are centre of the universe;

  – has long lunches;

  – has unlimited expense accounts;

  – brown-noses.

- The academic stereotype:

  – is theoretical/abstract;

241

- is egotistical/elitist;
- is serious;
- is prissy and precise;
- has an odd dress sense;
- is disorganised;
- is stubborn;
- is churlish;
- is sesquipedalian – they use overly long words;
- is highly intelligent, but lacking in common sense;
- is out of touch with the real world;
- lacks management and collaborative skills.

You may find the above lists amusing; however, we would suggest that if we had asked you to list the traits that you associated with any of these professions, you would have come up with a very similar list, providing, of course, that you are not a member of that profession itself. Stereotypes do tend to focus on negative, rather than positive, attributes, just as the media focuses on wrongdoing, the sad, the perverse and the downright horrible; good news is, sadly to say, just not newsworthy. Now think about a real person, a friend who is a member of one of these professions – we guess that when you think about it clearly and assess their merits, you will find that they are most probably nice, well-rounded individuals who actually exhibit very few of these traits. Nonetheless, if they introduced you to one of their professional colleagues, you are more likely to expect that colleague to fit your stereotype than to be just like your friend.

When you start to believe these rather negative collective truths about groups of people, you can start to find yourself disliking people you have never even met or spoken to. You may wish to reflect upon the stereotype of your profession as seen by an outsider. By doing so, you may start to understand why people look at you the way they do when you walk into the room.

Now let us consider our values and beliefs for a moment. We tend to interpret the behaviour of others through our own value systems. Imagine that you are observing one of your colleagues interact with a customer or a friend in an informal situation. Our values colour the way we interpret any situation and the motives we ascribe to the actions we see. For instance, we may feel:

- They are not mean, they are just thrifty.
- They are not brave, they are foolhardy.
- They are not open, they are naïve.
- They are not committed, they are obsessed.
- They are not sensitive, they are overemotional.
- They are not imaginative, they are unrealistic.
- They are not sceptical, they are cynical.
- They are not astute, they are cunning.
- They are not persuasive, they are manipulative.

Our interpretation tells us more about us than it does about the person we are observing. To truly understand someone's behaviour, we need to interpret it through their value system, rather than our own.

All in all, first impressions tell us more about society's collective opinion of various groups and our own prejudices and biases, rather than the person about whom we are making a judgement.

Making sense of it all

Just as we classify problems, opportunities and other business phenomena, we classify people. It is a type of shorthand for making sense of the world. From an evolutionary point of view, there is enormous survival value in an ability to make rapid judgements about people and situations. Imagine those days when we were walking the savannah plains and bumping into other living creatures; we had to make fairly instant decisions about whether they were friend or foe – our lives depended upon it. Analysing options and next steps was not a recipe for a long and fruitful life. Even today, despite years of education, development and sensitisation to political correctness, the sorting of people into 'in-groups' and 'out-groups' remains one of our primary ways of evaluating others. This is why first impressions are so important.

Human brains work with clusters of concepts, often referred to as 'neuronal groups'. Rather than building our impressions of the world by adding up the individual pieces of data, we make 'intuitive leaps'. Our brains are capable of jumping to conclusions because limited data is quickly matched against a number of 'templates' in the brain. So our natural tendency is not to say (unconsciously), 'This person or thing will remain unclassified until I have acquired enough evidence'; it is to say (unconsciously), 'What predefined pattern most closely matches my initial impression?'. This instant classification remains current until enough contrary evidence forces us to make the effort to reclassify. More often than not, the effort of reclassification is too difficult and, despite evidence to the contrary, we stick with our initial assessment, even when it is demonstrably wrong.

Practical advice

Stereotypical images need to be managed, not ignored. Overcoming them is difficult, but it is not impossible. Here are a few pointers:

- Make a deliberate effort to behave anti-'stereotype' for your profession – prove that you are different from the typical. Confront your stereotype:

- If you are an IT professional, for example, talk big picture, have a view about business matters in general, demonstrate a 'can do' attitude and that you have a sense of humour. Carry the *Financial Times* under your arm rather than *Computer Weekly*, and leave your anorak in the potting shed.

- If you are a librarian, let your hair down, both literally and metaphorically, wear some trendy clothes and tell a joke. Demonstrate flexibility in the use of your services.

- If you are an accountant, give people options, tell an entertaining story, or relate some amusing anecdotes. Wear a bright colours and trendy shoes.

- If you are a sales person, practise the art of actively listening without focusing on what you are going to say next. Answer questions directly and honestly, don't evade the question and give a balanced view. Save the garish clothes for your next fancy-dress party.

- If you are an academic, use short everyday words, praise rather than criticise the ideas of others and demonstrate humility. Work on your colour co-ordination, and avoid corduroy, elbow patches and brown shoes.

• Get things out in the open – discuss openly the traits, habits, routines, rituals, stories, myths, symbols, style, etc. that are associated with your profession. Articulating concerns, barriers and oddities makes them less powerful.

• Network and build personal relationships – when people have enough information about you as a unique individual, their stereotypical view will tend to fade into insignificance. Beware that this takes time and consistency of behaviour – socialisation is a long and slow process.

• Be seen as a forward-thinking, 'can do' person who is going places:

- Stop focusing on metrics and benchmarks, and start focusing on building relationships and trust.

- Don't overanalyse situations, learn to trust your gut and your heart.

- Talk about your organisation as a whole, where your industry is going, rather than your functional discipline.

- Stop focusing on the nitty-gritty of current issues, and start focusing on innovation and future directions.

- Stop talking about problems and start talking about possibilities.

- Stop being risk-averse and start making those big strategic decisions where there is no right answer or best practice to follow.

- Become a leader rather than a follower.

- Be likable, someone that others want to spend time with:

  - Be warm and friendly, keep smiling.

  - Always speak well of others; look for opportunities to say thank you, or well done.

  - Keep an open mind and be tolerant of others – reserve judgement and accept their values and beliefs.

  - Be open and honest, flexible and collaborative, patient and understanding.

  - Ask open, gently probing questions – be prepared to listen and learn. Share a little of yourself to encourage others to open up.

  - Always keep your cool and use humour to diffuse tension, or get difficult messages across.

  - Stop taking yourself too seriously, laugh at yourself; don't be touchy, prissy, precious, or easily offended.

- Develop allies and advocates and employ lobbying tactics – let your network do the work for you.

Further food for the curious

- Nicholson N. How Hardwired is Human Behaviour? *Harvard Business Review*, 1998:

  - An interesting insight into evolutionary psychology and our propensity to stereotype.

Things for you to work on now

Key questions to ask yourself

- What perceptions do you believe others may hold about you?

- Is there anything about your behaviour, the language you use or the way that you dress that reinforces their stereotypical image of you?

- How do you view other groups and to what extent does the way you think about their stereotype influence the way you approach and interact with them?

- How many hours a week do you dedicate to networking? How high does networking fall within your list of priorities?

- What is the first thing you do/say when you meet someone for the first time? Is your manner likely to support the stereotype of your profession, or is it markedly at odds with it? What impact are you trying to create?

Mini exercises you can try immediately

- Do your homework on your own stereotype – research the Internet, or ask a few trusted but honest allies what the stereotypical image is of your profession.

- Choose three aspects of your professional stereotype that you believe are most damaging to the way people might see and interact with you at work and in social situations (there may be different aspects for each).

- Choose two aspects of your stereotype that you believe could be beneficial to you when you interact with people at work and in social situations.

- For each of the aspects identified in the previous two points, think of one or two things you could do or say, or an aspect of dress, manner or body language that you could adopt every time you interact with people that will help them to see you in a more positive light. Make a policy of always practising these key behaviours – you will be amazed that after a couple of weeks they just come naturally to you.

- Make a list of your existing allies and advocates. Now make another list of potential allies and advocates. Consider how you could exploit your first list to turn your second list into a reality.

Links to other questions

You may want to take a look at:

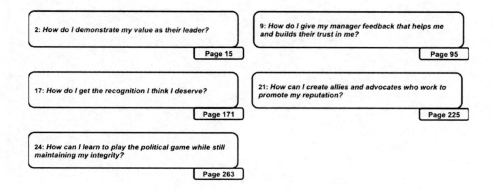

2: How do I demonstrate my value as their leader?

Page 15

9: How do I give my manager feedback that helps me and builds their trust in me?

Page 95

17: How do I get the recognition I think I deserve?

Page 171

21: How can I create allies and advocates who work to promote my reputation?

Page 225

24: How can I learn to play the political game while still maintaining my integrity?

Page 263

23: HOW CAN I BE SEEN AS SOMEONE WHO HELPS CHANGE HAPPEN?

Why should I be asking this question?

Nothing is permanent except change.

(Heraclitus, 500BC)

We are in transition to a world where change is continuous; not just episodic.

(Kotter, 2008)

Change is the one big certainty in our organisations. What makes us successful today is almost certain to be the root of our failure tomorrow. The problem is that when organisations are faced with instability in the environment, it generates uncertainty, which in turn leads to higher levels of stress and anxiety. This, in turn, leads to the very human reaction of falling back on established and familiar patterns and solutions. Paradoxically, the very time we most need to be flexible and accepting of change tends to be the time when we are least equipped to emotionally deal with the possibility and consequences of change.

In today's world, feeling contented with the status quo is a dangerous position to be in. If organisations don't change, they become extinct and if people don't change, they become irrelevant or surplus to requirements as far as their organisations are concerned.

The impact of the issue

It is a sad fact that most people and most organisations don't tend to seriously consider changing their behaviours until there is no other viable choice, and when you get to that point, it is invariably too late.

But simply saying we need to be more proactive, rather than reactive, is not very helpful. What organisations need is people who can shine a light into the darkness and illuminate a new way forward – to be the pathfinder for others – to lead the way to new behaviours and practices. Such people tend to be called change agents; they are the people who are skilled at asking the difficult questions that challenge existing ways of thinking and working. But it is not enough just to ask difficult questions – you have to do so in a positive way that excites people about an alternative future and ignites in them a passion to be part of that future.

All organisations need change agents, but being a change agent is not a role; you don't get appointed by HR. Being an agent for change is just something that some people can do and if you are one of those people, you are a precious asset and will be quickly recognised as such.

Making sense of it all

Change happens; our external environment can change in response to any number of independent, or related, variables over which we generally have little, or no, control. Our organisations then find themselves having to adapt to continue to function in that changing environment – the actions we take may be planned and deliberate, or we may just stumble into them almost by accident. It has always been so; the only new thing is that our external environment may be changing more quickly than it used to, or may be prone to more violent and unanticipated swings. What has not changed much is the way that managers and leaders react to change. In broad terms, there are four types of leadership response:

- *Defender* – leaders with this mind-set tend to see little, or no, uncertainty in the environment; they are comfortable and feel a level of immunity to the turmoil that appears to beset others. Their response, if any, is to make minor adjustments in organisational structures or processes:

  - History tells us that this defensive stance leads to extinction.

- *Reactor* – leaders with this mind-set see that change and uncertainty exist, but will not initiate any response until they have overwhelming evidence that inaction is no longer an option. At this stage, they may make substantial adjustments, but generally they are too late to gain advantage and the result of their actions is merely a slowing of the rate of their corporate decline. This mentality leads to a protracted struggle for survival and the best outcome is an extended life in the margins.

- *Nimble mimic* – these leaders see change and uncertainty, but are reluctant to make the necessary investment of resources to deal with them. Instead, they perfect the art of waiting for someone else to find a solution, and then rapidly adopt and adapt that solution for their own ends:

  - This sort of stance ensures survival and can even produce growth, but they are always playing catch-up and are always under threat from someone who can learn to copy better, faster or more cheaply.

- *Pioneer* – these leaders understand that change and uncertainty are constant companions. They continually experiment with new ways of responding to emerging trends. They are masters of intelligent opportunism. Pioneers have the ability to relate a proposed change to the business strategy or bigger picture and, in doing so, they can be instrumental in anchoring the change into new ways of working:

– Organisations and individuals who adopt this attitude will survive and prosper in any environment.

What we find interesting is that even companies which are, by nature, reactors or mimics still desire their managers to be pioneers. Indeed, a significant emphasis of many current leadership programmes is how to make managers more future-focused and innovative. It appears then that the most valuable management skill is not the ability to react to and manage through change, but rather the ability to anticipate movements in the market and have capacity in place to take advantage as it is happening.

If you can show yourself to have a pioneering attitude towards change, you will be an invaluable asset to your organisation.

Practical advice

There are no end of books that will help you understand the process of organisational change and the strategies that have been proven to be successful for others. But most of them start from the assumption that you know what needs to be done, and the main problem is how to make it happen successfully. Our question has a little wider focus – we recognise that your organisation needs people who can:

- see opportunities for change that others can't see – this means being able to look upwards and outwards and, in effect, see the money that others are leaving on the table;

- after having seen an opportunity, devise a strategy to deliver the benefits and reap the subsequent rewards for the organisation;

- galvanise people and resources behind an initiative and make something happen;

- remain focused on the main chance and take advantage of serendipity along the way.

We have studied people who appear to be adept at leveraging these benefits for their organisations and identified a number of common characteristics that drive their actions. If you want to be seen as someone who makes change happen, we suggest that you take every opportunity to model the following behaviours:

- *Be someone who knows where they are going* – understand what is important for the long-term health of the business, how your business creates customer value and what you and your department can do to increase customer value in that context. What does the business model look like and where do you fit into it? What new capabilities/approaches can help transform or renew your business model? Pick one or two things that will become your focus for the next 18 months to three years. Make sure that your thinking is aligned with that of your boss and that you both want, and are driving towards, the same goals:

  - Don't just blindly respond to short-term flavour-of-the-month initiatives – focus on things that will contribute to the wider, long-term goals of your organisation.

  - Focus on outcome – in all your discussions, pull the thinking back to the outcome, and create solid mental links between what is being done now and how it will build towards or enable the long-term goal.

  - Don't get locked into a *quality* mentality of *right first time*, or thinking that there is one best solution to any problem – that approach works well for business as usual, but not for organisational change. When you are dealing with change, you need a very flexible, iterative approach that values experimentation and recognises that failure is an essential component of success.

- *Bring the truth into the room* – when we are dealing with issues that involve change, there are always at least three agendas at play: rational, personal and social. People are always comfortable about sharing their rational concerns and agenda – cost, resources, growth, etc. They are less willing to share their personal and social concerns and agendas – yet we know that up to 80% of their decision making will be based on their personal and social agenda:

  - Have the courage to say the unsayable, to ask the forbidden questions, confront the 'taboos' of the organisation and challenge the 'eternal truths' that we all accept about how things work around here.

  - Don't shy away from uncomfortable conversations – they are both liberating and insightful.

  - Get people to articulate their fears – getting them out in the open makes them less powerful.

  - Get resistance out in the open – listen to people's concerns and issues – get them to engage in 'change talk'.

  - Agree the facts of the situation. Often business issues that are raised turn out to be just personal issues that are dressed up – get people to confront their own fears and give them a factual basis.

- *Utilise peer pressure* – work to create allies and advocates who will carry your message with passion and commitment:

  - Provide your followers with an igniting purpose – a question, task or vision that engages their hearts, as well as their minds, and gives them a way of making a contribution that can stand the test of time. You also need to engage their heads by calling upon the unique skills, knowledge and experience that they possess and only they can bring to the venture.

  - Recognise that change only happens when enough people think it is a good idea and they are prepared to invest their personal resources (and reputation) in the endeavour. You need to constantly expand your network of committed followers and connect them together, so that they can mutually support each other when you are not there.

- *Cultivate a predisposition towards action* – all great successes are built on the back of constant experimentation and frequent failure:

  – Start today – do something now and see where it takes you. It is mind-numbingly time-consuming to sit round and discuss, debate and delay. Often there are no right answers, only choices, so make a choice and *do something*. If it takes you closer to where you want to go, then do more of the same; if not, then do something else. If you do something, you always have the opportunity to move forward. If you don't do anything, you will always stand still or slip backwards.

  – Adopt a relentless focus on a few (maximum two or three) key outcomes that you want to achieve – link every decision you make to its ability to get you a step closer to one of those key outcomes. Avoid long wish lists of activities; they can be overwhelming and a sense of being overwhelmed stops action.

  – Be opportunistic! Often our actions have unintended, or unanticipated, consequences. Learn to sense those consequences and find ways of capitalising upon those that could have a positive impact on what you are trying to achieve.

  – If you think you need 'out-of-the-box' thinking, then get out of the box. Involve people from a different business unit, culture or industry; find people who see the world differently. Use their new eyes and ears to help you see new possibilities and to refine your own understanding of how you communicate about your vision and desired outcome.

- *Engage both hearts and minds* – it is increasingly clear that people don't change because they think it is a good idea – they change because they have made an emotional commitment:

  - Don't just communicate facts; let your passion show and don't be afraid of letting people see why something is so important to you.

  - Don't talk at people – rather engage in dialogue with them. Your aim is to gain committed behaviour, not compliant behaviour. When people are committed, they give generously of their time and resources, and they actively champion your cause, rather than watch from the sidelines.

  - Connect people together and give them the space to use their talents to find new and novel ways of rising to the challenges you identify.

  - Look for people who are full of ideas and dissatisfied with the way things are currently done. If you can harness their enthusiasm, they can be a valuable resource. But make sure that you pair them up with someone who is 100% aligned with what you are trying to achieve; otherwise you can find that the intellectually curious have wandered off down a different track. Passion combined with brains can produce great things, but generally you need someone else's hands on the steering wheel.

- *Deal with the resistors* – not everyone can, or will, become an ally or advocate. Change always produces winners and losers and just hoping that people will come around is not a great option:

  - Once you have a critical mass, some will follow the herd and get on side. You may need to neutralise others by bargaining with them or co-opting them onto the project. Find out what is important to them, so that you can understand their price and the potential value they can bring.

- It is important that you don't let the resistors take up too much of your time. Pick them off one at a time and try to limit your overall effort in this area to no more than 25% of your available time.

- If all else fails, make it clear that resistance is useless and propose a 'take it or leave it' deal. Be prepared to remove those who refuse to buy in.

- Ensure you operate 'fair process' and that you send a consistent message.

- *Celebrate your successes* – change is a tiring business and people need periods of rest and recuperation, so that they can get ready to fight the next battle:

  - Be generous with the way you recognise important contributions.

  - Learn about what is working well, particularly around critical interpersonal relationships.

Further food for the curious

- Kotter JP. *The Heart of Change*. Boston, Harvard Business Press (2002):

  - In the intervening years of research after the initial statement of the eight conditions, Kotter came to realise the importance of the human aspect and the need to appeal not only to the head, but also to the heart. This book is more rounded and contains more examples of his ideas at work in organisations.

- Kotter JP. *Our Iceberg is Melting*. London, MacMillan (2006):

  - This is a retelling of the *Heart of Change* as a metaphor. It is simple to read and engaging, while losing none of the theoretical underpinning of his work.

Things for you to work on now

Key questions to ask yourself

- What two things do our customers value most about what we do and how could we do those things better?

- If I had a completely free hand and no resource constraints, what are the two things I would change about the way we do our work?

- What two things give my team the most problems?

- Which problems never seem to get fixed and why?

- What are the big assumptions, 'eternal truths', about our company that nobody ever seems to challenge?

- What excites my team members and why?

- What drains the energy from my team members and why?

- What is the last thing our customers, or competitors, would think that we were capable of achieving and why?

Mini exercises you can try immediately

- Make sure that you understand the business model of your organisation and how your part of the business directly contributes to delivering the customer value proposition. Get to a level of understanding where you can sketch it on one side of A4, and explain how what you do contributes to the business as a whole.

- Reflect on the two or three big assumptions that underpin the business model. For each one, make a list of the behaviours that the assumption creates, and think about how those behaviours could change if one or more of those assumptions changed.

- Look at your major competitors, and see if you can work out what they are doing successfully that is different from you and how that could be incorporated into your own company's business model.

- Do a personal audit of your objectives for the next 12 months. How many of them are aimed at bringing about some fundamental change in your area of the organisation? For each one, identify the desired outcome and what impact it has on your customer value proposition, or how it contributes to accelerating the delivery of the business model.

Links to other questions

You may want to take a look at:

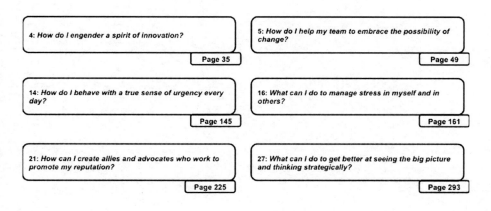

4: How do I engender a spirit of innovation?

Page 35

5: How do I help my team to embrace the possibility of change?

Page 49

14: How do I behave with a true sense of urgency every day?

Page 145

16: What can I do to manage stress in myself and in others?

Page 161

21: How can I create allies and advocates who work to promote my reputation?

Page 225

27: What can I do to get better at seeing the big picture and thinking strategically?

Page 293

24: HOW CAN I LEARN TO PLAY THE POLITICAL GAME WHILE STILL MAINTAINING MY INTEGRITY?

Why should I be asking this question?

Organisational politics are a fact of corporate life. All business professionals need to be adept at dealing with political situations; there is, however, no single formula for success. Politics are often messy, ambiguous and unpredictable; and, to top it all, being right is not enough. Outcomes in the political arena depend upon the subtle interactions and interplays between people. Each situation will be different and unique, and what proves successful in one situation may prove disastrous in the next. In essence, organisational politics is an art, rather than a science!

Political acumen is a key skill for anyone wanting to build and maintain their reputation – much of the theory and advice offered in the rest of this section will also contribute towards your ability to play the political game.

The impact of the issue

Ask anyone what words and phrases spring to mind when you mention the words 'organisational politics' and, nine times out of 10, you will get responses such as:

- doing deals;
- scoring points;
- personal agendas;
- getting one over on one's colleagues;

- secrecy and subterfuge;
- mafiosi tactics;
- win–lose.

But, like it or not, organisational politics is a part of corporate life. Organisations are communities of people and, where there is a community and social interaction, it is not long before political behaviour shows itself. All of us have to deal with organisational politics, but it is our choice whether we deal with them in a positive, or negative, way.

A positive view of organisational politics would be to say that it is about:

- influence;
- collaboration;
- building relationships;
- openness and honesty;
- being streetwise;
- win–win.

We believe that politics, when played in accordance with this more positive definition, are both constructive and beneficial, as opposed to the negative view that they are often destructive and harmful. We have often heard young managers say, 'I don't do politics', but that is not an option – we all do politics, but we have a choice about how we do them and how well we do them.

Making sense of it all

Researchers Baddeley and James studied leaders who had attained long-term political success within their organisation. They attributed their success to the following two key dimensions:

- Acting from an informed and knowledgeable position that demonstrates:

  - an understanding of the decision-making processes of their organisation;

  - an awareness of the overt and covert agendas of the key decision makers;

  - an innate understanding of who has the power and what gives one power;

  - a willingness to go above and beyond their job description;

  - an understanding of the style and culture of the organisation;

  - a sense of the meaning of 'politics' in the context of their organisation.

- Acting with integrity in so far as they tend to:

  - avoid psychological game-playing;

  - accept themselves and others for what are;

  - adopt win–win strategies for conflict management.

The model in Figure 14 utilises these two dimensions and is adapted from the work of Baddeley and James. Each quadrant of the model is illustrated with an animal analogy to create a political zoo. The *innocent sheep* acts with integrity, but hasn't a clue about what is going on in the organisational sense. The *clever fox* knows precisely what is going on, but uses this knowledge to exploit the weaknesses of others. The *inept baboon* neither acts with integrity nor knows what is going on. The *wise dolphin* represents the icon of political success.

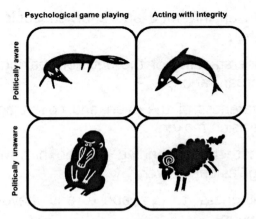

Figure 14: Political zoo[7]

The behaviour of the four animals is described below.

The *sheep* sees the world through simplistic eyes; they believe you are right if you are in a position of authority. They do what they are told, stick to the rules, are too busy to network and don't know how to build coalitions and alliances. They act with integrity, but are street-naïve.

The *fox* knows exactly what is going on, but uses this knowledge to exploit the weaknesses in others. They are self-centred with a charming veneer. They are manipulative and like games involving winners and losers, and love leading lambs to the slaughterhouse.

---

[7] The political zoo is an adaptation of the model developed by Simon Baddeley and Kim James in 'Owl, fox, donkey, sheep: political skills for managers' *Management Education and Development*, 1987, 18, pp. 3–19.

The *baboon* is not tuned into the grapevine; their antennae are blocked and they, therefore, end up conspiring with the powerless. They are emotionally illiterate, seeing things in black and white and not recognising when they are fighting a losing battle. They play games with people, but don't understand why they keep losing.

 The *dolphin* takes account of other people personally; they are excellent listeners and aware of others' viewpoints. They are non-defensive, open and share information. They use creativity and imagination to engineer win–win situations. They act from both an informed and ethical standpoint; they are both streetwise and virtuous.

What characterises the dolphin is calmness in a storm, a certainty about their own destiny and a thirst to learn from others. Dolphins may be busy, but not stressed or pressured; and they can always find the time to work alongside senior colleagues, or help others to learn. People have respect for them as model human beings first and as competent within their professional capacity second.

Practical advice

We will all behave like each of the four animals from time to time; however, it is about one's prime behaviour. We hope your aim would be to become a 'dolphin'. Here are a few examples of how the four animals would behave in various situations:

- *When in situations of conflict*:
    - The *dolphin* asks 'How can we work together to solve this one?'

- The *fox* asserts 'I am not prepared to change my position.'

- The *baboon* declares 'I can't agree and would prefer not to discuss it anyway.'

- The *sheep* mutters 'I concede the point and will accept whatever you say.'

- *When responding to or giving orders*:

  - The *dolphin* looks for opportunities to go beyond the call of duty' to extend their sphere of influence and to develop the potential in others.

  - The *fox* demands 'Do as you are told – it's my way or the high way'.

  - The *baboon* bleats 'That's outside my brief – I won't do it'.

  - The *sheep* says meekly 'I will do as you say'.

- *When communicating with others*:

  - The *dolphin* actively listens, is open and shares information.

  - The *fox* is dismissive of alternative viewpoints, looks for a fight and believes that information is power.

  - The *baboon* whinges and moans to others who are equally powerless.

  - The *sheep* keeps their head down and keeps quiet about anything potentially controversial.

- *When considering the phrase 'corporate politics'*:

  - The *dolphin* believes that corporate politics are a fact of life and are about influence, collaboration and achieving win–win.

  - The *fox* believes that corporate politics are a sport; it is about winners and losers and about coming out on top

  - it involves manipulation and exploitation to achieve one's own ends.

  - The *baboon* believes that corporate politics are a game, but doesn't understand why they keep losing it.

  - The *sheep* believes that they do not enter into the game of corporate politics – it is just everyone else!

If 'dolphinism' is your aim, the three single most important things you can do are as follows:

* Develop your network – build positive relationships with anyone and everyone; create allies and advocates, build coalitions and alliances. Use your network to find out what is going on, to acquire those nuggets of wisdom and to tap into that grapevine.

* Be someone that can be trusted – always do what you say you will do; never give people false hopes; if you can't guarantee, don't promise. Don't give empty promises like when you go on holiday, meet another couple and then go through the ritual of swapping phone numbers at the end of the holiday when neither party has any intention whatsoever of keeping in touch with the other. Remember, when it comes to trust, actions speak louder than words.

* Be generous – give a little of yourself to others: your time, your expertise, your knowledge, your help and your support without expecting anything in return. Look for the good in others, assume they have good intentions and stay curious to find out what these are, even when they are not obvious, or the person is behaving negatively. Be prepared to forgive, and offer people a face-saving route if they need to change their minds, or behave differently.

Further food for the curious

- Patching K and Chatham R. *Corporate Politics for IT Managers: How to get Streetwise*. Butterworth Heinemann, London (2000):

    - A good introduction to corporate politics, written with the IT manager in mind, but relevant to any discipline. It contains lots of cartoons to make it less serious.

- Baddeley S and James K. Owl, Fox, Donkey, Sheep: Political Skills for Managers. *Management Education and Development*, 1987, 18 (spring), pp. 3–19:

    - A short, but truly inspirational, paper.

Things for you to work on now

Key questions to ask yourself
• Within my current role at this point in time, which of the political 'animals' do I believe I behave most like and to which do I aspire to become?   • Do I always fulfil my promises; do my deeds always match my words?   • How extensive is my network and how much effort do I dedicate towards extending it?   • How aware am I of what goes on in the broader organisational context?   • Do I actively listen to others without judging?   • Do I openly share information?   • Do I do things for others without expecting anything in return?

Mini exercises you can try immediately

- Plan to invite to lunch someone who is important to you, but with whom you have had few dealings; repeat this activity each week for a month.

- Look for opportunities to do a good deed every day, e.g. if a colleagues is really busy, fetch them a coffee or sandwich, stop for a brief chat with the cleaner, the security guard or the car-park attendant, speak well of others when they are not present. In essence, learn to be generous with yourself – you will find it habit-forming.

- Next time you are just about to agree to do something, reflect for a moment. Do you really intend to do it, are you totally committed, would you move heaven and earth to deliver? If you cannot answer yes to these questions, think again before you commit. Always doing what you say is habit-forming, too.

Links to other questions

You may want to take a look at:

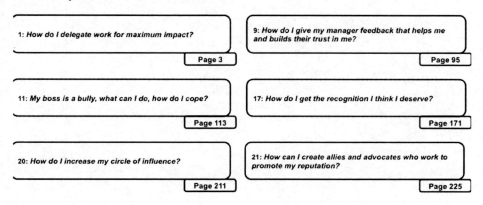

1: *How do I delegate work for maximum impact?*

Page 3

9: *How do I give my manager feedback that helps me and builds their trust in me?*

Page 95

11: *My boss is a bully, what can I do, how do I cope?*

Page 113

17: *How do I get the recognition I think I deserve?*

Page 171

20: *How do I increase my circle of influence?*

Page 211

21: *How can I create allies and advocates who work to promote my reputation?*

Page 225

272

HOW DO I MANAGE MY GROWTH?

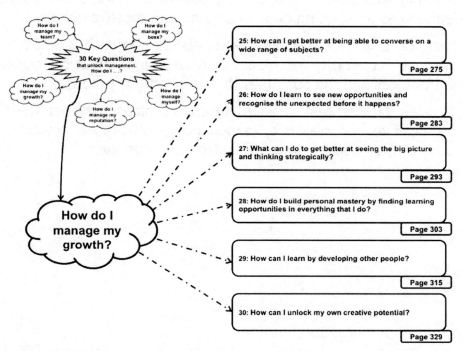

It is important to understand that you own your own career; your employer just affords you the opportunity to follow that career on their premises. This being the case, if you sit around waiting for your employer to develop you and your career, you will, as likely as not, wait a long time. Even the most enlightened of employers make a poor fist of career development, even if you are lucky enough to work for one of those organisations that trumpet their commitment to talent management – you have to get recognised as 'talent' before you can even start to ascend their greasy pole.

The next most important thing to recognise is that growth cannot happen without learning. Learning needs to be both discipline and industry-sector related, but, perhaps most importantly, we also need to learn how to function more effectively as human beings within complex social networks.

Learning is not an event, it is a process. Don't associate learning with attending a course, but rather think about your learning as an ongoing cycle of action and reflective enquiry.

Learning is a 24 x 7 activity; you need to approach it as such and be conscious of your own learning process, your preferences and the outcomes that your actions produce.

All life's experiences are learning opportunities, whether they be positive, or negative, experiences; the most powerful lessons often come from learning from our mistakes.

25: HOW CAN I GET BETTER AT BEING ABLE TO CONVERSE ON A WIDE RANGE OF SUBJECTS?

Why should I be asking this question?

Having consulted in many organisations around the world, we are tempted to divide people into one of two broad categories:

- those who are afraid to engage in a discussion because they have been made to feel that they have nothing of value to contribute;

- those who have an opinion on everything and will find any opportunity to share their opinions – this last class of people tends to be much better at transmitting than receiving.

Both groups are underperforming and both are contributing to a breakdown in dialogue. Dialogue is the oil that keeps a community from seizing up. When we engage in dialogue with others, who have different skills and perspectives than our own, we open up the possibility of seeing with new eyes and, hence, finding new and novel ways of working and being.

Dialogue is a mechanism for collaborative exploration of a topic; it is not a process of imposing your opinion on others.

Much of the debate that occurs in an organisation is adversarial in nature and debilitating in effect. Dialogue and open, enquiring conversation are key social skills that we all need to improve, as they are real drivers of individual and organisational development.

The bottom line is that:

You don't have to have an opinion to make an effective contribution to a discussion – in fact, a lot less opinion can take a conversation a long way.

The impact of the issue

Organisations and society work best when we have the desire to, and are comfortable with, engaging constructively with people whose attitudes and values are different from our own. To do this, we have to become comfortable with the idea of engaging with anyone on any topic. This level of comfort can only come if you work hard to develop the following key personal attributes. You must learn to:

- listen intently without judging;

- be open to new ideas;

- ask questions that cause others to reflect on what they are saying;

- offer suggestions that build on those of others;

- ask questions, or make comments, that encourage the exploration of connections between various strands of thought.

Far too many people see a conversation as an opportunity to show off their knowledge, or demonstrate their superiority – by doing so they shift the focus of the conversation away from the topic and towards themselves. A battle then ensues between individuals who verbally wrestle to gain their share of the limelight, or to impose their views, or beliefs, on others. In this mode, a good story needs to be capped by a better one and a good point is an opportunity to try to claim credit.

Being able to converse with anyone on unfamiliar topics is not just a 'nice-to-have social skill'; it is a critical driver of learning and personal growth. It underpins many of the organisational initiatives that we see around us.

How can we hope to 'understand the voice of the customer', 'become outcome oriented', or 'adopt a service culture', if we can't engage openly in non-judgemental conversations?

If we, as individuals, cannot get better at meaningful dialogue, our organisations cannot get better at serving their customers and constituents.

Making sense of it all

When you have an intractable problem at work, or in your personal life, who, if indeed anyone, do you turn to for advice, guidance or support?

There are numerous answers to this question, but whoever you do choose to turn to, we are pretty sure that you will turn to them because:

- you trust them;

- you respect them for their experience, wisdom, principles, and so on;

- you feel safe to share your problems with them;

- you are sure that they can offer you an insight that you could not have gained alone.

The remarkable thing is that the people who fit all the above conditions are always equally helpful, whatever the topic and whatever the problem. What is even more amazing is that they would be just as effective discussing an issue with regard to building a new molecule to increase the viscosity of oil, as they would discussing the implementation of a new HR policy.

You don't approach people because they have an opinion on a topic – or because they are likely to share your current opinion. You approach them because they can help you shed light on things that you had not thought of and, in so doing, they can help you see new ways of moving forward.

Alternatively, they may simply make you feel better by listening to you and empathising with your dilemma, or predicament. They do this by engaging you in dialogue – they listen, they ask questions, but they don't indulge themselves in judgemental statements. They can converse on any topic because the keys skills of true dialogue are:

- listening;
- being supportive;
- questioning;
- finding connections.

True dialogue is a mechanism for collaborative exploration of a subject, and an opportunity to share views and build on the insights of others:

- We all need to get better at dialogue and conversation.
- We need to become comfortable talking and listening to anyone.
- We need to broaden the range of people we interact with because, in doing so, we increase the range of our own experience.

If we can do these things, we give ourselves the opportunity to contribute to the enrichment of someone else's experience and, at the same time, we gain the added bonus of personal growth because we are sharpening an essential social skill.

Practical advice

We suggest the following things to work on to become better at joining and contributing to conversations:

- *Listening*: show that you are following the thread of the conversation with comments and questions, such as:
  - I think the same trend may be emerging in HR, Finance, etc.

- That's really interesting. I wonder if that solution is transferable to ...?

- How did you first notice ...?

- I wonder if others are seeing the same patterns?

- *Being supportive*: avoid being judgemental – even if you think something is off the wall, it may well be that, if the thought is developed further, you may see something you hadn't thought of. Avoid the use of the word 'BUT'; this is a put-down word. Replace it with the building word 'AND'. Try comments, such as:

  - That sounds great; and can you explain a little more about how you went about it?

  - Wow; and how did you hit upon an idea like that?

  - I really like this approach; and do you think it might work in my department?

  - I think that is a really interesting idea; and how do you think we could avoid the issue of ...?

- *Questioning*: try to think of future-focused, success-oriented questions that encourage the exploration of new possibilities, or challenge existing paradigms. Try questions of the form:

  - What would we need to put in place for that to happen?

  - How might our customers feel if we could do that?

  - What would the competition say if they thought we could do that?

  - What else might we be able to do if we crack this one?

  - Just how good could this get for us?

- *Finding connections*: look for big ideas in a conversation and then look for links between these ideas and other widely held ideas. Try questions and comments such as:

- I wonder if there is a connection between xxx and yyy?

- Might xxx have an impact on our ability to do yyy?

- If we could launch xxx in our key market, how might this impact our existing product lines?

- If we commit resources to this idea, what would be the potential knock-on impact on project xxx?

- Also look to connect at the social level; look for common interests, hobbies, support of the same football team, children of the same age, etc.

Being able to engage constructively with people is a real and valuable skill, but it takes more than just good questions. Your manner and body language are equally important:

- Be warm and friendly in your approach; smile and make good eye contact.

- Encourage your audience to talk and open up by asking gentle, probing questions.

- Give them time to think and respond, and signal that you are listening with encouraging noises and gestures.

- Use humour to oil the wheels of your conversation, to break any tension and to keep your audience interested and engaged.

- Vary the tone and pace of your speech.

- Keep an open, neutral posture, not too forward and in their face, and not too laid-back, or macho; don't fold your arms or cross your legs – this creates a barrier.

- Avoid putting your hands in your pockets – this will also prevent you adopting the annoying habit of jingling the loose change in your pocket.

- Practise your handshake; this needs to be firm, but not too firm; there is nothing worse than either a limp-fish or bone-crusher handshake.

You will find that, if you engage with people using the techniques above, you will be more at ease in any situation, and will really start to build your own knowledge base and be valued by others for your contribution to any situation.

Further food for the curious

- Pease A. *Body Language: How to Read Others' Thoughts by their Gestures*. Sheldon Press, London (1995):

  – An easy-to-read book that is both practical and insightful with lots of illustrations.

- Goleman D. *Emotional Intelligence*. Bantam Books (1995):

  – A very comprehensive text on the subject of emotional intelligence – one of the five emotional intelligences which Goleman describes is 'social skill'.

Things for you to work on now

Key questions to ask yourself

- How often do you turn to someone else for support, guidance or advice?

- How often does someone else turn to you for support, guidance or advice?

- Looking back over the past year, how broad is the range of subjects that you have conversed on?

- Looking back over the past year, how broad is the range of people who you have conversed with?

- When someone makes a suggestion, do you build on it with the words 'AND' this would mean ... or, inherently, criticise it with the words 'BUT' it could be difficult because ...?

Mini exercises you can try immediately

- Pick an organisational initiative that you know nothing about, ideally one that is being run by someone in a different department. Go and find them, tell them you would like to understand more about it and ask them if they have 30 minutes to explain it to you. Now practise your listening and questioning skills.

- Next time you run a meeting, keep a tally of the number of questions that people ask, as opposed to the number of statements that they make. If you find that the balance is skewed heavily toward statements, try to ask some exploratory questions that make them stop and think. See if you can subtly change the balance of the conversation by the way you conduct yourself.

- Next time you meet with someone new, take the time to find a common connection, e.g. a common interest or sport, or maybe you both have a teenage daughter.

Links to other questions

You may want to take a look at:

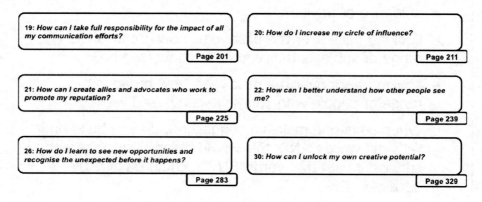

19: How can I take full responsibility for the impact of all my communication efforts?
Page 201

20: How do I increase my circle of influence?
Page 211

21: How can I create allies and advocates who work to promote my reputation?
Page 225

22: How can I better understand how other people see me?
Page 239

26: How do I learn to see new opportunities and recognise the unexpected before it happens?
Page 283

30: How can I unlock my own creative potential?
Page 329

26: HOW DO I LEARN TO SEE NEW OPPORTUNITIES AND RECOGNISE THE UNEXPECTED BEFORE IT HAPPENS?

Why should I be asking this question?

Try to remember when you first learned to drive a car. Quite apart from the fact that you certainly drove a lot more slowly, we can guarantee that, as you looked out of the windscreen, your point of focus was just beyond the end of the bonnet – maybe 10 to 15 metres ahead.

In all probability, your mind was telling you that the main perils lay immediately ahead of you and were already in your path. Later on, as an experienced driver, your focus probably shifted to 100 to 150 metres ahead. You learned not to watch the brake lights of the car ahead, but to look instead at the reflection of the brake lights of the car three cars ahead.

This shift of focus brought about a shift of behaviour. You started to look for things that were developing, or could develop, into dangers, rather than just reacting to things that had already become life-threatening.

As you become more experienced, you find that you can anticipate what is likely to happen based on patterns of activity that you have experienced before. Also, you continually, and subconsciously, store up new patterns and, consequently, become even more adept at recognising danger before it arises.

Yes, there is the odd moron who sits in their air-conditioned cocoon, totally oblivious of all other road users, but most of us have evolved beyond that. We all have the innate capacity to look ahead, anticipate potential futures and take appropriate action.

If we can do it in the fast-paced, and potentially lethal, area of car driving – why do we, apparently, find it so difficult to do it at work?

The impact of the issue

Our organisations are full of people running around like headless chickens, locked into an endless cycle of meetings. They are always reacting to the latest crisis, forever busy, but never having time to actually do anything.

Leaders moan that we need to be more proactive and less reactive, and then scream at you about the latest set of sales figures. Being proactive isn't just a catchy new-age management fad; it is your route to salvation and sanity.

Learning to look outwards and upwards is the key to seeing problems before they become major crises. Crisis situations throw you into reactive fire-fighting mode, dealing with the fallout and limiting the damage. They negatively impact productivity and morale, sap your energy and increase your stress levels.

We have always marvelled when watching Roger Federer at his peak playing in the finals at Wimbledon. He appeared to read the game so well that he had the ability to always be in the right place at just the right time; consequently, he never appeared to be moving very quickly or to be rushed into any manoeuvre.

That is the sign of greatness. The greats always have time to exceed expectations with time and energy to spare; they remain unruffled, have reserves of energy and make things look easy.

They are not superhuman. Yes, they may be exceptionally talented, they may have developed levels of technical prowess previously unseen – but, in all cases, what they share is that they are better at anticipating events than the people around them.

The ability to anticipate is rooted in the ability to read events as they are emerging; the good news is that we are all capable of doing this and it is a capability that can be learned and refined.

Making sense of it all

We live in a world of seemingly unlimited information – in the past, most of us have experienced data overload occasionally. Now, and in the future, it is likely to be a permanent state of being.

The good news is that our brains are naturally wired to protect us from data overload. The bad news is that they do this by filtering out what doesn't appear to be immediately relevant.

Of course, our brain's idea of relevance is based on what it has seen before. We look just long enough for our brain to recognise a pattern, then it says, 'Oh, I know what this is, it's one of them …' and then we stop looking.

To help us make sense of these phenomena, we will explore three key concepts:

- recognising new patterns;
- developing future memories;
- extending our experience across boundaries.

Recognising new patterns

The first step to seeing new opportunities is to learn to increase our ability to recognise new patterns; in effect, we first need to learn to see anew.

If we accept that our brain works on pattern recognition then the only way to increase our powers of perception is to increase the number of patterns that our brain uses to find a match. We need to work on constantly exposing our brain to new experiences and new sensations, and, at the same time, ask ourselves new and different questions about the experiences that we are having.

Young children do this naturally. Everything is new to them and everything new is associated with a barrage of inquiring questions: 'Why does that do ...? What would happen if? Why have I not got one of ...? Where did this come from? Who made ...? Where does this go at night?'.

Sadly, as we grow older, we lose our sense of wonder, we stop asking daft questions, and we start to limit our range of experiences by actively repeating only those things that have worked for us or pleased us in the past. In effect, our past becomes the limiting factor on our potential future.

Developing future memories

Secondly, we need to become a little more conscious about how our brain works and what it does with stuff. Current thinking about how the brain works suggests that it stores experiences as patterns (or, if you prefer, memories). The interesting thing is that it appears to make no differentiation between patterns of events that you have actually experienced and events that you have just mentally rehearsed.

This is an intriguing idea and has caused some neuroscientists to call this process creating *memories of the future*. This idea underpins organisational approaches, such as scenario planning; this is a process where we pose apparently unlikely questions and mentally grapple with (rehearse) how we might react if these events occurred. In doing so, the argument is that the brain now stores patterns of these events, as if we had actually experienced them.

Amazingly, although the events have not actually happened, the fact that we have thought about them is enough to store them away – we are, therefore, more likely to perceive them and attach relevance to them, should they actually happen. We are, in effect, storing memories of possible futures.

The message is that we can increase our ability to perceive not just by increasing our actual experience of a wider range of events, but also through mental rehearsal of how we might react in different circumstances.

Extending our experiences across boundaries

The third element of our journey to increased understanding is learning to stand in the shoes of others. So, in addition to taking steps to increase our own range of experiences, we can also try to tap into how other people might experience the same, or similar, circumstances. In effect, we need to take every opportunity we can to experience the world through the eyes of others.

Many researchers in the field of organisational development and innovation development are now calling this capacity 'boundary spanning' – stepping across the artificial boundaries of organisational or social structure to experience the world as others see it.

It turns out that boundary spanning is one of the most important factors in increasing the innovative capacity of an organisation. When we engage with people from different departments, different companies, different industries and different cultures, we start to see and experience different aspects of a situation. When we are unhampered by the limitations of past experience, we can start to see dimensions of potential solutions that would otherwise be hidden from us.

Other people see things differently and, therefore, can see different solutions to problems that we have found to be intractable. As we increase our exposure to these alternate ways of seeing and being, we also increase our ability to sense triggers in our environment that can alert us to things before they happen. In effect, we are increasing our ability to anticipate events before they hit us.

So it turns out that there are two key skills associated with being able to anticipate the unexpected and recognise new opportunities:

- Get better at seeing things that are currently within your sphere of activity, but that you are currently unaware of, or you are in the practice of ignoring.

- Broaden your general ability to perceive by learning to see through the eyes of others.

Practical advice

We have seen that, if you can populate your brain with more experiences and hence more patterns, you will increase the chance of your brain finding relevance in the indicators in the environment and, hence, you increase your powers of perception.

Try doing some of the following things:

- Find opportunities to spend time working in other departments and look to rotate your staff through various roles and departments.

- Volunteer to serve on cross-functional initiatives, whole-organisation changes, etc.

- Take an interest in what other departments are doing and try to understand the values that underpin their initiatives.

- Understand the end-to-end nature of the processes that your department is engaged in. Where do the inputs come from, where do your outputs go and how are they used? Think along the time line, as well as the process flow.

- When you have a particularly challenging problem, try to simulate the various alternative solutions. You can do this by:

- role play;

- structured walk-throughs;

- problem brainstorming sessions – if you do this, make sure you have a very wide range of experience and backgrounds in the group;

- computer simulations.

- If your industry is changing, or facing new competitors, try using the techniques of scenario planning. Develop a range of questions that challenge the basic assumptions of your industry and then work through these questions in a mixed group.

- Stand back and ask the big questions 'What is the purpose of this?' and 'Why do we do it this way?' or even 'What would happen if we didn't do it at all?'

We have also seen that putting yourself in the shoes of others is a key way of seeing differently. Try to build some of the following boundary-spanning activities into your routine:

- Get into the habit of having lunch, or coffee, with people from different professions, different scientific disciplines, or different departments from you.

- Attend conferences on topics that attract people from different industries, or professions. Use the opportunity to network; talk to them and make lasting connections. Don't waste this valuable opportunity by spending the time checking your e-mail and catching up with the issues of the day back at the ranch.

- Increase the breadth of your reading. If you are an engineer, try reading some popular literature explaining developments in biotechnology, genetics or finance.

- Read eclectic journals, such as *Harvard Business Review*, *Nature*, *The Economist* and *Fast Company*.

- Take up a new hobby, one that is likely to expose you to different cultures and ways of thinking. For example, if you are an engineer, try your hand at amateur dramatics.

- Consider some form of higher education, but do it in a discipline where you have no experience. For instance, if you have a background as a physical scientist, go and study the history of art, or something so different that it will give you a whole new perspective.

Further food for the curious

- Hayashi A. When to Trust your Gut. *Harvard Business Review at Large*, Feb. 2001:

  – A short, yet excellent, article that provides examples of 'out-of-the-box' thinking and practical advice as to how to sharpen your intuition.

Things for you to work on now

Key questions to ask yourself

- What is your horizon? How often and how far do you think ahead? How much of your time is spent dealing with day-to-day issues versus planning, or developing yourself for the future?

- When did you last take a whole day out for thinking about the future/scenario planning?

- When you attend a conference or training course, can you tear yourself away from your e-mail and make the most of the opportunity to meet people, make new connections and 'boundary span'?

- How often do you connect with people from: other departments; other organisations; other disciplines; other industry sectors?

- Do you have a vision for your department in, say, five years' time?

- Do you know where your company is headed? Could you readily articulate your company's vision and strategy for the future?

Mini exercises you can try immediately

- Next time you attend a conference, or training course, set up an 'out-of-office' reply and take an e-mail vacation. Your organisation will not collapse in a heap without you. Maximise the opportunity and spend every waking minute of your time networking and building 'boundary-spanning' relationships for the future.

- Plan, each week, to have lunch, or coffee, with someone from a different area within your organisation.

- Each month, take a whole day out to consider the future – what will you be doing, how will your department be organised, what new processes will there need to be in, say, three years' time?

- Paint a mental picture of your industry sector in five years' time.

Links to other questions

You may want to take a look at:

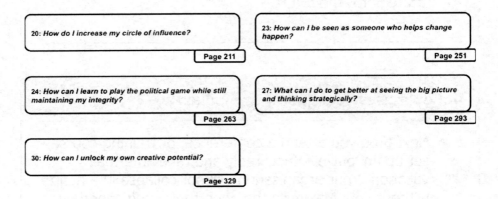

20: *How do I increase my circle of influence?*

Page 211

23: *How can I be seen as someone who helps change happen?*

Page 251

24: *How can I learn to play the political game while still maintaining my integrity?*

Page 263

27: *What can I do to get better at seeing the big picture and thinking strategically?*

Page 293

30: *How can I unlock my own creative potential?*

Page 329

27: WHAT CAN I DO TO GET BETTER AT SEEING THE BIG PICTURE AND THINKING STRATEGICALLY?

Why should I be asking this question?

Surveys show that *strategic thinking* is one of the top three capabilities that is valued and looked for in senior leaders.

Most management competency frameworks include strategic thinking, so this is something that interviewers try to identify during the job selection process – but it is one of the things that interview candidates have most difficulty understanding, discussing and giving practical examples that demonstrate their capability.

Organisations cannot survive by just aimlessly repeating what they did last year, or even last month. We need to be able to respond to changing circumstances, take advantage of emerging trends and constantly find new ways of delighting our customers with new levels of service and products that were previously unimaginable.

To this end, a fundamental capability for all managers is the ability to initiate and bring about change. But an organisation needs its change initiatives to be aligned towards a common purpose – that purpose is articulated in the business strategy and each manager needs to be able to internalise that strategy to the extent where it provides a guiding framework for all their decision making.

The impact of the issue

We have all seen organisations being torn apart by parochial decision making that puts the narrow needs of a function above the broad goals of the organisation. All too often, we witness local decision making that can only hope to serve the ends of local leadership.

Strategic thinkers are people who can think holistically and see beyond the limits of the current issue. They take a broad perspective on how a proposed course of action can contribute to the achievement of the long-term goals of an organisation as a whole, as well as resolving the immediate local problem.

When you are busy and stressed, and faced with a critical problem, it is difficult to find either the time, or the perspective, to see beyond the bounds of the immediate, but the strategic thinker always takes the broader perspective and the longer-term view.

The way you demonstrate strategic thinking is to focus on things that can contribute to bringing about long-term objectives. You should always use this perspective as the basis for your decision making. When you fix things with an eye to the long-term impacts, or consequences, they tend to stay fixed. On the other hand, if you make your decisions based solely on the impact in the here and now, the problems have a nasty habit of coming right back again.

The more managers we can get to behave in this manner, the greater the decision-making alignment of the organisation and the more effective it becomes.

Making sense of it all

If you Google 'strategic thinking', you will get in excess of five million hits. If you take a little time to investigate some of the hits, you will quickly notice that the content is long on business strategy and the process of crafting winning strategies, and very short on explanation of the different sort of thinking that is needed.

It would appear that most experts think that strategic thinking is what you do in order to create a business strategy. But when you go for a job interview and the HR representative tells you that they really need someone who can think strategically, they are not saying they expect you to work up their business strategy – no, that's what the Board does:

- So what do they mean when they say they want a strategic thinker?

- What is strategic thinking and how is it different from the rest of the thinking we do?

- Does it need some elaborate process?

- Can it only be done when you are consciously formulating strategy?

An important skill of strategic thought is the ability to take a different view of a situation. But not just any different view – what you need is a view that allows you clear sight of your objective, where you are trying to get to, while at the same time letting you see the terrain that stands between you and your objective. A good way to visualise this sort of view is to think of the experience of walking a maze.

As you enter a maze, you do so with no clear view of where you are trying to get to. You know you want to get to the middle, but you cannot see the middle and you have no idea where it is or how to get there. So each time you come to a junction, you are faced with having to make a choice; without any plan or overall route, you can only make random choices. Each choice has the effect of opening or closing options but without any feedback on the success of the previous choice.

If, on the other hand you were provided with a plan view of the maze taken from above, you would have no difficulty in seeing the most direct route to the centre. It seems obvious, but when you know what your objective is, and when you can see that objective in a broader context, decision making becomes much easier and your route to success more sure and direct.

This is a great metaphor for strategic thinking – sadly, though, many managers behave as if they are in a maze with no overall plan of what the maze or their objective looks like. Far too much organisational decision making appears to be random, with no guidance from a consistent objective, or set of guiding principles.

Most of the time, most of our thinking is what might be termed analytical and forward pass. We start with the problem and work forwards through logical steps until we find a potential solution. This form of thinking is so deeply ingrained in us through our education and experience that many people think that it is the only valid way to think, and that any other process is not real thinking.

But there is another way to think – Stephen Covey calls it 'backwards thinking' or 'beginning with the end in mind'; he sets this out in his *The 7 Habits of Highly Effective People*. Others call it systems thinking, backward-pass thinking, intuition or synthesis. Whatever you call it, we can depict the process as follows (*see Figure 15*):

- We make an intuitive leap from 'a' – to an attractive, but as yet unimagined, outcome 'd'.

- We then work backwards, asking ourselves – 'What do we need to put in place now to make this outcome more likely to come about in the future?'.

The important thing to realise is that the future state 'd' does not yet exist, nor is there any certainty that it will ever exist.

The leap we make is not about predicting a future that will happen, but of imagining a future that we would find beneficial.

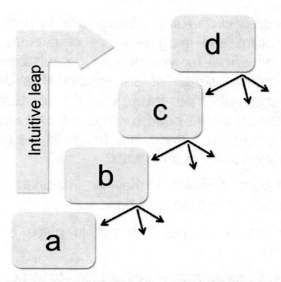

Figure 15: Backward-pass thinking

When we start to work backwards from 'd', we are not doing detailed planning of the steps we need to close the gap, but rather putting in place capabilities that make the realisation of this future more probable than the possible alternatives.

We are, in effect, taking steps to create the future rather than waiting for someone else's future to happen and then having to react to it.

Key to this sort of thinking is the recognition that we operate within complex, adaptive self-organising systems and that a fundamental property of such systems is 'emergence'. New and unpredictable properties emerge as self-organising systems adapt to their environment.

So the actions we put in place will have both intended and unintended consequences. A key skill is, therefore, to be alert to the emergence of new trends and to intelligently and opportunistically grasp these possibilities for the overall benefit of our organisations as a whole.

If we accept this definition of strategic thinking, then the core skills that we need to develop are as follows:

- *Outcome-focused thinking* – being able to project yourself into the future and imagine a set of circumstances that would be beneficial for you or your organisation. You then need to craft a series of statements that describe the characteristics of that future's state in terms of the capabilities you would need to create it and what it would feel like once you got there. Key to this is the ability to see every situation in its wider context.

- *Backward-pass thinking* – having imagined a desirable future, constantly asking questions such as:

  - What would we need to put in place to make this happen?

- *Intelligent opportunism* – being alert to emerging trends and taking advantage of them.

To complete the process of strategic thinking, ultimate decision making needs to be grounded in a set of core principles that place a higher value on promoting action to realise the desired outcomes than on merely taking action to resolve the symptoms of the problem that you are faced with.

Practical advice

In order to get better at taking an outcome-focused view of a situation, try the following techniques:

- Write a summary of a book you have just read on a single page of A4. This will require you to identify the governing thought of the book – what is the key message that everyone should take from reading this book?

- Next time you visit a new city, imagine that you have been asked to write one paragraph for a travel brochure giving the potential visitor an impression of what they might experience. Again, the key to this task lies not in descriptive detail, but rather in your ability to discern a unique characteristic of a city and to convey that in a compelling manner, so that others might be captivated by the impressions you have conveyed. Your message needs to be emotionally compelling, but anchored in an achievable reality.

In order to get better at backward-pass thinking, try to incorporate some of the following ideas into the way you tackle change:

- First, start with the visionary purpose – what do you want things to look like at some point in the future? – this can be as far-fetched as you like; in fact the wackier the better.

- Next, list and quantify the benefits you are seeking by creating this future.

- Then, consider which parts of the organisation will be involved in delivering the identified benefits.

- Finally, identify the capabilities that would need to be in place to bring about this environment, and outcomes that you could create.

- Now you may refine your visionary purpose into something that would sound more potentially realistic.

In order to attune yourself to spot emergent factors and behave with intelligent opportunism, try the following techniques:

- Paint a vision for your industry in 10 years' time.

- Consider the generic technological capabilities that exist today, and consider how you could harness them to the advantage of your organisation.

- Consider examples of competitive advantage gained in other industries. What are the common themes? How could any of these be applied to your industry?

- Always remember to think of the possibilities, rather than the problems. Reflect on the famous quote from Thomas

Edison: 'I did not fail: I just succeeded in finding 100 ways not to make a light bulb'.

Now that you are on your way to developing the three core skills of strategic thinking, you need to align your decision making around the core principles of achieving the desired outcomes and focusing on root causes rather than symptoms. You will know that you have succeeded in this when:

- you are leading the way rather than following, or copying, that of a competitor;

- you have provided direction and inspiration rather than prescription and rigidity;

- the people around you are excited by possibilities and choices;

- there is a positive atmosphere and people feel liberated, rather than constrained;

- things are starting to happen and change for the better.

Further food for the curious

- Collins J. Level 5 Leadership: The triumph of humility and fierce resolve. *Harvard Business Review*, Jan. 2001:

  - An excellent article about their research into what catapults a company from merely good to truly great.

- Covey S. *The 7 Habits of Highly Effective People*. Simon & Schuster UK Ltd, London (2004):

  - An excellent insight into the process of strategic thinking and what makes one person highly effective in their role.

Things for you to work on now

Key questions to ask yourself

- What is the most radical/wacky idea that I have ever had?

- How comfortable am I with taking risks?

- How much do I rely upon past experience, the tried and tested, or best practice?

- How comfortable am I with ambiguity, uncertainty and complexity?

- How prepared am I to put my neck on the line for what I believe in?

- How prepared am I to follow my gut instinct, or what my heart tells me?

- How much time do I dedicate to 'strategic thinking'? If I am honest with myself, do I prefer to focus on day-to-day issues?

Mini exercises you can try immediately

- Write down the strategic direction of your organisation in one simple, easy-to-understand sentence.

- Within the context of the strategic direction of your organisation, write down your purpose, again in one easy and simple-to-understand sentence.

- Within the context of the above, think of three initiatives that would make a difference to your

> organisation for the better – be opportunistic, be off the wall. These may only be small initiatives, but they are all that is needed at this stage, as long as they fulfil all the other criteria.
>
> - Take out a subscription to a magazine, such as *New Scientist* or *HBR*.

Links to other questions

You may want to take a look at:

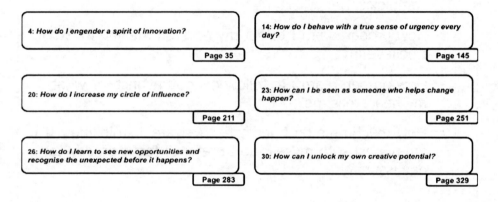

4: *How do I engender a spirit of innovation?*

Page 35

14: *How do I behave with a true sense of urgency every day?*

Page 145

20: *How do I increase my circle of influence?*

Page 211

23: *How can I be seen as someone who helps change happen?*

Page 251

26: *How do I learn to see new opportunities and recognise the unexpected before it happens?*

Page 283

30: *How can I unlock my own creative potential?*

Page 329

28: HOW DO I BUILD PERSONAL MASTERY BY FINDING LEARNING OPPORTUNITIES IN EVERYTHING THAT I DO?

Why should I be asking this question?

There is an old adage that says:

Practice makes perfect.

The reality is that practice just makes you better at doing what you are doing and more certain that what you are doing is right.

Without appropriate feedback and reflective thought, we can never hope to get truly better at doing anything. The learning process is a simple one.

We take action, we observe the results, reflect on why things turned out the way they did, and then we think about how we can modify our behaviour next time to get different or better results.

This is termed the *learning loop* and was articulated neatly by David Kolb in 1984.

As you can see from Figure 16, in order for us to learn, experience has to be backed up by reflection, which, in turn, allows us to make generalisations and formulate concepts that can then be applied to new situations.

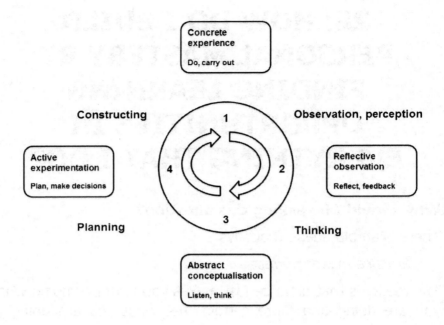

Figure 16: Learning loop

The thing that makes all of this work is *feedback* – information that we sense from the real world that gives us a sense of how things are playing out. Feedback is a critical element for learning and growth.

So, if you want to achieve personal mastery at anything, you need to look for feedback on your current performance and then reflect on what that feedback is telling you.

Everything we do is an opportunity to learn and grow, but unless you get feedback, you will never be able to take full advantage of these precious learning opportunities.

The impact of the issue

So we know that we need feedback, but, sadly, feedback is not always easy to come by. Often the consequences of our decisions or actions do not show up until weeks, or even months, later. The outcomes, when they do arise, are all too often somewhere else along the value chain and, therefore, not visible to us.

This causes a big problem in our feedback loop and it shows itself as follows:

- We meet a situation. Our brain recognises a pattern in the events and says, 'Oh, this is one of them'. If you have met the situation before, you are likely to remember what you did last time.

- Since you know that you are right and that you did the right thing last time, the obvious conclusion is that you didn't do it well enough last time, or that you should have done it faster or more vigorously.

- So we do the same thing again, but harder. The consequence is that we repeat solutions that fail and in many cases we keep repeating them ad infinitum because we never get feedback on the outcome, or consequences, of our actions.

The scenario we have just explained is just as likely to show up in the way we handle our relationships as it is in the way we play out our organisational responsibilities. Day after day, we always do what we always did, we always get the same results, we don't question those results, or witness the outcomes, and we don't take personal responsibility for those outcomes.

The result is that our leaders shake their heads in dismay and wonder why the same problems keep cropping up time after time, and why the competition appears to be more nimble and more innovative. The answer is that we don't need to get better at what we are doing; we need to get better at understanding why we are doing what we are doing and recognising when we need to start doing something different.

Making sense of it all

The following mini case study helps to put this issue into context.

> *This story is about Anne, a middle manager in the operations department of a large FMCG (fast-moving consumer goods) organisation. Anne was bright, hardworking, highly professional and well respected by her peers. She ran her department well and could be relied upon to do what was right and deliver a great quality service.*
>
> *Anne was approaching 40 and well contented with her job, her life and her achievements. Anne came to the attention of the HR department and was offered the opportunity of a one-year sabbatical to go back to university and do a master's degree, paid for by the organisation. She was excited by the prospect and prepared herself for the challenge. Just a couple of weeks into the course, Anne realised that the challenge was not to learn new stuff, but rather to learn new ways of looking at all stuff. She had to examine everything she knew and question why she thought about things the way that she did.*
>
> *With this new sense of 'self' came the crushing realisation that she did not have 15 years' experience of management – what she had was one year's experience repeated 15 times. Eventually, she came out of the programme knowing new things, seeing all things differently, and having a new sense of her own value and a commitment always to try to see everything as if she were seeing it for the first time.*

The above story illustrates nicely that, paradoxically, personal mastery does not necessarily come from striving to perfect what you currently know. Anne's breakthrough came when she realised that the big pay-off came through learning how to learn better and more quickly, rather than learning more.

Personal mastery and development comes through learning new ways of learning and embedding the desire to learn in everything that you do. As we saw from Kolb's learning cycle, (shown in Figure 16), learning is kick-started by new experiences.

So the way really to get better is by grappling with things you don't know. You need to challenge what you think you know and how you came to be so certain about it. You need to spend more than half of your available time striving, however imperfectly, to seize the unknown.

Practical advice

We will split our advice into two parts:

- Get better and achieve mastery in what you are currently doing.
- Get better at learning, so that you can achieve mastery in something new.

First some tips on how to become a superstar at what you are currently doing.

- Set yourself performance goals for all the important things that you have to do.
- Monitor your own success rate against your personal performance goals. What is your personal best?
- Get into the habit of visualising what it would feel like to set a new personal best:
  - How would you need to prepare differently?
  - What would you have to do differently?
  - How will you know when you have achieved something new?
- Ask yourself how others would assess your performance. Ask people for feedback on the following indicators:
  - What is it like to work with you?

- How do you make people feel?
- What one or two things would they really like to change about how you do what you do?

Now we need to turn our attention to doing things differently and also to doing different things.

In terms of doing things differently, our message is a simple one; every hour spent on up-front thinking and reflecting with an enquiring mind will pay big dividends and could save you 100 hours down the road, mopping up the consequential issues of a bodged job, or dealing with the quick fix when it fails. This up-front hour should be spent:

- considering alternative approaches;

- putting yourself in the shoes of the person, or people, who will receive the output of your efforts; ask yourself what is important to them and how they would want you to improve what you are doing;

- asking yourself, if this will fix things in such a way that they are likely to stay fixed;

- ensuring that you are addressing the root cause, rather than merely the symptoms.

You also need to find every opportunity you can to do something different. Our basic rule of thumb is that when looking for a new challenge, you should try to aim for something that is 50% familiar and 50% completely unknown. You need the 50% familiarity, or you are likely to freeze and become unable to act. The 50% unknown forces you to think new things and imagine new solutions.

When you approach a new challenge, start by asking yourself:

- What is different or new about this situation, problem or request? Then:

- Look for new angles.

- What are the big assumptions that underpin your thinking about this situation? Are those assumptions still valid?

- If you were coming at this for the first time with no prior knowledge, how would you react?

- What would be the first thing that made an impression on you?

- What would world-class performance on this issue look and feel like?

- How far are you away from providing world-class service?

- What is the single biggest barrier to success?

- What don't you know about this situation? Is the lack of that knowledge a roadblock that will stop progress or merely a speed bump that will slow you down? Then:

  - If you are facing a roadblock – can you find someone else who has the knowledge you need?

You also need to adopt a rigorous approach to creating opportunities to be different. We suggest that, at the start of each week, you choose one event that you may be called upon to repeat a number of times; for example, chairing a meeting, meeting a customer, or, maybe, briefing a team member on a task.

Then pick one aspect of the task; for example, planning for the task itself, how you use questions to steer the meeting, how you build rapport, or how you check on understanding.

Whatever you decide to focus on, make sure that you do the following things:

- Be conscious of the thing you are trying to practise.

- Monitor your own feelings and internal struggles as you carry out your task.

- Monitor the reaction and behaviour of the people you are dealing with:
  - Were they at ease and receptive?
  - Were they following your train of thought?
  - Could they feed back to you an understanding of what you wanted?
  - Had you engaged both their hearts and minds, or just one aspect?
  - Did you get the level of contribution from them that you had hoped for?
- Now think about the outcomes you were hoping to create, and use those outcomes as feedback to guide your learning about the effectiveness of your new strategy:
  - How confident and natural did you feel as you used the technique?
  - What went really well?
  - What could have gone better?
  - What one or two things that you did appeared to resonate with the people you were working with? What got them excited?
  - Did the energy you created produce a positive result?
  - If you could immediately repeat the same exercise with the same people – what would you do differently and why?

Keep a brief log (bullet points only) of what you tried, and what you observed happening, as a result of what you tried. Capture how you felt, as well as what you did. Later in the day, when you are relaxed, review your personal log and identify:

  - two things that you will try to do more of;
  - two things that you will try to do less of.

Notice that there is a consistent set of themes in all of our advice about personal mastery. It is all about:

- finding ways of getting feedback;

- reflecting on what the feedback tells you about yourself and your impact;

- using your new understanding to modify what you do and how you think.

The process that we have described above looks pretty straightforward, but, in our experience, the facet that people have most difficulty with is reflection. Our advice would be to get yourself a coach, or trusted adviser. It is important to understand that, when choosing a coach, you are not looking for someone who can tell you what to do. You are looking for someone who can listen to your experiences and then ask you really good questions, questions that make you think and that kick-start your learning process.

The key to achieving personal mastery in anything is reflection and learning and the courage to try something new. If you want to achieve mastery in everything you do, you have to find learning opportunities in everything that you do.

By all means take pride in doing something well – but always remain alert to the possibility that maybe you could have done it even better. It is the quest for continuous improvement that marks out the star performers.

Further food for the curious

- Goleman D. *Emotional Intelligence*. Bantam Books (1995):

  - A very comprehensive text on the subject of emotional intelligence – one of the five emotional intelligences that Goleman describes is 'motivating yourself to achieve peak performance'.

- Taylor D. *The Naked Leader*. Capstone, Oxford (2002):

   –   An easy read with many poignant truths and practical tips.

Things for you to work on now

Key questions to ask yourself

- How do I judge and measure my own performance?

- When did I last think anew, rather than follow the tried and tested path?

- How much of my time does fire-fighting and rework consume?

- When did I last actively seek feedback on my performance?

Mini exercises you can try immediately

- Start to keep a personal diary of learning – jot down things that you do that work well and things that don't work quite so well. How did you recognise that they were working, or not working?

- Set aside some quiet time to review your learning diary and reflect on how you can change one or two of the things you do. Make a plan of how you will change those things and be rigorous about following through on your planned actions.

- Ask for feedback from your staff, your boss, your peers and your customers. Ask them what they value most about your style and approach and what they value least.

- Get yourself a coach and be prepared to have at least three coaching sessions.

- Set yourself three personal performance goals. How will you measure your progress and how will you know when you have achieved these goals?

- Understand that you can also improve performance by eliminating some behaviours – identify two things that you are currently doing that are getting in the way of improved performance – vow to stop doing them.

- Once you have succeeded with these three, set yourself another three.

Links to other questions

You may want to take a look at:

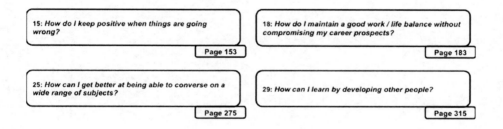

15: *How do I keep positive when things are going wrong?*

Page 153

18: *How do I maintain a good work / life balance without compromising my career prospects?*

Page 183

25: *How can I get better at being able to converse on a wide range of subjects?*

Page 275

29: *How can I learn by developing other people?*

Page 315

29: HOW CAN I LEARN BY DEVELOPING OTHER PEOPLE?

Why should I be asking this question?

If you really want to understand and know something, teaching it to someone else is the fastest and most effective way. The act of trying to help others understand causes you to look at an issue in more depth; as you try to put yourself in their place, you will be forced to answer questions that you had not thought of before and you will start to look at problems from completely different angles.

This is not a new idea.

To teach is to learn twice

Joseph Joubert (1754–1824)

Seeing things through the eyes of other people, and grappling anew with ideas that you had stopped questioning are sure-fire ways of kick-starting your own learning process.

The message is clear; you learn most when you help others to learn. This is because to help others learn, you have to see with their eyes, understand how they think and re-examine things that you may not have questioned for years.

The development of the people in your team is a fundamental role of management. But it is more than just altruism; it is your own route to self-development.

The impact of the issue

Far too many people in our organisations believe that, in order to succeed, everyone else must fail. Sadly, this mental model is reinforced by endless reality TV shows that depict hapless people being evicted, or fired, while the alpha male (or female) tramples over the broken bodies in their quest for personal glory.

Don't get us wrong; we have no problem with competition or with the idea of winners. Nor is this about being nice or being weak; this is about helping others and, by doing, so helping yourself.

The bottom line is that when you take the time to develop others, you are making a big investment in developing yourself.

When you expand your own potential and that of the people around you, great things can happen and it will show in the way that you and your team perform.

Making sense of it all

Abraham Lincoln was a wise man, but he was patently mistaken in thinking that all men are created equal. Self-evidently we are not equal; some of us can run faster, jump higher or think more quickly than others. It is not a crime to be less able than someone else; it is, however, a terrible waste not to perform to the best of our own ability.

The key to attaining your own potential is learning. We are beginning to understand that learning need not be an individual event; it can, and should, be a team sport. You should strive to learn with, and through, other people.

When people fail to learn, they will inevitably operate below their capability. Many things can get in the way of learning; maybe you have a lack of challenge, or lack of respect for your peers, or your leadership. Sometimes a feeling of despair, or lack of self-worth, can get in the way and make you feel that you have reached your limit.

Whatever the reason, the chances are that the roots of underperformance lie not with your innate ability, but rather with a lack of alignment between what you find yourself doing and what truly motivates you.

The following case study, although extreme, is typical of the work experience for many.

This story is about Ben, a middle manager, working within the IT department in the public sector. Ben was an old hand – he had flitted from job to job and eventually landed as the Data Manager – a role that kept him away from the actual data and its organisation, but, instead, saw him setting data policy and standards and sitting on various committees.

Ben was relatively well liked on a personal level, but, as far as his work contribution was concerned, he was considered by almost everyone as a 'total waste of space'. To add to this, he had something of a drink problem and there was only about a one-hour window each day when he functioned halfway normally – this was from 11.30 am to 12.30 pm, when he had recovered sufficiently from the night before and not yet had a chance to pop out for another drink.

Each night at 5.30 pm, Ben would go home, get changed and pop to the local community club, not to drink, but to run it. Ben had grown the club from nothing, did all the fund-raising, arranged all the functions and outings, managed the building, did the accounts, ran the bar – basically Ben was the alpha and the omega of this institution.

Clearly Ben was a well-motivated and extremely able individual who only came alive after 5.30 pm each day.

The real tragedy is – why could successive managers not awaken, or stimulate, his interest and harness his innate qualities during normal working hours? During the day he did just enough to get by and had stopped learning, or contributing. But in his other life, he was an inspiration, he developed capability in himself and others and had a purpose.

The story above does not depict a lack of ability, motivation, or, necessarily, a lack of direct supervision. What it does display is an almost criminal waste of human resource; from the point of view of both the individual and the organisation.

We have deliberately painted an extreme case, but we suggest that all of us have at some time performed well below our capability because we have got ourselves stuck in a rut. We end up doing the same old things in the same old ways, rather than looking for opportunities to see differently, to be different and to learn new things.

Over the decades, numerous studies have set out to discover what makes people happy and fulfilled at work. The research almost always focuses on three variables: ability, values and life interests. One recent study found life interests to be paramount. The researchers argued that while ability can make you feel competent and you can be contented with the rewards that you receive, only life interests will keep most people happy and fulfilled over the long term.

They defined these life interests as long-held, emotionally driven passions: the things we truly love doing and, if injected into our working day, are likely to increase job satisfaction and improve our motivation. In their *Harvard Business Review* paper, Butler and Waldroop describe eight 'deeply embedded life interests' or DELIs for short; they suggest that one, two or three of these drive most of us. They are as follows:

- Application of technology – people with this life interest are intrigued by the inner workings of things. They are the ones who want to know how it works because the technology excites them, as does the possibility that it could be tinkered with and improved.

- Quantitative analysis – people with this life interest gravitate towards numbers. They love running the numbers and see it as the best way to figure out business solutions.

- Theory development and conceptual thinking people enjoy thinking and talking about abstract ideas, the 'why' interests them far more than the 'how'. They like thinking about situations from the '30,000-foot' level.

- Creative production – people with this life interest are frequently seen as imaginative, out-of-the-box thinkers. They thrive on newness and may take little interest in things that are already established.

- Counselling and mentoring – these people are drawn towards teaching and guiding others towards better performance; they are drawn to work situations that allow them to help others grow and improve.

- Managing people and relationships – people with this life interest prefer to work with, and through, people to accomplish the goals of the business. They thrive in line-management positions.

- Enterprise control – people with this life interest are happiest when they have ultimate decision-making authority. They feel great when they are in charge of making things happen.

- Influence through language and ideas – for people with this life interest, effective communication is more than a skill; it is a passion. They feel most fulfilled when writing or speaking; enjoyment comes from storytelling, negotiating, or persuading.

If you can understand your own DELI or DELIs, you will be better able to recognise the things that will inspire and drive you to do something new. Doing something new will, inevitably, involve engaging with others, so that you are involved in the process of co-creation and, hence, learning with and through other people.

Practical advice

Know your own mind and be aware of your own DELIs. These are the things that inspire and motivate you – they drive your passion for learning and they structure and give meaning to the way you learn.

Choose the one or two DELIs that you think come closest to capturing what drives you. Then read the specific advice for your DELI given below, and think of ways you can adopt and adapt the advice to your particular circumstances.

If your DELI centres on the application of technology – we suggest that you look for ways to:

- Engage with people to better understand how your business processes work. What are the key points of leverage that you can work on to make things more effective?

- Look at the systems and technologies that support your area of the business. Which areas work well? Which areas are not working so well, and why? If you could change one thing, what would it be?

- Engage with your information systems (IS) function and get to know the business or systems analyst that works on your part of the business. They tend to think differently than you and use different tool sets. Find out how they set about planning and analysing systems and what information they use when redesigning processes to make them more efficient and effective. Make sure that you create an environment that allows you to have a regular dialogue. Find out which new technology is most admired by your IS colleagues, and explore together how such a technology might be harnessed in your area.

- Try to develop a 'let's take this apart and solve it' mind-set. Encourage the people you work with to ask questions about why something works, rather than just how to use it.

If your DELI centres on quantitative analysis – we suggest that you look for ways to:

- Engage with your colleagues in the finance department to see how they build financial models of the business, or how they evaluate the potential business impact of different strategic business programmes.

- Look at how you currently forecast growth, or return on investment. Can you find a better way of modelling these decisions?

- Look at how you currently produce estimates for the revenue-generating potential of new products. Do you include an assessment of risk, or factor in the probability of launch failure? Do you use single-point estimates, or some form of statistical range? Can you find a better way of modelling these factors and can you build in some sensitivity analysis?

- Read up on decision-analysis theory. Can you use decision theory in any of the decisions that you have to make? How can you use numbers to compensate for subjectivity? Can you produce a better model that provides better unbiased data to inform the decision makers in your organisation?

If your DELI centres on theory development and conceptual thinking – we suggest that you look for ways to:

- Construct a high-level process view for your area of the business. Identify areas that currently constrain action.

- Map out the monthly sales-forecasting process and show how you can improve the view of the sales funnel.

- Build a benefits-realisation model for a key programme that is ongoing in your area.

- Pick an area of concern for your organisation – for example, workplace injuries, high turnover of staff, etc. Examine all the available data, and see if you can build a robust model that explains things that are driving the phenomena and, hence, propose possible interventions.

If your DELI centres on creative production – we suggest that you look for ways to:

- Get involved with your marketing people – see how they craft a design brief and how they put together an advertising campaign. See how you can transfer your new insight into your current job.

- Research the idea of *design thinking* – start to take a more holistic view about the service you provide and try to visualise it in terms of customer needs. Build this sort of thinking into the way you brief your team members on a new task.

- Get involved on the organising committee of a major social event for your organisation; for example, the Christmas ball, or the annual sales event off-site. These are always great vehicles for unconstrained creative thinking and they get you noticed.

If your DELI centres on counselling and mentoring – we suggest that you look for ways to:

- Put yourself forward as a coach for people on the talent programme.

- Find a mentor for yourself.

- Offer to be a mentor for one of your more junior colleagues.

- Get involved with your company's induction programme – offer to be a buddy for new arrivals.

- Talk to your HR department about the possibility of getting trained up to administer and debrief people on some of the personality diagnostic tools that they use for recruitment.

- Work with HR to get involved with any 360-degree assessment tools that they use, or leadership profiling tools.

- Consider some self-development by taking courses on behavioural psychology, or neurolinguistic programming.

If your DELI centres on managing people and relationships – we suggest that you look for ways to:

- Work with your HR partner to identify people for the talent programme, or to build the succession plan.

- Get involved with the people side of any organisational change initiatives. Get trained up on change management, behavioural interviewing and other related topics.

- If your organisation has to restructure, or make people redundant, don't shy away from these tough managerial challenges – step up to the plate and be the lead manager for your area. It is hard, it hurts, you will lose sleep – but working with people when they are at their most vulnerable will teach you a lot about yourself and will really make you draw upon your core values.

- Really get to know every nuance of your annual appraisal process, and make sure that when you do appraisals on your staff, you are a model that others should strive to emulate.

- Offer to be the management representative on grievance panels and disciplinary hearings. When you see things that have gone hopelessly out of control, you will learn so much that helps you avoid similar pitfalls.

If your DELI centres on enterprise control – we suggest that you look for ways to:

- Work with your boss to better understand how they make decisions and how decisions are made at board level. Try to get them to delegate tasks to you that will help you develop your decision-making capabilities.

- Volunteer to project- or programme-manage key initiatives. Make sure that you get trained up in the key methods and tools that are associated with project or programme management in your organisation.

- Get involved in building business cases for new products, or initiatives.

- Always volunteer for any cross-functional or inter-organisational projects.

- Work with your finance partner to fully understand the business planning cycle.

- Get your boss to talk you through their input to the strategic planning process. See if you can help them pull together the initial analysis that underpins their input.

- Get involved in sales planning, or setting sales targets and commission structures.

If your DELI centres on influencing through language and ideas – we suggest that you look for ways to:

- Talk to your public relations (PR) department and volunteer for media training. You would be amazed at how few people want to do this and how scary, yet fulfilling, it can be.

- Next time your organisation undertakes a major change initiative, see if you can get on the advisory committee. Volunteer to put together briefing documents and conduct cascade briefings.

- Write articles for your company newsletter. Offer to write for professional journals. Work with your PR department to identify publishing opportunities. Form a working relationship with someone senior in your PR department who can guide you and help you improve the impact of your written communication in style and format.

- Volunteer to lead or be a member of any project, or programme, that has multiple powerful stakeholders in different functions and geographic regions within your organisation. The more you can work with different cultures, the better you will become at influencing.

The ideas we have suggested above are not meant to be prescriptive. We suggest that you look at them and use them as inspiration to craft your own set of actions to try out.

Further food for the curious

- Butler T and Waldroop J. Job Sculpting: The art of retaining your best people. *Harvard Business Review*, Sept./Oct. 1999:

  - An excellent paper providing both insight and practical advice in relation to motivating and developing people in the workplace.

Things for you to work on now

Key questions to ask yourself
<ul><li>What is/are your top one, two or three DELIs?</li><li>To what extent does your current role build on and play to the strengths of your DELIs?</li><li>How do you feel about this?</li><li>How well do you understand the hearts and the minds of the people that work with you and for you?</li><li>Could you identify their DELIs?</li><li>To what extent do their respective roles satisfy their DELIs?</li><li>What can you do to help them better understand themselves, so that they can perform better?</li><li>How much time and effort do you spend helping others to learn new ways of thinking and new ways of looking</li></ul>

at problems?

- What have you learned in the last week as a direct result of helping others to learn?

- What emphasis did you place on learning during the last appraisal cycle?

Mini exercises you can try immediately

- Determine what your DELIs are and how they give shape to your decision making. What determines the priorities you place upon learning?

- Talk to each member of your team and ascertain how happy and fulfilled they feel in their current role. Share with them the concept of DELIs, and try to discover what makes them tick and what their aspirations are for their future.

- When you have completed this exercise with each member of your team, use these insights to identify one area where you can work together to learn and use your DELIs to see situations differently.

- Consider how you could redefine, or enhance, your role to ensure you utilise your strengths to the full and are able to exercise your DELIs as much as possible.

Links to other questions

You may want to take a look at:

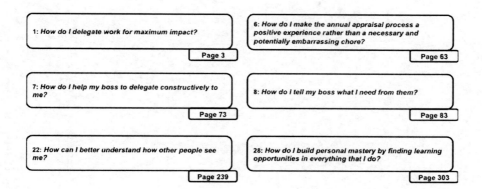

1: How do I delegate work for maximum impact?

Page 3

6: How do I make the annual appraisal process a positive experience rather than a necessary and potentially embarrassing chore?

Page 63

7: How do I help my boss to delegate constructively to me?

Page 73

8: How do I tell my boss what I need from them?

Page 83

22: How can I better understand how other people see me?

Page 239

28: How do I build personal mastery by finding learning opportunities in everything that I do?

Page 303

30: HOW CAN I UNLOCK MY OWN CREATIVE POTENTIAL?

Why should I be asking this question?

Creativity is associated with originality of thought, or inventiveness. The dictionary might say 'having or showing imagination'.

Whenever we interact with a representative of an organisation, whether that be the receptionist at a hotel, the guy from the IT help desk, or the sales rep of another company, we would like them to show a little imagination in the way they deal with us.

What we want them to understand is that we are individuals with unique needs and that their role is not to make us fit their preferred process or product, but rather to seek to understand our unique needs and then use their imagination and creativity to tailor their service to fulfil our needs.

We do not want to conform to their one-size-fits-all approach. We want our size, and we want it delivered in a way that gives us a sporting chance of achieving the outcome that we desire.

The impact of the issue

How often do you feel frustrated, or even angry, at the service, or lack of, that you receive? We constantly hear the words 'No, you can't have that', or 'We only serve that after 11 am', or 'That's against the rules', and so on. What we want is a positive 'can do' attitude; we want to hear what can be done, rather than what can't be done; we want people to think outside of the box and offer us alternatives and options; and we don't want bureaucracy, red tape and rules just for the sake of them.

We want, however briefly, to be the focus of attention, and we want to feel that the service we receive is aimed first and foremost at meeting our specific and unique needs. We want to be made to feel that we matter, that the service-giver understands our needs and is prepared to go out of their way in order to fulfil those needs

Basically, it is not enough that we get a slick and efficient process – we also want to see the imagination, flair and creativity that make us feel special and good about what we are getting.

What we want from others, we should also strive to deliver ourselves. There is also the added bonus that when you are creative, you almost always feel more fulfilled.

Making sense of it all

While we cannot all aspire to the intuitive ability of some of the great chief executives who can turn a company around overnight, we can maximise our own creative potential by opening our minds and harnessing the collective abilities of those around us.

Some people are naturally ideas-oriented, while others are more practical in their approach. Ideas people tend to be more imaginative; for them, ideas come cheaply and those ideas do not have to be either practical or realistic; it is volume that counts. Practical people, on the other hand, instinctively go into evaluation mode and can spot that one good idea out of 100 and turn it into a practical reality; for them it's quality that counts.

The process of bringing a new product to market, for example, requires both types of thinking and sets of abilities, as illustrated by the model in Figure 17.

Such a process requires collaboration among different types of people; people who see the world in inherently different ways. They need to work together constructively and creatively; in order to do this, they must value and respect each other's skills and talents. However, all too often, such differences in style and approach result in unproductive conflict among people who do not innately understand one another. Disputes become personal and, as a consequence, the symbiosis of the creative/innovative process breaks down.

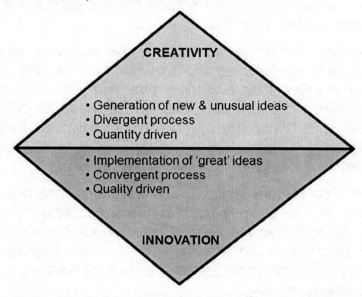

CREATIVITY

• Generation of new & unusual ideas
• Divergent process
• Quantity driven

• Implementation of 'great' ideas
• Convergent process
• Quality driven

INNOVATION

Figure 17: Creativity/innovation process

To be creative, you must first be open to the idea that things could be different and that, often, what may appear at the outset to be a great solution is, in effect, just a convenient one.

To be innovative, you must be brave enough to challenge authority and accepted wisdom; to have the courage and conviction to run with that novel or unusual idea.

Consider the following mini case.

Jill was the IT manager of a retail bank and one day she was asked to extend the bank's services to a 24 hours a day, seven days a week operation. This was neither practical nor feasible, but instead of saying 'no', or giving a prohibitively high estimate for the work, Jill asked the business why it wanted to go 24 x 7.

The business explained that it had been the first telephone bank and for a couple of years this had been their unique selling proposition (USP).

However, many other banks had subsequently followed suit. They now needed a new USP and the business saw a 24 x 7 operation as providing this.

Jill confirmed that she understood the rationale behind the request and again asked more questions. This dialogue gave her more information and more time to think of alternatives. She asked the business if they would want to offer a full service throughout the night, what volumes they were anticipating and whether the data needed to be 'up to the minute', or if it mattered if it was a few hours old.

Armed with the answers to these questions, she was able to suggest an alternative solution that would address the business issue; to download the data as of 6 pm each evening onto a large personal computer and run a basic enquiry service overnight until the main systems came back on stream at 8 am the following morning.

The business thought this was perfectly adequate and were truly amazed at the speed and affordability of the solution delivered. They ran with this option on a trial basis for a period of three months, monitoring the volumes and types of activity. After this time and armed with more data, they agreed a more permanent and robust solution offering a full service, but only between the hours of 7 am and 9 pm, seven days per week. This trial and error process allowed them to formulate a different, but better, solution than was originally envisaged; and Jill became the heroine, rather than the villain, as is often the case with many IT managers in similar situations.

What key skills and talents did Jill portray? She demonstrated the ability to:

- ask gentle, probing questions to get to the 'nub' of the issue, the root cause;
- actively listen without making judgement, or being critical;
- focus on the real business issue, rather than an ill-informed and inappropriate solution;
- use her intuition to think of an alternative solution that addressed the real problem;
- collaborate with the business to find a win–win solution.

So you see, creativity in most organisational contexts is not about being a naturally gifted genius, but rather being willing to ask questions, listen carefully and then challenge the accepted way of doing things.

You unlock your creative side by letting go of the fears that trap you where you are, by looking beyond the ordinary and the obvious and asking questions that reveal possibilities, rather than emphasising limitations.

Practical advice

In order to unlock your creativity, the two most important skills you need to develop are:

- your emotional intelligence:
    - understanding yourself, your style, values, strengths and weaknesses, behaviour, image and reputation;
    - understanding others, valuing and appreciating differences;
    - demonstrating empathy for others and being able to put yourself in their shoes, appreciate their perspective;

> – the social skill to build rapport, to question and listen, and build upon the ideas and thoughts of others.

- your intuition:

  > – the ability to detect patterns, or make connections that have not been made before, that others have overlooked or mistaken for random noise;
  >
  > – listening to our subconscious – drawing on rules and patterns that we can't quite articulate.

Because the focus of this question is on increasing personal creativity, we will concentrate our advice on the creative, divergent phase of identifying ideas and possibilities, rather than on the innovative, convergent phase of narrowing down the possibilities and homing in on a course of action.

When in creative mode, it is important to remember the following key rules:

- Begin with an easily understandable goal statement. A statement beginning with 'To …', which is no more than 12 words in length and that would be understandable by a child of eight years of age.

- Remember that anything and everything goes – every idea is written down; the objective is to capture as many ideas as possible, the wackier the better. No idea should be critiqued, judged or discarded during the creative process.

- Use building, encouraging words, such as 'AND', rather than condemning or closing words, such as 'BUT'. Spark off and build upon the ideas of others; think laterally.

- Take sufficient time – research shows that ideas seem to peak and decline, and then spring back to life again, as illustrated in Figure 18.

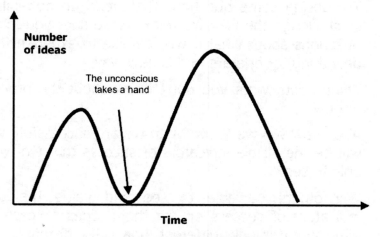

Figure 18: Ideas time line

- The key insight from Figure 18 is that most of the time we close down on ideas' generation before we get into our second phase of creativity. So the question you need to be asking is, 'Have we have run out of ideas because we have exhausted all possibilities or have we stopped because our unconscious mind is having a rest?' Here are a few things that you can try to jump-start the ideas generation process:

  – Try the technique of word association to develop new channels of thought. Choose three or four verbs, or nouns, at random and then look for the associations between these words. Develop these themes and finally link back to your original goal statement.

  – Select several analogies that capture the essence of your goal. Produce actual solutions to the analytical goal; now translate these back to your actual goal statement.

  – Generate some 'get fired' ideas, i.e. ones which would solve, or reduce, the problem, but that are so outlandish that your work colleagues may seriously consider your sanity if you presented them in a serious business meeting.

- Try posing some questions that open up possibilities, or challenge the way we think. Make sure you include questions about what it will feel like to experience this new thing, or operate in this new way.

- Think about what you don't know about the problem, or goal.

- Ask, 'How will we know when we are successful? What will be the visible indicators of success that we will be able to see?'

- Will others be able to see and value the same indicators of success or, for them, does success look different? If it looks different, how is it different?

- If we can fix this issue, what other opportunities might it open up?

In an organisational sense, creativity isn't about being a naturally gifted genius or prodigy. It comes from asking questions, seeing possibilities and having the courage to try something new and different.

If you want to open yourself up to creativity, you need to open yourself up to new things and new ways of working and being. Never say never. Always ask why. And never dismiss anything as silly or irrelevant.

Think off the wall, weird, wacky, way out, out of the box; as Arthur C Clarke put it so succinctly:

> *Any sufficiently advanced technology is indistinguishable from magic.*

Further food for the curious

- Goleman D. *Emotional Intelligence*. Bantam Books (1995):

  - A very comprehensive text on the subject of emotional intelligence.

- Hayashi A. When to Trust your Gut. *Harvard Business Review at Large*, Feb. 2001:

  - A short, yet excellent, article exploring and helping to explain the mechanics of 'gut' instinct.

- Leonard D and Straus S. Putting your Company's Whole Brain to Work. *Harvard Business Review*, July/Aug. 1997):

  - A well-constructed article focusing on the business imperative to innovate and how to harness the different thinking styles in a process of 'creative abrasion'.

Things for you to work on now

Key questions to ask yourself

- When did you last place yourself in an unusual situation?

- How open is your mind? How quick are you to judge the ideas of others, or close down thinking in order to arrive at a decision?

- In collaborative situations, what sort of words do you use and what effect do they have on the dynamic of the group?

- When working in a group, how much of your time do you spend getting your point of view across and heard? Compare this with how much time you spend appreciating the ideas of others and asking questions that help others to contribute ideas?

- What gives you the best feeling – being right, or helping others give voice to new, or radical, ideas?

- How do you feel when people meet your ideas with negative comments about why they won't work, or how they have been tried before?

- How often do you display a 'can do' attitude, rather than a negative (it's going to be difficult, costly, risky, non-standard, etc.) attitude? What impact does your response have on the creativity of others?

Mini exercises you can try immediately

- Practise brainstorming – list 50 ways in which your company can adopt more environmentally sustainable practices. When you start to run out of ideas, try some of the techniques we listed previously to boost your ideas' generation capacity.

- The next time you are in a collaborative situation, observe the different behaviours that are produced when someone responds with 'AND ...', rather than 'BUT ...'. Which of these words open up creativity and which of them close it down? What other words and phrases have the same sort of effect on your group? Monitor what goes on in the group and see if you can change the dynamic of the whole group by the interventions that you make, rather than the ideas that you contribute.

- Place yourself in an unusual situation – for example, if you are a research and development scientist for a food manufacturer, try serving in your works canteen for a day. The idea is to hear the voice of the consumer and to see how people actually engage with your products, or services.

- If you are faced with a particularly difficult challenge – go and ask someone who you are absolutely convinced knows nothing about your challenge and could not possibly have anything of value to contribute. Listen carefully to their daft questions and ideas. Then go away and ask yourself why you think they are so daft. You may get a real surprise.

Links to other questions

You may want to take a look at:

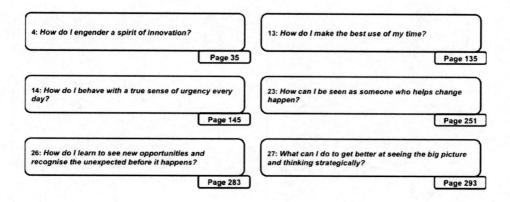

4: *How do I engender a spirit of innovation?*

Page 35

13: *How do I make the best use of my time?*

Page 135

14: *How do I behave with a true sense of urgency every day?*

Page 145

23: *How can I be seen as someone who helps change happen?*

Page 251

26: *How do I learn to see new opportunities and recognise the unexpected before it happens?*

Page 283

27: *What can I do to get better at seeing the big picture and thinking strategically?*

Page 293

ITG RESOURCES

IT Governance Ltd. sources, creates and delivers products and services to meet the real-world, evolving IT governance needs of today's organisations, directors, managers and practitioners.

The ITG website (*www.itgovernance.co.uk*) is the international one-stop-shop for corporate and IT governance information, advice, guidance, books, tools, training and consultancy.

http://www.itgovernance.co.uk/catalog/511 is the information page on our website for our soft skills management resources.

Other Websites

Books and tools published by IT Governance Publishing (ITGP) are available from all business booksellers and are also immediately available from the following websites:

www.itgovernance.co.uk/catalog/355 provides information and online purchasing facilities for every currently available book published by ITGP.

www.itgovernance.eu is our euro-denominated website which ships from Benelux and has a growing range of books in European languages other than English.

www.itgovernanceusa.com is a US$-based website that delivers the full range of IT Governance products to North America, and ships from within the continental US.

www.itgovernanceasia.com provides a selected range of ITGP products specifically for customers in South Asia.

www.27001.com is the IT Governance Ltd. website that deals specifically with information security management, and ships from within the continental US.

Pocket Guides

For full details of the entire range of pocket guides, simply follow the links at *www.itgovernance.co.uk/publishing.aspx*.

Toolkits

ITG's unique range of toolkits includes the IT Governance Framework Toolkit, which contains all the tools and guidance that you will need in order to develop and implement an appropriate IT governance framework for your organisation. Full details can be found at *www.itgovernance.co.uk/ products/519*.

For a free paper on how to use the proprietary Calder-Moir IT Governance Framework, and for a free trial version of the toolkit, see *www.itgovernance.co.uk/calder_moir.aspx*.

There is also a wide range of toolkits to simplify implementation of management systems, such as an ISO/IEC 27001 ISMS or a BS25999 BCMS, and these can all be viewed and purchased online at: *http://www.itgovernance.co.uk/catalog/1*.

Best Practice Reports

ITG's range of Best Practice Reports is now at *www.itgovernance.co.uk/best-practice-reports.aspx*. These offer you essential, pertinent, expertly researched information on a number of key issues including Web 2.0 and Green IT.

Training and Consultancy

IT Governance also offers training and consultancy services across the entire spectrum of disciplines in the information governance arena. Details of training courses can be accessed at *www.itgovernance.co.uk/training.aspx* and descriptions of our consultancy services can be found at *http://www.itgovernance.co.uk/consulting.aspx*. Why not contact us to see how we could help you and your organisation?

Newsletter

IT governance is one of the hottest topics in business today, not least because it is also the fastest moving, so what better way to keep up than by subscribing to ITG's free monthly newsletter *Sentinel*? It provides monthly updates and resources across the whole spectrum of IT governance subject matter, including risk management, information security, ITIL and IT service management, project governance, compliance and so much more. Subscribe for your free copy at: *www.itgovernance.co.uk/newsletter.aspx*.